THE MODERN NATIONS IN

HISTORICAL PERSPECTIVE

ROBIN W. WINKS, *General Editor*

The volumes in this series deal with individual nations or groups of closely related nations throughout the world, summarizing the chief historical trends and influences that have contributed to each nation's present-day character, problems, and behavior. Recent data are incorporated with established historical background to achieve a fresh synthesis and original interpretation.

JOHN C. CAIRNS, the author of this volume in the Modern Nations in Historical Perspective series, was schooled in England, Canada, and the United States. Presently Professor of History at the University of Toronto, he has published articles on various aspects of modern French history, and is currently at work on a book on the end of the Third French Republic.

FRANCE

JOHN C. CAIRNS

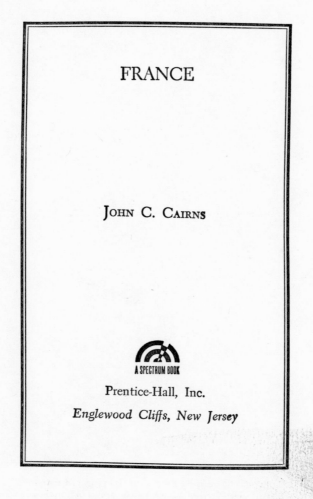

A SPECTRUM BOOK

Prentice-Hall, Inc.

Englewood Cliffs, New Jersey

Current printing (last number):
10 9 8 7 6 5 4 3 2

To the bright and unforgettable memory of my sister

This book is a brief introduction to France, her history, her civilization, her problems, and her role in the world. It may be arbitrary; I hope it is not unfair. No doubt much here proposed, borrowed, summarized, interpreted, and alluded to will invite dissent. The complexity of French life and society is a challenge and warning to any foreigner. The folly of essaying some study of even a small part of it may be read in the eyes of one's French friends almost before one has quite spelled out the purpose that has brought one to France. Fortunately for me, I never had occasion to betray the intent which has now become this small book, since it never occurred to me that I would be writing it. Yet now that it is done, despite its faults, I hope that a few who may happen to see it will accept it as my thanks for the kindness and friendship which my stays in France, while working on other things, have brought me.

I should of course acknowledge my indebtedness to the wisdom, the skepticism, or whatever one may call it, of the Duc de la Rochefoucauld, from whose *Maximes* have been borrowed the epigraphs for each chapter.

My thanks are due also to Robin Winks, Stanley Hoffmann, and some others whose criticisms were much to the point.

But above all I owe my thanks to Fernand Ernstein, without whose delightful companionship over the years the memory of the Third and the realities of the Fourth and Fifth Republics would have been less attractive to me, and who, should he read these pages, will quite likely disagree with almost everything in them.

J.C.C.

CONTENTS

ix

"Vieille France, accablée d'Histoire, meurtrie de guerres et de révolutions, allant et venant sans relâche de la grandeur au déclin, mais redressée, de siècle en siècle, par le génie du renouveau."

—Charles de Gaulle

ONE

FRANCE, THE FRENCH,

AND THE GENERAL

"On n'est jamais si heureux ni si malheureux qu'on s'imagine."

The twentieth century has grown accustomed to the rise and fall of nations. The First World War swept away old and powerful regimes which had been bulwarks of the European order. The Second World War proved to be hardly less cataclysmic. No state was cast down more rudely than the Republic of France. A quarter century before, it had suffered and endured to triumph at last as the very heart of the allied coalition against the Central Powers. In the summer of 1940 it sustained the most sudden and unmitigated military disaster a major nation has known in modern times. In a matter of weeks the land was overrun from the Vosges to the Atlantic, from the Channel to the Pyrenees. For four years thereafter France struggled confusedly and in shackles to survive and to reorganize herself. Liberated by armies from without and a rising Resistance from within, she continued the search for a political and social consensus which eluded her always. Though the French slowly rebuilt their economy to achieve at least a partial rationalization of it, they found no unity on domestic, foreign, or colonial problems. Beneath the burden and discord of imperial retreat, they appeared to be approaching civil strife. And yet on the verge of this incoherence, in 1958, a majority of them rallied to the strong, if ambiguous, leadership of a man who had stood apart from their most recent quarrels. Almost as suddenly the French Republic seemed to recover its sense of unity and purpose. Though the way led across territory still fraught with the danger of civil-military rebellion, France followed this man and under his direction emerged in the 1960s as the ambitious candidate for the leadership of western Europe and as the center of what many continued to hope would be a far-flung cultural community around the globe.

The Prestige of the Fifth Republic

France is undeniably a great state, though not, by the standards of the United States and the Soviet Union, a great power. As the twentieth century advanced, Europe's authority was eclipsed. The role that France and other European states had taken in the world was assumed increasingly by non-European nations having populations at least four times that of the Republic. Nonetheless, after falling so low, the prestige of the French state grew rapidly after 1958, out of all proportion to the size, wealth, and strength of its people. The voice of France was listened to with respect once more. Her actions and declarations carried an authority undefinable in the ordinary terms of military might, mere numbers, or territories held. When Charles de Gaulle proclaimed that France would "undertake great actions, assume great proportions, and greatly serve her own interest and that of the human race as well," there were skeptical smiles but less and less disbelief. Under the Fourth Republic such a declaration would have seemed almost ridiculous. Under the Fifth this sense of purpose won a serious, if grudging, attention from other nations.

A large part of this new prestige was owing to the nature of the Fifth Republic's first President. More than any other single being he had re-created France's title to greatness. He did not, however, create the claims of France: he merely reasserted them and by an extraordinary manipulation of domestic and world politics made them something more than words. Those who came after him would not lightly abandon them. Frenchmen had seen in this century how such claims to place and authority might be quickly lost, and how long and arduous is the task of reconstituting them. In the tough and mostly unprincipled politics of the international arena, the claims of France were for many years ineptly presented, weakly supported and roughly considered. It might well turn out to be de Gaulle's principal achievement that he showed his countrymen how to maximize their potential, how to abandon untenable commitments, and how to pursue a striking new role for France in Europe and the world which was essentially in the historic tradition of which they had almost seemed to despair.

Nature alone gave France a certain title to greatness. Her situation on the far western edge of the Eurasian land mass was never more important than in the twentieth century. Washed by the Mediterranean, the Atlantic, and the Channel, France has maritime interests of the first order. Strategically, her position is very strong. The Pyreneean barrier commands the road from Spain. The eastern frontiers from Switzerland to the Flanders coast open out into the wooded hills and the great continental plain. Yet the position has its fundamental weakness too. Seagirt and yet with lengthy land frontiers, some of them classic invasion routes, France is at once vulnerable to an enemy and indispensable to an ally. Even more than the British Isles, she dominates the western approaches to the heart of Europe. She has paid for her superior situation by becoming more easily the victim of her continental neighbors from time to time. Geography and the twentieth century imposed heavy responsibilities upon this country. Those who sometimes took advantage of France's periodic weaknesses at other times cursed them. The English-speaking world lived in a state of ambivalence about French power—uneasy when it was manifestly great, unhappy when it was in eclipse. Old republics and old allies, France and the United States made ritual appeals to the Lafayette tradition, but they never lived it.

A decade after the Liberation the Fourth Republic was at the point of lowest prestige. Both London and Washington demanded that it assume a more positive attitude toward creation of a European defense system. The humiliation of Prime Minister Joseph Laniel by Winston Churchill and Dwight Eisenhower at the Bermuda conference of December 1953 opened an era of ultimatums and provoked the resentment of a nation beset by imperial war. Claude Bourdet might proclaim *"C'est Cambronne qu'il nous faut,"* but Cambronne's word (*"merde!"*) had not turned the tide at Waterloo. Something more constructive was needed to restore the dignity of France *vis-à-vis* her western partners. It came in 1958 with the return to power of de Gaulle. Thereafter the mood changed. If Cambronne's word was not quite spoken, its sense was communicated repeatedly to Washington, London, and Moscow. Backed by something closer to national consensus than any leader of the Fourth Republic had ever enjoyed, the General sought to realize the position that France by her geography, her experience, and her history naturally embodies—that and a great deal more—even in a world of superpowers. The era of ultimatums came to an end. From Paris where, as he would so often maintain, "we see the world as it is," went forth political and diplomatic initiatives which often disturbed or stunned "the Anglo-Saxons." It was unquestionably a brilliant performance, but it would be wrong to suppose that it was mere bravado and illusion. It focused world attention on France. It compelled the United States to be infinitely more deferential than it had been. It delighted the French. The question was posed, however, as to whether those who ruled the Republic after this man would be able to put forward France's claims as forcefully as he had done.

Land and Resources

As nations go, the French population is not large. Its homeland is relatively small. Continental France and her immediate appendages, though more than twice the size of the United Kingdom, are less than one-fifteenth the size of the United States. By 1964 the population was unofficially estimated at more than 48 million, having risen by about 19 per cent since the end of the Second World War. More than 700,000 Europeans from North Africa took refuge in such cities as Marseille and Toulouse after 1961. But even so, all the provincial urban centers of France are dwarfed by the capital. Marseille, with 783,738, according to the March 1962 census, therefore not including the whole influx from Algeria), was far behind the 2,811,179 that Paris officially claimed. No other city approached Marseille: Lyon was far behind with 535,784; Toulouse with 330,570 (again, before the refugees poured in); Nice with 294,976; and Bordeaux with 254,122. Most Frenchmen are scattered across the countryside in small towns and villages. Yet these figures are slightly misleading in that they do not consider those living so close to urban centers as really constituting part of the largest towns. Thus it might be more realistic to put the population of Greater Paris at well over seven million, or nearly one-sixth of the whole nation. And this is a principal fact of France: the extraordinary focusing of almost every activity and interest upon the capital, a phenomenon not seen perhaps, as Ernst Robert Curtius noted, since ancient Rome. By any standard, Paris represents one of the most splendid examples of the urban civilization of the West.

France grows steadily more populous and more urban. This was not always so. From the mid-nineteenth to the mid-twentieth century Frenchmen deliberately (to maintain their standard of living) or accidentally (as the result of war) failed to keep pace with the rapid population growth of continental Europe. Only since 1945 has there been a substantial increase of births over deaths. The 48 millions estimated in 1964 had already passed the prediction made three years earlier for 1970. Long-range forecasters predicted about 100 millions by 2040. Many factors could intervene to upset such reckonings. But a dramatic reversal of the demographic pattern was under way. The France of 40 millions, so long a constant, belongs to the past. Of 1964's 48 millions, about 32 per cent were children and adolescents, 58 per cent adults, and 10 per cent old people. France, that is to say, is a young country, with a heavy burden laid upon its adult population.

The land is varied and wealthy. Most of it is a great plain, which extends like a giant arc from the Aquitaine Basin in the southwest up through the Paris Basin to the great North European Plain, and from the Languedoc plain bordering the Mediterranean sweeps up the Rhône-Saône valley toward the Vosges mountains. Venturing beyond the Ile de France and the sometimes depressing industrial northeast, the traveler discovers the mountainous regions of ancient Hercynian formations, the Armorican Massif of Brittany, the Ardennes and Vosges wooded slopes in the east, the great Central Massif, and, further east, lying against the Swiss and Italian frontiers, the Jura and the western Alps of later formation, like the Pyrenees along the Spanish frontier. Four major river systems irrigate the land: the Rhône-Saône flowing from Switzerland down to the Mediterranean; the Garonne from the Pyrenees northwest to the Atlantic; the Loire from the Central Massif north toward the Paris Basin, then cutting due west to the Atlantic; and the Seine, flowing northwest out of the Central Massif to the Channel. Often swift-currented, subject to seasonal rainfall, these rivers, with the exception of the Seine system, are not of much navigational use, although traffic may be observed even on the hurrying Rhône. And of course the mighty Rhine, forming the Franco-German border for more than 100 miles north from Basle, is a commercial highway of the first magnitude, the source of irrigation of the Alsatian plain.

Of all the river systems, the Seine is the most useful. With its criss-crossing canals, it provides an important transportation route for northern industry. In all, there were 4,761 miles of navigable waterways in use in France during 1961, including 2,841 miles of canals. About 25 per cent of all goods were moved by water. Thus the rivers of France are not only handsome, as the tourist who has shot the Tarn gorge rapids knows, but also functional. Together with three basic regional climates—oceanic in the west and northwest, Mediterranean in the south, and mountain—the rivers assure France a variety of crops and a richness of diet which is the envy of the world. In addition, the more than thirty hydroelectric dams built since the Liberation, plus half as many steam plants, had by 1962 raised French electric power production from 18 billion kilowatt-hours to more than 83 billion.

Other transportation facilities are excellent. The nationalized railroad system (*Société national des chemins de fer*) recovered rapidly from wartime destruction to become one of the most modern in the world. More than 65 per cent of the roadbed was electrified by 1964. Speeds in excess of 100 miles per hour were routine on express runs out of Paris. Road building was less spectacular; express highway construction had fallen lamentably behind the needs of a nation in which the number of cars had quadrupled in the decade 1954-1964, notably in the Paris region where city traffic has tended to reach the point of paralysis. The merchant marine, with a total tonnage of nearly 5 millions (in excess of 100 gross tons) ranked far behind that of Great Britain or Norway, but boasted the largest passenger liner afloat in the mid-1960s, "France." Finally, in Air France, the French claimed the world's longest network (about 329,000 miles), handling more than 3 million passengers a year.

France has become an increasingly important industrial power. About half the gross national product comes from this source. In no major industrial production does France lead the world, but in many industries she ranks very respectably indeed. Iron and steel manufacturing flourish in Flanders and Lorraine. A growing aluminum production is centered in the Alpine and Pyreneean areas, where hydro-electric and natural-gas resources lie. French textiles hold fourth place in world production, wool manufacture third place, cotton manufacture second place in Europe. Around Paris, Lyon, Dijon, and Lille is grouped a burgeoning electrical and electronic industry. Widely scattered, the chemical industry rates sixth in the world. Shipyards prosper modestly on all three seacoasts. Located in the Paris area and the southwest, the aircraft industry is a successful fourth in the world. Ranking fourth also is the French automobile industry, small by American standards, but with an annual output in good years exceeding one million passenger cars.

Most French petroleum comes from the Sahara fields, but below the Garonne some 3 million metric tons are produced annually. Even with the North African resources, of course, France remains dependent upon other imports here. As the first uranium producer in Western Europe, she had a plutonium production center operating at Marcoule as early as 1958; three power stations were in operation there, two others were established at Chinon. As for older sources of energy, coal mines in the northeast made up 50 per cent of French production, those in Lorraine another 25 per cent, and those in the center and south another 25 per cent. Though France claimed the highest man-day output of all Common Market producers, many mines had to be closed as inefficient. These losses might well be made good by such resources as the great Rance river tidal power plant in Brittany, the solar furnace at Mont-Louis near Tours, and the natural-gas fields in the southwest at Lacq.

Change and Society

Only yesterday France was viewed as a society resisting change, immensely conservative, uninterested in the outside world. There was a measure of truth in that view, but it is and always was too simple, too neat, and too much untrue. If the French have been constant in their fundamental impulses, they have also, as Alexis de Tocqueville pointed out, been changeable and so revolutionary in habits and thought as to startle even themselves. His analysis seemed as apt under the Fifth Republic as under the Second Empire of Louis Napoleon.

Mere statistics proclaimed the movement of French society, and none better than those concerning the family unit. Before 1939 the birth rate was so low (averaging 600,000 annually) that, had it remained constant, the population would have declined to 30 million by 1985. What could explain the reversal of this downward trend, particularly among the urban middle classes, remained a matter for debate. A certain cult of youth, an appeal to produce children was launched by the Government of Marshal Philippe Pétain in the immediate aftermath of the 1940 disaster. Even before that, the previous regime had introduced a *Code de la famille* in July 1939. Thus, whether the explanation lay with family allowances or some less definable alteration of outlook and ambition, the regimes after 1939 systematically encouraged larger families. Allowances were especially generous to those having more than four children. Although the age limit for payment was normally 15 years, in the case of children who were still students payment might be made until they were 20 years old. And so France continued to protect and encourage development of what the bourgeoisie cared to call her "elite."

The position of women in society altered markedly during the first half of the century. In law the wife may be considered head of the family. After 1946 women had the same franchise as men and were equally eligible for public office. Equal work in France brought equal rates of pay. Discrimination on the basis of sex was outlawed. By the 1960s more than 40 per cent of women between 15 and 64 were employed. An increasing number of wives work, young mothers placing their children in nurseries at two years. Frenchwomen might still submit to forms of domestic slavery that North American women had almost forgotten ever existed. But the tyranny of lining up daily at little shops to buy every little item began to yield slightly under the Fifth Republic with the introduction of (bitterly resented) supermarkets in big cities. The possibility of stocking perishable produce in the home appeared, as sales of refrigerators rose (by 1964 one for every four homes). Even intransigent husbands began to relinquish their God-given privileges and performed a few domestic tasks in a situation where, as everywhere else in the West, that symbol of bourgeois status and female exploitation, the underpaid *bonne*, was threatened with extinction. The television and telephone, like the vacuum cleaner, the washing machine, and the automobile, were transforming the lives of Frenchwomen of many classes. And though women of a certain station have always been unsurpassed for chic, any tourist in France after 1945 would notice remarkable progress year by year in the appearance of the general female populace. Mass production in the garment industry, development of the cosmetic industry, and high-pressure advertising in the expanding mass media held out the desired image, which a booming industry rendered increasingly attainable.

A society so rightly solicitous of its womenfolk's well-being did not entirely neglect the principal breadwinner. But although men profited no less by the automobile, were entertained as much by television, and were increasingly aware of the delights of bathtubs and showers, indoor water closets, and the dubious pleasures of packaged foods, their situation changed less dramatically than that of their women. Legally there was less to win; domestically there was more to lose. If men still filled the municipal councils and the national legislature, peopled the administration and staffed the schools, they also continued to bear arms, support the burden of taxpaying and, on the average, bring home pay envelopes markedly less fat than those of the working population in the United States. Small shopkeepers resisted innovations tending to eliminate their independent but inefficient activity. Many men not enjoying the freedom and slavery of self-employment were slow to share in the profits of an expanding economy. All the same, the conditions of life were better. Strikes and demonstrations, though sometimes bitter and violent, lacked the brooding character of class war which existed before 1939. The attitudes of labor and management had evolved; the role of the state was less partial and the cause of social welfare no longer in dispute. Social mobility existed in France, but although the sunny Côte d'Azur might be host to the vacationing industrialist, the shopkeeper, and the worker, their worlds remained an infinite distance apart.

There was a constant drain of the rural population to the expanding cities of France (1.3 million in 1955-1962). Despite François Mauriac's dictum that "Cybèle has more worshippers in France than Christ," the lure of the city did not diminish. Yet when the traveler quit the sprawling suburbs of Paris he might be pardoned for concluding falsely that France remained a predominantly rural paradise. Of the total of 136 million acres, 112 were devoted to agriculture. More than half of French farmers worked their own lands; one-third were tenants; the rest were *métayers* (share tenants or sharecroppers). The basic unit remained the family farm (from 12 to 120 acres, averaging about 36.3). Two-thirds of the French farms covered only 15 per cent of the country's farmland, and a few great estates covered very large areas. Beyond rural exodus, the most significant feature after 1945 was mechanization of agriculture and agricultural cooperation.

In the first years of the Fifth Republic half a million tractors existed where there were 30,000 in 1939. Buying on credit invaded the country-side; the truck replaced the mule; the television aerial became ubiquitous. As mass-produced goods filtered into the village, the rural artisan declined. Mechanization led many young people to seek employment in a newly created rural branch of industry, or to commute long distances to the city. Physical mobility of this kind, plus the invasion of the countryside by summer vacationers, tended to break down rural insularity. Among the farmers themselves there was increasing readiness to work together for common interests. An increasing articulateness found expression not through elected representatives but through direct action. With agricultural schools, research institutes, and experimental stations developing, and with the Government abetting modernization of techniques and seeking markets outside France, the old image of the narrow-minded, wholly insular peasant culture of France was at least on the wane.

Whatever its destination, French society was on the move. Not more than a generation ago some Frenchmen were looking longingly back to the *belle époque*, golden years before the catastrophe of 1914-1918. This nostalgia was dying. The very old might still remember sadly other days and other styles. But France in the 1960s looked forward. A greater mood of hopefulness was to be seen among the working class, spurred on by the fact of some material gain, the successes of collective action, by increased leisure and more accessible entertainment and travel. Factory workers were less cramped, less doctrinally militant, less bitter. The machine-shop uni-form was less a social badge or political indicator than a utilitarian con-venience. Moderately prosperous middle-class people who had always gone to stay with country cousins for the holidays now inspected the isles of Greece or tramped through Edinburgh Castle, skied at St. Moritz or even ventured to Leningrad. Some were so curious as to venture to America. Personal and corporate horizons had broadened; the unprogressive peasant was disappearing, the blinkered urban provincial decreasing.

Still the barriers of a far from equalitarian educational system impeded accessibility to the mythical "careers open to talent." An unjust distribu-tion of the national wealth perpetuated social rifts. French society con-tinued to observe rites and distinctions, which no older society ever re-nounces all at once. Attitudes of suspicion toward foreigners, of crippling pride in one's own systems and habits remained to give character to this society, while languishing in the assaults of the generalized western culture of the post-1945 world. France, as President de Gaulle so often insisted, must be France. Happily, this was so, and no one observing this society doubted its quality and its distinctiveness.

Government and Politics

Strong, prosperous, healthy, and moving forward, the Fifth Republic nevertheless presented an uncertain picture politically. How serious its condition was might be difficult to say, for across the political structure of the state lay the shadow of Charles de Gaulle. The heroic responsibilities borne by this man after 1958 had almost completely obscured the political state of mind of the people. They had welcomed him back, not unanimously but with a sense of colossal relief. During the Second World War, de Gaulle had imposed his will to represent France upon Frenchmen and the wartime allied powers; and then, refusing to play the political game as the Republic had so long played it, had withdrawn into reflection, abortive political action, and a long vigil of bitter expectancy. In the summer of 1958 France took him back on his own terms, gave him the authority he demanded, not because she trusted him more for the passage of a dozen years (his popularity at the close of 1957 was low), but because the hour was late. He was asked to save the Republic from the consequences of its divisions, irresponsibilities, illusions; he promised vaguely to bind up its fresh wounds and reconcile its opposites. As it turned out, he could only save France from total chaos, and there were to be moments when it seemed as if this staggering task alone was beyond even his strength.

His success by the summer of 1962 had delivered the nation fully into his hands, and he was virtually free to give it the direction he wished. No other political voice could seriously challenge his. Those who dared stand against him or make proposals counter to his, even in private, were stingingly rebuked in public. The whole radio and television apparatus was in his control. An observer might have been puzzled by the passivity with which all this had been accepted by the French people. The nation had never been Gaullist, and there was no reason to think it became so after 1958. Yet repeatedly it accepted de Gaulle. Mass apathy is a difficult condition to determine and to account for. How can one measure the shouts and cries of an enthusiastic crowd in one provincial town square against the sullenly shuttered windows of a village through which the presidential caravan passes at speed? All that was certain was that the alternatives to de Gaulle did not seem realistic or attractive. And following the President's stunning election victory in November 1962, political opposition to him was almost totally eclipsed. The mass of the nation was ready to follow wherever he led.

By that date parliamentary institutions in France had not been in such unhappy straits in a century. Condemned by the record of 24 cabinets set up and cast down in the fourteen years after the Liberation, parliament had lost the public confidence. It had failed to alter the Third Republic's device of government by means of shifting alliances. Ministerial instability postponed decisions and encouraged military and civil proconsuls in the Empire to make policy without reference, or in flagrant opposition, to Paris. The authority of the legislature and of the executive branch declined;

the plight of the French State grew more embarrassing. Opinion was almost unanimous in condemning the incoherence of the system. By the summer of 1958 parliament's store of credit was close to being exhausted. Events thereafter offered few occasions to build it up again. The President cultivated certain parliamentarians privately, but he seldom lost an opportunity publicly to denigrate the parliamentary regime. The politicians of the old parties were driven farther from the cabinet, their places being taken by outsiders. Whatever he intended for France once he had left office, the Chief of State clearly had no wish to revive what he called the "regime of misfortune."

Many expected that parliament would assert itself once the war in Algeria came to an end. This did not happen. Instead the National Assembly was overwhelmed by deputies proclaiming allegiance to de Gaulle. Their election successes in 1962 made him the greatest vote-getter in French history and confirmed the subordination of the legislature. The quasi-presidential regime seemed firmly established, dependent upon a man who proclaimed himself "guarantor of the destiny of France and the Republic, entrusted therefore with heavy duties and possessing extensive rights." No republican ever conducted himself more regally; no authoritarian had ever been so self-denying concerning possible political opposition rising against him; no Chief of State ever dealt so severely with the Army and at the same time was so careful of its well-being and sensitive to its misfortunes. Though immensely contemptuous of ordinary men, de Gaulle paradoxically drew strength from the crowds he constantly sought out in the towns and villages of France. Capable of treating his closest collaborators as mere servants, he used them as lightning conductors for public displeasure. He revealed only what he wished to reveal. Oracular ambiguity was his chosen weapon and a lofty romantic mood his ultimate refuge. No ruler of France ever had a more profound sense of mission. Few had more spectacular successes—certainly not when hedged about, as even Charles de Gaulle was hedged about, by the institutions of a modern constitutional system.

So large did this President loom that it was possible to forget the existence of other political institutions in the Fifth Republic. Increase of the executive power has been a continuous process under every French regime, but the constitution of 1958 established no dictatorship. Being invested as the last Premier of the Fourth Republic in June of that year, de Gaulle promised to guarantee in the new constitution he would submit to the nation the principles of universal suffrage, separation of powers, and governmental responsibility to the legislature. His own tenure of office as President was to suggest the limited value of his promise to maintain complete separation between the offices of Chief of State and Prime Minister, but it was far from certain that his successor would have any such control over the Prime Minister as his extraordinary character and prestige gave him. Even though parliament had by 1962 been reduced to a condition of extreme weakness, no constitutional text forbade the revival of a more active role once the presidential Elysée Palace was occupied by a lesser figure, the Hotel Matignon by a more independent head of government, and the Palais Bourbon by an Assembly majority owing nothing to vague but crucial attachment to the charismatic first President of the Fifth Republic. Whether this would be a constructive role, breaking with the irresponsible record of the Third and Fourth Republics, when parliament terrified governments by destroying them or threatening to do so, was quite another matter. What might happen once public opinion broke free from its apathy under de Gaulle (or its instinctive reaction during every crisis to follow him, when he threatened resignation, rather than the deputies who had become the scapegoat for the nation's misfortunes) no one could predict.

But the evaporation of this majority support in the nation would create a new situation. Both President and parliament could claim a national mandate by virtue of their election. In the event of differences of interpretation of this mandate, however, the position of the Prime Minister (chosen by the President, responsible to the legislature) would be both delicate and potentially far more powerful than had been realized under de Gaulle. No President could ever again be so aloof from mere politics, no parliament so supine or frustrated. Doubtless the nation approved this strengthening of the offices of Chief of State and Prime Minister, and those who filled them after de Gaulle and his servants would not readily relinquish their potential authority. Much of the future of the regime rested on the extent to which France would be capable of achieving a social and political consensus. In the 1960s it was not at all clear that the Fifth Republic was closer to this attainment than the Third and Fourth had been. Public opinion was supine. The failure of parties to regroup promised further parliamentary incoherence. On the far Left, if not on the far Right, subsisted antidemocratic blocs, hostile to the regime. The Socialists were reluctant to overcome internal divisions, to live down their compromises under both the Fourth and Fifth Republics, and to adopt a less doctrinaire approach. The Radicals and their neighbors remained casualties of their own civil wars of the Fourth Republic, looking both forward and backward. The Popular Republicans, likewise victims of the disintegration of the center, could only hope to profit tomorrow from the collapse of Gaullism. What the massive bloc of Gaullists would stand for after de Gaulle was impossible to guess. Short of some constitutional revision, there could be no return to the Assembly excesses of the Fourth Republic. Moreover, the country would be unlikely to tolerate them. And yet the revival of parliamentary life was certain, and the prospect at least conceivable of fresh, acrimonious multiparty struggles which could make the Gaullist era appear splendidly restful by comparison.

Foreign Policy

The mysteries of the French political system, especially under the Third and Fourth Republics, doubtless sprang from inherent intricacies not easily grasped by those accustomed to political practices in the English-speaking world. But the mysteries of French foreign policy were more obviously the result of failure on the part of outside observers to try to see things as they appeared to the French. If proud nations never make easy partners, their sensitivity is bound to be keener when they are on the way up from misfortune, and when at the same time they are being stripped of those imperial trappings which somehow had survived the major misfortune. Such was the case of France, struck down in 1940 on her own battlefields and liberated four years later, only to fail to master that imperial revolt suffered by every colonial nation, but which her own humiliation made all the more desirable to overcome. It is the tragedy of the international state system that the ambitions of nations, however comprehensible and valid in their own context and terms, do not often coincide. And it was the fate of the French after 1945 to have to make their way against a tide of opinion in the English-speaking world, which quite failed to accept or even understand the premises from which they started. Errors, misunderstandings, and stupidities occurred on every side, of course, but it may be that France was too severely condemned for a policy of self-interest which, after all, every state must follow in a world where there is no arbiter but the small voice of reason and the ultimate reality of brute force.

After the Napoleonic epic the French tended to stay at home in Europe. Although they were gradually committed to an active colonialism in the nineteenth century, they had no enthusiasm for it as a people and they became emotionally involved in it only as it approached its dramatic end. If they succumbed to war in Europe in 1854 and 1870, they resisted the temptation more often. Secure as a great people, concerned with their own social and political problems, they sought friends and allies before 1914, but no trial of strength. Yet having been forced to fight, having survived at frightful cost, they believed themselves robbed of the guarantees in victory which alone could strengthen them, given their obvious condition of relative decline among the great states. So they went forward bearing a burden of international responsibility implied by the victory of 1918 out of all proportion to their physical strength or their moral commitment to the task. Whatever may be the just distribution of blame for the collapse of the European democracies in the following twenty years, the French found themselves reluctantly consigned to a struggle which swiftly turned to catastrophe. They went down to defeat largely unaided by their friends and former allies. They were rescued largely by the efforts of those same forces. The task of restoring France to her rightful place as a power was thus to be doubly difficult, not least because the principal victors of 1945 were agreed that France was "finished" for some time to come and would have to work her passage back.

Liberated, she asserted her views as if never defeated, but the attempt to reestablish her authority in Europe by dismantling the German state was as unsuccessful in 1945 as it had been in 1919. Any hope that Great Britain would bind herself closely to continental Europe was equally ill-founded. The Soviet threat, domestic and international, both denied France an ally in the East and guaranteed the reemergence of a strong Germany. Thus France had no choice but to seek out Europe, a course urged upon her by certain internationally-minded Frenchmen, the reluctant British, and the exasperated Americans who sought both to shore up Europe against the Russian thrust and to assist Europeans to revive and help themselves. But Europe meant the West German Republic, and although it was not difficult to enter into close economic relations with the Germans, the French hung back from military agreements. The result was browbeating from Washington and London and a renewed humiliation of France. And when finally in 1955 she accepted the military agreements involving Germany and the principle of the European Common Market, and an eventual European Community in the Rome Treaties of 1957, her commitment to a series of forlorn and debilitating colonial wars was robbing the state of coherence and the nation of authority both in Europe and in the rest of the world. The Fourth Republic never resolved these problems. It suffered criticism from outside for the costly battle to retain part of its empire and for failure to contribute to the defense of the western world; it moved toward internal schism and even collapse into civil war.

The irony was that this incipient collapse of the French state in 1958 threatened at the moment when the economic and financial condition of the country had vastly improved, when the European idea had gained considerable ground, and when the nation had begun seriously to contemplate a negotiated end to the imperial dilemma. Indeed it was this threat to end the war in Algeria that precipitated the Fourth Republic's collapse, opening the way for General de Gaulle. Thus he inherited both the strength and the weakness of the previous regime, and turned both to account. Rallying the majority of a now profoundly worried people as no one had done before, he mastered civil and military disobedience and set out to reconstitute the authority of France *and* of Europe. Americans who hoped that de Gaulle would bring the Fifth Republic to accept a heavier part of the defense of the West were doomed to disenchantment. The General served notice that French power must be properly restored before being placed in the service of a redefined Atlantic Alliance, no less after the conclusion of the Algerian war than before. Renouncing neither the United Nations nor the North Atlantic Treaty Organization, he badgered both and refused to fulfill France's obligations to them. In effect he called the American bluff of threatening "agonizing reappraisal," which had so humiliated the Fourth Republic, and, secure in the conviction that the United States would not withdraw from Europe for some time to come, actively set about to awaken Europe to its potential strength and independence of the Americans, and to accustom Europeans to the idea of a renewed French political, military, and cultural primacy.

Utterly skeptical of supranational hopes and schemes, he believed deeply in the future of the nation state, the identity of France's fortunes with those of a great Europe of fatherlands, and the necessity for Europe, led by France, to constitute a great third power between the Anglo-American and Communist groupings. Suspicious of American intentions in Europe, determined to break American military control of the free world's defense system, the General nevertheless lined up with the United States in the confrontation with the USSR over Cuba. Intransigent about western rights in Berlin, he nevertheless believed that with time, firmness, and patient handling Russia might be brought to withdraw from eastern Europe as the United States would from western Europe. The Fifth Republic was practicing a tough, completely cynical "cabinet" foreign policy. The *politique de grandeur* had nothing Napoleonic about it in the sense of seeking an imperial control of Europe. It sought rather to arouse France from her long lethargy, to quicken an old Jacobin concept of being not only master of one's destiny but the rescuer of Europe from the toils of former defeats and present external controls. While it was made possible by American commitments to Europe, it insisted upon American sins and errors, relied upon American strength to strike attitudes of defiance of the Soviet Union which found favor in Germany, and used the momentary good relations with Germany to underpin rejection of a British partnership in Europe because England was bound primarily to the American notion of an Atlantic Community.

At once intensely French and European, the General's foreign policy was conducted with a daring and brilliance his successors might well lack. But it was inconceivable that the goals of this policy, rooted in the historic tradition of the national past, would be abandoned. His successors could fail (as de Gaulle could fail), if they (or he) blundered by giving clear proof that the interests of France were being pursued at the expense of Europe. They could fail also if such a policy were pressed to the point where a French consensus refused to follow it, feeling it to be harmful not only to Europe but to France herself. It had not been unchallenged within France; opposition might well continue in proportion to the degree of conflict incurred with European states or the United States. Finally, this *politique de grandeur* could truly become the policy of the Fifth or any later Republic only when the domestic structure of the regime had become regularized, when a coherent political system and a rationalized economic and social system had been brought into being.

"The French nation is at peace," the President declared in January 1964. "It is at peace within itself, where the political struggles have no profound reality, where subversion has been dispelled, where the social divisions are becoming blurred thanks to the general prosperity and to a growing and necessary equity in distributing the fruits of national progress. . . . This situation, so new for France, allows her to consider and deal serenely with the important matters concerning her." In some measure this was true. In some measure it was all too true. In some measure it was merely what Charles de Gaulle wished to be true. But it could never be entirely true. One day the nation would have to reopen the national dialogue at every level and assume responsibilities set aside for many years. Though the Republic had been saved, the way, as always, lay uphill.

TWO

LONG JOURNEY FROM THE PAST

"Les occasions nous font connaître aux autres, et encore plus à nous-mêmes."

Sometimes the French seem infinitely self-regarding. What, one wonders, interests them more than their own history? Not a year passes without a spate of new popular histories and historical biographies. The tourist wandering from bookstall to bookstall along the Seine is struck by the repetitive titles on Louis XV or the ill-fated King of Rome, on the Renaissance splendors of the reign of Francis I or the apparently tranquil harmonies of the pre-1914 era. Some offer the "inside" story of a royal mistress's influence or purport to solve some historical mystery; many are indicative merely of a normal commercial urge; few will survive as literature, biography, or history. Like the more serious and more solid historical scholarship, which flourishes in contemporary France, they reflect the preoccupation with the national historical image.

It is a truism that the past weighs on the French. Historic quarrels have been astonishingly echoed in present politics. Current problems have been hopelessly distorted by being misinterpreted in terms of issues of former days. Perhaps more than most peoples the French have considered themselves and the rest of the world in the light of the past. Americans no doubt invoke the memory of Jefferson, Lincoln, or Wilson; there are Britons who recall Cromwell, Pitt, or Gladstone. But one of the numerous premiers of the Third Republic actually sought to achieve a physical resemblance to Danton. At least until 1939, possibly as late as 1958, an inflexibility stemming from attachment to tradition dogged the French regimes. It may be that, while the historic moorings of the nation remain secure, France is prepared to consider her problems more pragmatically. And yet what statesman in the long annals of this land ever evoked more movingly than did the founder of the Fifth Republic the dominant symbols of the common past: "night falling over Notre Dame, the majesty of evening at Versailles, the Arc de Triomphe in the sun, conquered colors shuddering in the vault of the Invalides"?

Beginnings

Origins are imprecise. The tendency of the history of France, like its time of beginning, must always be a matter of interpretation. Faced with a now immense historiography and denied any gift of foresight, living in a century that perhaps dreams of larger societies but continues to light tapers on the altar of the national state, we may say simply that the history of France has been a quest for unity. So obvious a theme scarcely distinguishes the French past from that of any other nation, but surely the recurrent schisms in France have by their periodicity and intensity marked out this quest as being more elusive than that of any other great people. No one can say quite when it began, but most would agree that it became the pursuit of the kings of France. And this unfinished quest was their legacy to the many regimes that followed them.

This dominant tendency can hardly be discerned in the most distant past. In the first millennium before Christ, France was a crossroads of agricultural peoples, migrant and diverse, until Celtic invaders assumed the role of overlords and imposed some rough common culture. In time they gave the land its name of Gaul and its various and quarreling inhabitants the dialects which approximated unity of tongue. But it was the Romans who first imposed a measure of administrative unity and urban civilization upon this tribal people. Descendants of the Greek merchants from Asia Minor who had founded a trading settlement at Marseille about 600 B.C. called in the Romans to protect them against marauding tribes, and a century later, in 52 B.C., the Roman governor of Gaul, Julius Caesar, defeated the local opposition led by Vercingetorix at the battle of Alisia. Thus protection of Gaul from outside invaders turned to conquest. A vulgarized Latin tongue spread across the land century by century and the beginnings of Christian conversion were known before the great Roman Empire itself began to crumble and the occupation forces were withdrawn. These linguistic and religious innovations, together with the network of roads marked out across France as far as the Channel coast, were the memorial to this first attempt to impose unity.

The barbarian invasions of western Europe caused a breakdown of such elementary coherence as the Roman centuries had brought. But by about A.D. 500 one of these northern tribes, the Salian Franks, had subdued most of France, settled down in the north and east, embraced an alliance proffered by the Church and accepted its faith, and begun to extend Frankish rule and the Christian religion by fire and the sword. Clovis, their king, was thus the founder of the first great French dynasty, the Merovingian. But there was no notion of a centralized monarchy. The Frankish people were unknown to the Gallo-Roman tribes who lived across much of southern and western France. This diversity was increased by the partitioning of Clovis's domains among his heirs. Constant strife and a long line of weak Merovingian kings destroyed the house, increased political decentralization, and finally in 752 gave rise to a new dynasty from the ranks of the powerful Mayors of the Palace. The most famous of these Carolingian monarchs was Charlemagne. Crowned Emperor at Christmas, A.D. 800, he was a militant ally of the Church, and the short-lived ruler of a "united Europe." Under his rule industry, commerce, and religion flourished. There was an elementary dispensation of royal justice, but neither linguistic nor administrative unity. And the area of France was only a part of a great Frankish empire, which fell apart after Charlemagne's death. Thus his empire would become historically more relevant to the idea of a united Europe than of a united France, though in the second half of the twentieth century the one might be thought of as closely connected with the other.

After 814 the imperial power dwindled. Charles the Great's descendants divided and subdivided his domain. Norse invasions and regional revolts troubled the grandson ruling that part of the empire most closely approximating what is now France. The process of politico-military decentralization continued to sap the royal authority, increase the power of local lords, and give rise to the loose arrangements of territorial possession and military dependency known as feudalism. Lords and vassals presided over a population of farmers in a society sharply divided into classes according to function. Only the most nominal legal formality bound the disparate provinces together. The idea of France scarcely existed as the first Christian millennium drew to its close, with the last Carolingians confined to the small lands around Laon in the northeast. But, as it happened, the dispersal of authority had run its course with the Carolingian line. In 987 a usurper, Hugh Capet, Duke of Francia, was elected king by his peers. Francia was large, but the Duke's control of it limited. The land was wealthy, but allegiance to his person was uncertain and revenues few. Yet from this unlikely center was to grow a united kingdom of France.

The Church assisted this new royal house to establish its claim, to survive the challenge of powerful vassals, and, in collaboration with the growing urban classes, to extend direct control over the whole country. The Capetians profited from quarrels among their nobles which prevented any combined revolt powerful enough to overthrow the monarchy, and they annexed their vassals' lands as the opportunity presented itself. They offered royal protection against noble depredations and steadily increased the extent and sway of royal justice emanating from the town of Paris. Thus the king's lands and authority steadily encroached upon the territory and independence of his vassals. The Albigensian heresy in the south provoked Rome to preach a crusade in 1209 and thus opened the way to royal destruction of a dangerously powerful provincial autonomy. The territorial encroachments of the English in the west were less conclusively dealt with. The precise territorial limits of the realm, especially in the east, remained undefined. But economically the kingdom prospered. With the growth of a measure of administrative authority, commerce revived. Lands were cleared, grain and wine production was revolutionized, wool and cloth manufacture flourished, and towns proliferated as the merchant and

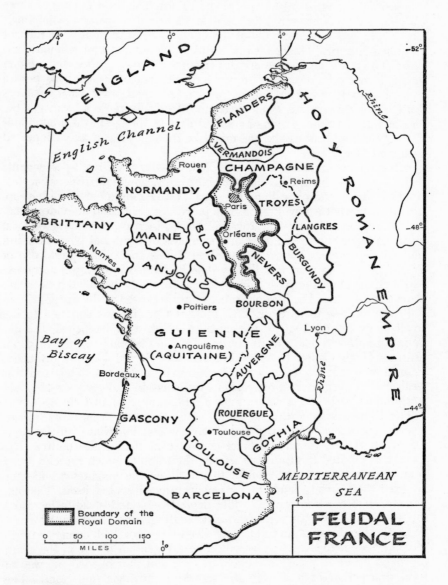

FEUDAL
FRANCE

Boundary of the
Royal Domain

0   50   100   150
MILES

artisan classes expanded. Not later than 1302, representatives of these towns met with nobles and clergy in an Estates-General. Until 1328 the Capetians continued to wear down the feudal power, sometimes disciplined their ally the Church and insisted upon the primacy of the secular rule, created the beginnings of a modern administrative system, crusaded against infidel and heretic, and held off the English. It was not possible for them to impose a uniformity of customs or language upon France. Though Paris had the original palace of the Louvre, the beginnings of a great university, and a splendid cathedral, it was still only the center of a great royal domain and not yet the capital of a nation.

Capetian and Valois

Early in the fourteenth century, the House of Capet, its direct line exhausted, handed the kingdom over to a younger branch of the family. The Valois kings inherited an established but by no means wholly unchallenged dynastic system. In 1338, these new rulers were launched upon a sea of troubles when their efforts to bring still semi-independent provinces, such as Aquitaine, under their control. Here they collided with English ambitions, and there ensued a hundred years of intermittent war. Even worse than the cessions of territory made to the English before the final French victory in 1453 were the riots, revolts, and civil war the monarchy endured. Monarchical incompetence caused aristocratic rivalries and violence, treasonable collaboration with the enemy, and the loss of Paris itself by the French king. By 1422 the Valois inheritance was sadly divided, the land devastated, the population starved and butchered. Thereafter, however, owing to the extraordinary appearance of the Maid of Orleans, and the reorganization of the king's army, to English domestic difficulties and the end of English alliance with the Duke of Burgundy, the tide turned. By mid-century, of all the English conquests only Calais remained. And in the end, if the war had been paid for by the common people, it was lost by the French nobility (defeated in battle, superseded by mercenaries, replaced by commoners, antiquated by gunpowder). The triumph of the crown over foreigner and vassal was apparently complete. Its fiscal, administrative, and territorial reach had lengthened. Even the economic ravages of the war and the mid-fourteenth century Black Death were being obliterated by 1453. Despite fresh industrial and commercial rivalries from other lands, reviving France competed successfully. The great crisis of the Hundred Years War was overcome, and the slow progress toward unity resumed.

Over the next century the House of Valois concentrated upon putting down the dukes of Burgundy and Brittany and incorporating their lands in France, upon fixing something approaching a royal absolutism upon the country (curbing the Papacy and the Church in France, opposing democratic tendencies in the Estates-General), and upon engaging in wars in Italy. By the time Francis I died in 1547, after a brilliant reign of epic triumphs and defeats in the field, France was a great state ruled by a powerful prince. The process of reducing feudalism, subordinating the clergy, and attaching the bourgeoisie to the royal authority was far advanced. Royal power had been challenged by antitax leagues and rebellious townsmen, local assemblies and dissident aristocracy. It had dealt successfully with each. But a period of great personal weakness in the line of succession in the sixteenth century, along with a vast European religious upheaval, seemed swiftly to reverse the movement toward unity that had characterized the French past. The premature death of Henry II in a tournament left his wife Catherine de Médicis to struggle with the politico-religious agitation of the Reformation era. A quarter of a century before, Francis I had vainly ordered the heresy exterminated. After 1559 the temptation to seize power during Catherine's regency, and the various failings of her wretched sons, condemned the kingdom to a generation of strife. A triangular contest ensued, bedeviled by fanaticism and the impotencies of this ambitious woman's unlikely offspring.

From Civil War to Absolutism

The conclusion of a long period of warfare with the Habsburg Empire in that same year 1559 was the signal for renewed attacks upon the Huguenots of France, Protestant followers of the exiled John Calvin. Both noble and bourgeois from the manufacturing towns of the south and west, the Huguenots defended themselves after royal efforts to find a solution collapsed under Catholic militancy and Protestant demands for liberty of worship. From 1562 to 1598 some eight religious wars occurred, fanatic and murderous, in which foreigners took a hand on behalf of Catholic or Protestant, in which Catholic and Protestant joined to drive out the foreigner, and in which much of France was laid waste. In the extraordinary welter of events, the Valois line ran out with the death of Catherine's last son; a Catholic faction masked its royal ambition as the defense of popular sovereignty and elective monarchy; and the Protestant prince Henry of Navarre, the lawful heir to the vacant throne, finally triumphed as the supporter of divine-right monarchy. Moderate Catholics rallied to him against the destructive fanaticism of Catholic extremists and their Spanish supporters. Though adopting the Catholic confession for political reasons, Henry granted full religious and civil liberties to the Huguenots, guaranteeing them with fortified towns. And thus, having come to the brink of total disruption, the most responsible leaders of France closed ranks, placed the survival of the State before particularist ambition and religious conviction, and rallied to the royal standard. In all this long crisis, it should be noted, the various initiatives lay with the crown and the nobility. The Estates-General (which had first represented both town and countryside in the meeting at Tours, 1484) met infrequently, developed no taxation or legislative authority, and thus gave no leadership to the country. Such unity as France knew by 1610, when Henry IV was struck down by an assassin, was largely the result of the imposition of authority from above.

In the time of fresh troubles which opened up thereafter, it was thanks to the wisdom and ruthlessness of two servants of the crown, Cardinals Richelieu and Mazarin, that the monarchy retained its position and the State its unity. Identifying religious liberty with political powers independent of the royal government, the Huguenots fought off persecution but were stripped of their peculiar privileges of self-government and self-defense. The factious nobility were disciplined and put down. The development of a royal army and a royal administration continued. Increasingly, all roads led to Paris. Against this all-pervading centralized authority of the State occurred a last revolt, the Fronde, from 1648 to 1653. A confused episode, part aristocratic, part bourgeois, an unlikely coalition of nobles and magistrates resentful of the trend toward absolutism, the Fronde collapsed in incoherence. It was the last serious challenge to the monarchy before the outbreak of the great revolution in the next century And it was the prelude to that age of splendor and direct royal rule associated with the reign of Louis XIV.

The legend of Henry IV in French history is that of a wise, fatherly man, slightly rakish but benign, skeptical in religion but solicitous of his subjects' welfare, not very convincingly identified with some vague "Great Design" for Europe; above all, the unifier and healer after a generation of civil wars. The legend of Louis XIV—king at the age of 5, assuming direct control of the state at the age of 24, on Mazarin's death in 1661—is of a great and industrious monarch, a warrior who expanded the eastern frontiers of France, a celebrated patron of all the arts, the creator of a brilliant court the like of which the world had never seen and would never see again, the very symbol of the *ancien régime* at its greatest, when France was the center of the civilized world. Whatever his faults and failures toward the end of the longest reign in French history, Louis has appeared as the finest expression of the monarchical principle, and his memory was long invoked by those Frenchmen unable to accept the end of monarchy in their country. To them this golden age appeared prestigious and harmonious, characterized by unity and firm direction, graced by achievement in the arts, socially stable, militarily secure.

The reality was of course more complex. Absolutism certainly flourished and criticism made itself heard with difficulty. Particularist provincial, municipal, and religious liberties were largely put down. But if the Huguenots were persecuted and suppressed, many regional administrative, legal, and commercial institutions continued to survive and resist the unifying activities of the intendants appointed to guarantee order, dispense justice, and collect revenues. Mere distance and the problems of communication limited the royal power. Though the Estates-General was in eclipse, potential opposition continued to exist in the *parlements* of France, where the royal edicts must be registered to have the force of law. The various councils might offer only advisory opinions to the king, but even the hard-working and capable Louis XIV could not oversee all the business of state. The extension and stabilization of France's frontiers were successful;

the attempt to dominate western Europe was ultimately ruinous. Even the constructive achievements in industry, agriculture, and commerce begun by Henry IV did not provide a foundation adequate to so variegated a striving as Louis and his ministers pursued. Richelieu and Louis's intendant of finance, Colbert, worked to build the maritime, colonial, and commercial strength of France; the overweening military commitments in Europe did not serve such a policy, and the country was stretched to breaking point. All the same, France under Louis XIV was undeniably the greatest power in Europe. Over-all, the cause of French unity was advanced.

Moreover, the French dominion in the realm of culture was secure. The legacy of the age was rich: the plays of Racine, Corneille, and Molière; the philosophy of Descartes and Pascal; the palaces and gardens of Le Brun, Mansart, and Le Nôtre; the music of Lully and Rameau; the canvases of Claude Lorrain, Poussin, and Le Nain; the wisdom of La Fontaine and Bayle. . . . These things would last and, long after Louis XIV and his times were only a glittering historical memory, they would become increasingly accessible to a nation, constituting an element of a unity still far from complete in the seventeenth century.

But there was another side to the coin. When he died in 1715, this mightiest of the kings of France left behind another legacy. Having reduced the nobility in power and political pretensions, he had nevertheless permitted them to retain privileged social status and financial immunity. Thus he failed both to eliminate their ambitions entirely and to set the State on a secure financial foundation. It is by no means certain that this was beyond his grasp. Complete religious uniformity and orthodoxy, however, was not his to impose, and his successor was to be troubled by outbreaks both of confessional quarrels and of disputes between the Church and civil authorities. Possibly most fateful of all was the continued existence of the *parlements*, relics from the thirteenth century, twelve in all, numbering about 2,000 magistrates, formerly middle-class lawyers but now aristocrats owing their place to birth and purchase. Led by the most important of them, the *parlement* of Paris, these venal institutions, with powers in the areas of religion, morals, commerce and industry, reasserted the claims their fear of Louis XIV had muted. The infancy of Louis XV and the consequent Regency after 1715 provided the initial opportunity for their activity; the incapacities of the mature king encouraged it; and the final disastrous financial straits of the crown under Louis XVI permitted them to bring the *ancien régime* to an end by 1789. In the name of Jansenism and the Gallican liberties of France, they opposed the Church. In the name of the rights of Frenchmen, they prevented reform by the central government. The criticism Louis XIV had known in the later years of his reign increased under his successors. And it was by no means confined to a still restive aristocracy which, led by these magistrates so lately translated from the Third, or common, Estate, sought to restrain the powers of the crown, hedge it about with aristocratic controls and provincial rights, in the memory of a well-balanced medieval constitution which in fact had never existed. The *parlements* fostered discontent, eroded the foundations of the Bourbon absolutism, and called the administration and the Church into question, but they really only turned to account the climate of opinion associated with the Enlightenment.

Enlightenment and Revolution

Eighteenth-century France is famous not only for its extension of the age of elegance that Louis XIV's reign had begun, but also for the literary movement of inquiry, criticism, and proposed reform that was known throughout Europe but best represented in France. The *philosophes*, heirs of such men as Bayle and Fénelon, were many and varied, as unlike as Voltaire and Rousseau. They were not of a single generation. Their social origins were not the same. Their purposes were many, their targets diverse. Some were well known, many quite obscure. If they had any common general attitude, it was probably this: that men ought to be governed by right reason, that what was not reasonable ought not to be tolerated, and that if human affairs were conducted properly by wise and reasonable men the prospects for a good life on earth would be far brighter than the world had ever known. Not all were critics of the social and political order; not all were enemies of absolutism; not all were friends of the poor, enemies of the rich. But some were. Their impact on their times has been much debated. Few, save ardent foes of the Revolution, would now hold them responsible for it. Many would insist that they helped to cause a general questioning of the structure of society and politics that made the Revolution thinkable by 1789. The influence of some of them in the course of the Revolution is certain. Whatever they were for their own times, they have seemed in retrospect to belong to that goodly company of enlightened men, articulate and literate, who dare question present practices and ridicule human follies and crimes, and who believe that the future can be made better in every way.

In those days, other voices seemed to prevail. The *philosophes* had their critics. The established order did not lack defenders. But the debate opened fresh fissures in the nation, and the struggle for authority moved on across the century. France lived on her capital, the State by financial expedients. The nobility sought power equivalent to their privilege; the middle classes, social status commensurate with their wealth and talents. The peasantry suffered an increasingly exiguous landlord class in search of higher incomes. Conditions varied greatly even among the vast mass of farmers, but evidently something was wrong in the kingdom. The most grievous losses were sustained in colonial wars with England; the power of the State ebbed; the brilliance of the court faded. By the time Louis XV, after not quite sixty years on the throne, rotted to his death in 1774 and the young Louis XVI committed France to the cause of the Thirteen Colonies, the monarchy was shakier than it had been in two centuries. If no revolutionary impulse could be discerned, a troubled mood of expectancy hung over the land. After so much discussion, so much protest against injustice, incapacity, and intolerance, the only question was: What kind of change, by whom, and for whom?

The great Revolution came in almost by the back door. It began long before the famous events of 1789. Though its reception may have been prepared, its nature and course were quite unforeseen. The nobles, who resisted all efforts of the crown to eliminate their financially privileged position, sought to curb the monarchy, but hardly to destroy it. The bourgeoisie, who refused to continue loans to the State, wanted a rationalization of government and a constitutional settlement recognizing itself, but no collapse of the conservative monarchical system. They combined to bring the king to summon the Estates-General, which had not met since 1614, but their purposes were quite at odds. Having achieved this royal acquiescence, they immediately fell to struggling for control of the parliament thus called for the spring of 1789. The peasant masses of the nation hoped for relief from tax burdens, royal or noble, through the beneficence of the king; they did not dream of cutting off his head. The monarchy hoped for fresh monies from the Estates-General; it was not ready to consider the fundamental rearrangement of the social and political structure of France. Within weeks or months the magnitude of what was happening became clear.

When the deputies of the three estates assembled at Versailles that May, the ephemeral bourgeois-noble alliance had fallen apart. Confronted with the crown's insistence upon sitting and voting by estates, and thus by the impossibility of making their double representation prevail against clergy and aristocracy, the middle-class deputies stunningly announced the doctrine of popular sovereignty and their own mandate to speak for the nation. In a moment the theoretical underpinning of the monarchy was assaulted mortally. Perhaps the crown might have saved itself by dispersing these rebellious deputies with armed force. But it hesitated and capitulated, ordering all three estates to sit together. Thus the claims of the Third Estate triumphed, the neo-feudal dreams of the aristocracy vanished, and the historic foundations of the regime crumbled before the determined lawyers and their liberal allies of the first two estates. When the Paris crowd swept through the streets on July 14 to storm the Bastille and when rural burnings of title-deeds and murders of government officials indicated peasant determination to destroy agrarian oppression, the monarchy survived but the three-class division of the country quickly disappeared. In all these actions, in the Declaration of the Rights of Man and of the Citizen, and in the constitution reluctantly accepted by Louis in September 1791, the very basis of the French community was changed. Not common ties of loyalty to the crown, but the dogma of liberty, equality, and fraternity bound the nation. In fact, however, the search for unity was as incomplete as before, and fresh divisions loomed ahead.

At first it was a middle-class revolution, supported by insurrection in the capital and disturbances in the provinces. The objective was creation of a moderate constitutional monarchy. Why the first settlement of 1789-

1791 proved short-lived will always be a matter for debate. Partly it was that the Assembly, brought to Paris and working under the eye of the radical city, slipped to the left. Partly it was the suspicions evoked by the obvious conservatism of the deputies of 1789. Partly it was the revolution's failure to solve the financial crisis, the bread problem, and the problem of an untrustworthy monarch encouraging outside intervention by fellow monarchs hostile to these events. The need for revenues occasioned confiscation of Church lands, nationalization of the clergy, and a total reorganization of the ecclesiastical structure. Thus were foreign fears heightened and the king's treasonable activity increased. Into this uncertain situation were injected new class fears, a more evident articulation of the advanced views of the Enlightenment, and the warlike counsels of *émigré* nobles who had fled France. Conservative Europe, led by the Emperor of Austria (brother of Queen Marie Antoinette), hesitated. But by the spring of 1792 the loosely associated group in the French Assembly known as the Girondins had concluded that war would determine the real attitude of the king, destroy the *émigrés*, silence the dissident clerical and conservative elements in the country, and ruin their political rivals further to the left by rallying the people to a patriotic struggle.

It did not turn out that way. The French declaration of war on Austria resulted in military reverses, a still worsening economic situation, counterrevolutionary outbreaks in the provinces, and the triumph of political radicalism and popular extremism. By the end of 1792 the military situation had improved, but the monarchical experiment had collapsed in urban massacres, political strife, and creation of the new French Republic. Shortly, both Louis and his queen were sent to the guillotine, events that sickened Europe and revealed the unsuspected intensity of the storm that had so long loomed on the horizon. The year 1789 had separated forever the old world from the new. But the spilling of royal blood was no panacea. Western France was in rebellion, food shortages caused riots, the state was always financially stricken, and amidst cries of treachery and intrigue in the new parliament, the National Convention, the Girondins went down before the attack from the left-wing Jacobin party. By then, the late spring of 1793, renewed foreign invasion of France plus the internal dissidence had brought formation of the Revolutionary Tribunal and the Committee of Public Safety, which would use it to compel unity through terror. Backed by the capital, the Jacobin dictatorship (elected out of the Convention) led by Robespierre set about instituting a highly centralized military, financial, economic, and political reorganization of the country. Enforced by every means, this was the real Terror. Lasting until Robespierre's fall in the summer of 1794, it saved France from disruption and defeat.

Revolution to Empire

In five years the country had moved from the *ancien régime*, through a conservative constitutional settlement characterized by the rule of the well-

THE
NAPOLEONIC
EMPIRE
AT ITS HEIGHT

France and the Revolutionary acquisitions to 1799.

French acquisitions under Napoleon.

French satellite states under Napoleon.

0   200   400
MILES

to-do, to a radical left-wing dictatorship cowing the Convention and governing without a constitution. The pendulum had swung from central-ized to decentralized and back to highly centralized administration. The Revolution had moved steadily left. But military success in 1794 and the collapse of the Jacobin dictatorship brought a reaction. The highly demo-cratic constitution drawn up by the Convention in 1793 was never put into practice; it remained as a statement of radical republican goals and beliefs to haunt the nineteenth and twentieth centuries. The constitution of 1795 was far more moderate, and until 1799 France was ruled again by the moderates. So much history had of course thrown up enemies to the Right and to the Left. Intermittently the war with Europe continued; the civil war inside France was not mastered. Political quarrels, intrigues, financial difficulties, and frequent insurrectionary outbreaks finally wore down this regime of the Directory. Caught between the fires of disgruntled Jacobins and even more radical groups on the Left, and the clerical, royalist, peasant forces on the Right, the Directors were steadily more dependent on the new and powerful army of the Revolution. This instrument of a new ex-ternal ambition that had been awakened in the French people was hence-forth the arbiter of the situation. Called upon to quash an election or put down a municipal outbreak, quite apart from clearing France of the for-eigner and carrying the war into Italy or Egypt, it ended by exacting the price of military dictatorship in return for the guarantee of domestic tran-quility. The brilliant young general who intrigued with the Directors to achieve this outcome against the elected representatives of the nation in 1799 was Napoleon Bonaparte.

With this man—First Consul, Consul for Life, and finally in 1804 Em-peror of the French—the Revolution reached its climax and its end. Ten years of political and social experimentation had given the French material to interpret in a hundred ways for two centuries to come, as mere history, as politics, and as sociology. The debate on the Revolution, begun almost with its outbreak, would only intensify as the years went on. It was so rich an experience that every kind of argument could be drawn from its evidence. Ideologies scarcely foreshadowed then would claim ancestors from its kaleidoscopic events. Its proclaimed ideals of 1789—the sov-ereignty of the people, the liberty, equality, and fraternity of the individual —however interpreted or misinterpreted in its course, were to glow ever afterward in the history of France and of the western world. And by that light—or against it—much of the subsequent events of the nation was to be played out. But then, in 1799, it was clear only that the people were more or less willingly renouncing their revolutionary role in return for a guarantee of their major achievement. Bonaparte was to sum up the striving for unity by putting an end to politics, identifying himself with the will of the nation, and imposing the most highly centralized legal and administrative system that the French had ever known.

He did the things the kings of France, and the people themselves before him, had never been able to do: reform the finances of the State, regularize the situation of the Church within the State and grant freedom of worship, and to some great extent heal schism in the body social. Though he was guilty of violating many ideals of the Revolution by acts of intolerance, injustice, oppression, and simple inhumanity, this many-sided genius attached the nation to himself as no other ruler had ever done. Though he promised peace, he brought war, and the nation did not abandon him. A restless seeker after glory and a European hegemony for his adopted fatherland, the Corsican Emperor drove on through masterly campaigns to shatter the peace for a decade. He was seldom defeated, yet his victories were never final. To conservative Europe he represented the Revolution in arms. Losses were heavy, the dictatorship weighed on France. Opposition manifested itself among the political classes and brought reprisals. But on the whole he did not lose the loyalty of the rural masses. Though he abandoned them or their sons in Egypt, deserted them in the catastrophe of the Russian winter before Moscow, marched and countermarched them across the continent until the last fighting retreat over the borders of France itself in the spring of 1814, they stuck by him. After the exile on Elba, they followed him again in that romantic final episode that ended in rout and collapse. Sent to the South Atlantic, this extraordinary man, so full of glory and so wholly self-deceiving, relived his life for those around him and created the legend that would haunt the French nation long after he died on that miserable island in 1821.

Like the great Revolution itself, the Napoleonic episode would be a matter of much dispute. Possibly Bonaparte was the greatest ruler France ever knew. Certainly he appeared to both sum up and impose that unity in the general pursuit of which so much of the history of France had unfolded. That he was the Revolution, as he claimed, would be infinitely more difficult to propose. It was indeed not he who mirrored its complexities but the history of the country after he had gone.

THREE

TURBULENT ERA:

1814-1914

"Il doit y avoir une certaine proportion entre les actions et les desseins si on veut tirer tous les effets qu'elles peuvent produire."

The capital into which troops of the great allied coalition came that spring of 1814 was the heart of a unified state. Though about to be modestly rectified in two peace treaties, the boundaries of France had long since been established by her kings. Stripped of her revolutionary and Napoleonic conquest in Europe, she returned to them naturally. Though the Emperor had fallen, the centralized administrative apparatus remained; it was the logical extension of the former, imperfect royal bureaucracy, momentarily relaxed after 1789, tightened up by the Jacobin dictatorship, again slackened by the Directory, and then thoroughly reorganized and disciplined by Bonaparte. Regional variations prevailed, but the particularist legal, political, and economic institutions and customs, which had survived all through the *ancien régime,* were gone forever. In the millennium now ended the linguistic dichotomy of spoken Romance had disappeared, "Langue d'Oc" or "Provençal" giving way to the French which grew out of the dialect of the Ile de France in the north; from the seventeenth century the French language was assured of national acceptance, and although regional and local *patois* would continue to exist down through the twentieth century, the progress of education and growth of national information media assured an increasing uniformity of speech. Pockets of resistance, demonstrations of independence, celebrations of local customs, and the remembrance of the historic past suggested that the individualistic characteristics of this people had not died. But the patriotism proclaimed and demonstrated in the Revolution was a fact.

A definition of the national consensus in religious, social, economic, or political terms would, on the other hand, have been quite impossible. Not a little of the fascination of the Revolution derived from its mirroring every point of view. There were divine-right monarchists, constitutional monarchists, parliamentary monarchists. In the antimonarchical camp were conservative republicans terrified of the radicals and the popular masses behind them, survivors or heirs of the great purgings of 1793-1794; beyond the Jacobin radicals again were those who had taken the communist doctrines of the eighteenth century for their rough creed and who had momentarily looked to the ill-fated Babouvist conspiracy of 1796 as the instrument by which to destroy the bourgeois oligarchy that had replaced the aristocratic-monarchist regime. In the towns, and even in the country-side, there were the God-fearing and the godless, those who accepted the general optimism of the Enlightenment and those who condemned it as dangerous blasphemy. In short, France in 1814 remained greatly divided. It was a much more complicated matter than a struggle between the Red and the Black, or *"les deux Frances,"* and the nineteenth century was to underline the multiplicity of points of view which the collapse of the *ancien régime* and the revolutionary experience had brought to the surface.

Restoration

The political break of 1814 was not really forced upon France by the allies; it was not demanded by France herself, despite all the groans in the last months of the regime. Rather it was inflicted upon the country by Bonaparte's inability to abandon his conquests. Relentlessly he drove toward total defeat, making abdication inevitable and the recall of the Bourbons desirable. And thus, although there was *a* restoration there was no restoration of the prerevolutionary situation. Supported by the allies, summoned by opportunist politicians and a royalist-controlled press, the brother of the executed king styled himself "Louis, by the grace of God, King of France and Navarre." He accepted no conditions, but he granted them in a royal Charter: a two-chamber legislature; no taxation without legislative assent; equality before the law; trial by jury; judicial independence; freedom of person, press, and religion; recognition of the national debt, the titles, pensions, and honors of the Empire; confirmation of those who had bought nationalized lands; and the principle of social mobility. Louis XVIII in this manner sanctified the major part of the Revolution settlement. There was no going back, unless in mere ceremony. The Restoration was a mighty compromise with the Revolution, only slightly masked by this wise and weary monarch's "resumption" of his task "in the eighteenth year of our reign." Many had made their peace with the Revolution years before: returning *émigré* exiles, the Church itself in 1802. But even so tolerant a solution was bound to dissatisfy substantial sections of opinion: the quarreling republicans Bonaparte had silenced, the un-forgiving nobility and clergy, the veterans hit now by financial economies dictated by the State's circumstances. Whatever the new regime did would bring criticism and opposition. How slight was its serious support Napoleon's Hundred Days revealed in 1815. And the effect of that disastrous foray was the embitterment of fresh defeat, an obvious imposition of Louis on France by the allies, a punitive peace treaty, bloody reprisals in a White Terror, and such a reactionary Chamber of Deputies as made its dissolution on allied advice essential after the unlikely spectacle of this tiny extreme royalist political oligarchy's claiming the right of parliamentary government.

Louis XVIII never admitted the proposition. The fundamental question of where sovereignty lay remained clouded. The Revolution's basic assertion of popular sovereignty was not denied but ignored. Between the far Right and the far Left the king picked his cautious way, leaning to center Left and then to center Right, managing elections through the administrative system. The political class, composed of those paying the highest direct taxes, remained small; the opponents of the regime, from fanatic Ultras to secret societies, were many. The Government remained suspect on all sides. Yet this unimpressive regime either effected or presided over the recovery of France and her reemergence as a power in Europe. Although there were some political outrages and demonstrations, both left and right, a kind of balance was held. Though elections were managed and majorities acquired by the crown, the development of parliamentary practice was important in a land that had known nothing but the experiments of the Revolution. Neither theocrats nor liberals accepted the system, but the country as a whole did. Bourgeoisie and peasantry did well enough, and liberties were assured. When Louis died in 1824 he had in a way realized his determination not to be king of two peoples. But in retrospect it would seem that he had also achieved little more than a respite and a postponement of some fundamental confrontations.

His brother and successor, Charles X, was not so tolerant, so tired, or so lucky. By 1830 he had pulled the royal house down on his head, having frightened the middle classes into believing that he intended to destroy the Revolution settlement and put the clock all the way back. The political system was no more oligarchical than it had been, but this man's notorious extreme rightist views encouraged reaction. Passage of a bill to indemnify all (royalist or republican) who had been dispossessed during the Revolution may well have been intended to close the account books forever; reduction of the interest on government bonds to produce the necessary funds hardly pleased the propertied bondholders; the Left objected to compensating *émigré* traitors, the Right complained of the insufficiency of the measure. More ominous were the clerical reaction and the pretensions of the Church, already felt in the previous reign. A European religious revival was reflected in Charles's return to Rheims for a traditional coronation ritual. Jesuit propaganda, assaults on the Napoleonic concordat with Rome, a law to punish sacrilege with life imprisonment or death, the reaching out for control of education all alarmed the liberals, collided with the Enlightenment tradition, and created a climate of hostility to the regime. By 1827 the Left was set on a collision course with the crown. Defeated in the elections of that year, Charles retreated by appointing a moderate ministry to suit the Chamber, withdrew press censorship, dampened clerical enthusiasms, and proposed elective local government. It was not enough. His dissolution of the National Guard for *lèse majesté* and a now coincident onslaught of industrial and agricultural depression fed the discontent. Determining to have his way, he then appointed extremist ministers in defiance of the Chamber. The battle lines formed, each side reaching out into the uncertain territory where sovereignty lay. Dissolution and new elections brought his stunning defeat. He then followed with another dissolution and ordinances recreating censorship and so limiting the franchise as to strike at the bourgeoisie. This was fatal. Riots ensued, the Government had neither the wit nor the strength to stamp them out, and the political class stepped in to conrol the Revolution. Thus a self-constituted provisional Government took over Paris, Charles abdicated, and the Duke of Orleans became lieutenant general of the realm. If depression had not caused these events, it helped to make them acceptable. The coincidence of bad times, clerical reaction, and middle-class fears had destroyed the compromise of 1814.

July Monarchy

The revolutionaries were a richly assorted band, the reflection once more of the diversity of the Revolution: workers and students recalling 1792 or worse, Imperial soldiers, defenders of the Orleanist ambitions, former servants of Louis XVIII, moderate republicans like the aged Lafayette, who had deserted the Revolution. But the propertied and political class had no intention of watching the country slide leftward or Europe intervene to suppress a republic. Acting swiftly, they won over Lafayette to the idea of an Orleanist monarchy under the tricolor, bound by a contractual agreement between crown and people, deprived of any shred of divine right. Civil liberties were redefined in the new Charter, and the settlement was accepted in the name of the nation by the two chambers sitting as the National Assembly. Thus popular sovereignty was recognized (and the franchise slightly widened), but the principle of ministerial responsibility to parliament (despite the right of the Deputies to impeach before the Peers) was not. The rift between the nation and its Government continued.

France accepted the new regime quietly. Louis Philippe was a popular monarch with the respectable classes at least, but outside the consensus were the ranks of the discontented: unrepentant defenders of Charles X (Deputies who refused the oath of allegiance or who lost their seats; prefects, mayors, generals, and diplomats who were dismissed) and embittered republicans of many kinds. The regime was liberal but by no means democratic. If hereditary peerage was suppressed, the upper chamber was crown-appointed. The old nobility abandoned public service. France was governed by a combination of king, bureaucracy, and a small oligarchy of the propertied, commercial, industrial, and professional classes. In the early years, a continuing industrial distress provoked riots and savage government intervention on behalf of the industrial bourgeoisie. Radical republicans were driven underground; between the workers and the middle classes a profound class consciousness developed. Liberalism and socialism began to part company within the Enlightenment tradition to which both belonged. On the one hand secret societies and political clubs organized, talked, planned, and occasionally demonstrated against the regime; on the other, a political opposition within the Chamber demanded liberal reform. In a sense, 1830 was the final consolidation of the middle-class Revolution. The great bourgeoisie proved as selfish as the old aristocracy, as politically exclusive and unwilling to share power. They had, as Tocqueville said, taken government up as a trade.

In foreign affairs the regime was cautious. It shied away from adventures, reassured Europe of its conservatism, and backed down when challenged (as by Great Britain in the Mediterranean in 1840). It pursued the Algerian conquest barely begun by Charles X, it pushed out into the Pacific Ocean. In literature, music, art, and thought, France under the July Monarchy offered a wealthy display, as it had under the previous monarchy: the religious revival of the early century survived, but it was less obviously allied to conservatism. Though liberalism tended to identify with the established order, its socialist and humanitarian components took on a life of their own. Romanticism ceased to serve reaction, though it might celebrate the idealized medieval past. Realism held up the unattractive commercialism and injustices of the time, to which the many prophets of some social and political utopia replied with their various recipes. In the comic and bitter cartoons of Daumier, the withering sociological analysis of Fourier, and the monumental, detailed portraits of Balzac the follies and the style of the age were revealed. In industry, agriculture, and transportation, progress was perhaps slow but certainly marked by the end of the reign. Those who governed the country thought less of the Industrial Revolution than of agrarian and commercial wellbeing. If time was wasted in the area of government (with a failure to draw the inevitable conclusion about the political implications of popular sovereignty), it was squandered here too. Productivity failed to keep pace with even a modest population increase; the standard of living fell. Thus, once more, depression would provide the setting for political revolt.

Unity was as remote as ever. Old opposition was replaced by new. The crown itself was again bitterly assailed in the public press, pilloried and ridiculed as the symbol of the new oligarchy. Those who manipulated elections in its name said plainly that they were servants of Order, possessing the indispensable Might and Right. Like François Guizot, they radiated confidence and set their face against change. Less despotic, possibly, than short-sighted and incompetent, they knew of no way to channel discontent and meet grievances honestly. Thus opposition loomed larger: the receding Empire took on enchantment, the myth of St. Helena beckoned in a modernized version, despite the comic failures of Napoleon's nephew to overthrow Louis Philippe. The Emperor's body being brought back to the Invalides in 1840 was not a guarantee but a challenge. Clustered in the inhospitable cities, immigrant peasants swelled the army of the uneasy poor. The parliamentary opposition that could not be defeated or bought vainly demanded electoral reform; the political clubs staged protests. Crop failures and soaring food prices from 1846 to 1848 sharpened the mood of discontent. Even the revived and supposedly conservative National Guard demanded reform. Too late, in February 1848 the king sacrificed Guizot to the general outcry. Street riots turned to revolution when shots were exchanged with royal troops, and barricades appeared. Slow to realize what was happening, reluctant to shed blood, the king abdicated and the monarchy ended, as it happened, forever—a scapegoat for profound divisions in the body social and for the refusal of those whom the Revolution had placed in power to admit that it was more than a temporally circumscribed event or that its principles were universally applicable.

Revolution, Republic, and Empire

Occasioned by accident, the revolution of 1848 was caused by the stubborn *immobilisme* of a small ruling class in a changing world. Easily swept aside, the regime was less easily replaced. The working class had helped tumble the throne, but it had neither the class consciousness, the numbers, nor the organization to do more. The various social critics and reformers enjoyed a power of analysis that outstripped their practical capacities. Without much difficulty, therefore, all the heterogeneous groups of monarchists and republicans, socialists and moderates, friends of the Church and foes, backed the provisional Government formed about deputies of the old opposition. Momentarily their vague social program of promising the right to work stifled street violence in the capital. This and the instituting of universal suffrage was the extent of their liberalism; in a nation of landed peasants universal suffrage was the guarantee of a most conservative settlement. Between February and June the character of this ad hoc Republic became more evident, the outlook of the political leaders more plain. The depression, deepened by these events, intensified mutual suspicions between bourgeois and worker, and brought a flood of provincial needy to the capital in search of work or at least enrollment in the Government's relief program. It was the hope of the radical republican Minister of the Interior that by replacing all the old prefects by republican *commissaires* he could carry the rural districts against the clergy's and the local notables's influence; it was the fervent hope of his more conservative colleagues that he could not. The spring elections proved them right. Half the new constituent assembly was monarchist, most of it was thoroughly conservative. The vote was a vote against Paris, against the memory of July 14, let alone 1793-1794, against the income tax, and against the right to work. Demonstrations and agitation in the capital mounted; the leaders of revolutionary clubs were arrested if they did not flee the country. And in June the assembly and its leaders decided to have done, ordering the despairing poor into the Army or back to the provinces from which they had come. The result was a great leaderless revolt, and then its savage suppression by troops. The slaughter of the June Days, the executions and transportations that followed, created a myth of working-class solidarity. It deepened urban social schism, underlined peasant and army conservatism, and opened the way to the destruction of this fragile democracy.

Again, the crowded and contradictory past pressed upon France in the shape of the constitution of this Second Republic. Popular sovereignty was enshrined in the Assembly's election by universal male suffrage; separation of powers in the popular election of a President. The ministers could not be held responsible to the Assembly; the President could not dissolve the Assembly. All this evoked the first phase of the Revolution. The election of Louis Napoleon Bonaparte as President in December 1848 recalled the last. He was thought by republicans to be politically safe, and by monarchists biding their time, politically opportune. He was neither. Unlike his uncle, he was not a soldier. He was a dynast, an unsuccessful adventurer, a cunning politician. Faced with an Assembly that favored the Church, disfranchised a third of the electorate, and curbed the press, he shrewdly appealed directly to the rural population as the representative of a glorious tradition, to the business classes as the guarantee of stability, and to the whole country as the champion against a legislative would-be oligarchy. Refused a constitutional revision by the Assembly to afford him a renewal of his four-year term, having made certain of the administration, the Army, and the police, he dissolved the Assembly, arrested his victims, and seized the State by coup. If bloodshed was minimal, imprisonments and transportations far exceeded the threat of opposition to him. This was a mistake. Confirmed in these violent acts by plebiscite (once more, an echo from a half century before), he reshaped the constitution, took a firm grip on bureaucracy and politics, carried his cause to the country and, backed by an overwhelming plebiscite, reestablished the Empire in December 1852. Yet again, the price of order and prosperity seemed to be in making an end to politics. But although monarchists, socialists, radical republicans, and the working class were hostile, the great mass of France was content.

The debate on the Second Empire—what it was, where it was going— has never ended. In eighteen years the regime showed many faces. It began as a dictatorship, backed by force, supported by plebiscite, tempered by state-managed and strictly circumscribed political trappings. Whether by original design and according to the Emperor's deepest desires or not, it evolved after 1860 toward a liberal parliamentary system with the Government responsible to the legislature. The early press laws were dismantled; the republican opposition made headway and the authoritarians around Napoleon III lost ground and sustained electoral defeats. To the end, despite all the changes and all the failures abroad, the man himself carried a vast popular support in the country. Of his many and contradictory advisors, none were more significant than the intellectual followers of the utopian Henri Saint-Simon, as the expansion of credit, the growth of banking, and the development of railways and industry showed. Though the State merely watched over an unprogressive agriculture, it encouraged business and spent money on public works, of which Baron Haussmann's ruthless reconstruction of the capital was the most notable example. It was a prosperous time, in which the bourgeois plutocracy flourished, the monarchists watched and waited, and the unforgiving republicans suffered or plotted or waited for more propitious days. The Empire had its cultural boasts to place beside the record of muted class hatreds, scandals, and injustices. The music of Offenbach, the paintings of Courbet and Millet (not to mention those like Edouard Manet, then ridiculed, creating the Impressionist school), the novels of Flaubert and Hugo, and the continuing history of Michelet, a republican enemy of the regime—these too were part of the era. And when the Congress of Paris assembled in 1856 to mark the end of the unhappy Crimean War, France had not stood so high since 1810.

This regime may well have satisfied France better than any she had known since 1789, but obviously discontents were many, and increased as time ran out. Disease struck at the wine and silk industries, the American Civil War at the cotton. The wealthy who had done so well out of the imperial encouragement of expanding credit lost confidence, withdrew their funds, and permitted financial orthodoxy to overwhelm the bank most closely identified with the Government. The Opposition, though ultimately impotent, launched its thunderbolts. Aging and in declining health, the Emperor was pulled this way and that by diverse advisors and compelled at last to get rid of those who had first given the Empire such shape as it had. But above all, though Napoleon successfully pursued colonial expansion, it was his foreign policy that turned everything to disaster. By supporting Piedmont and the cause of Italian nationalism in 1859-1860, he alienated Austria, the Papacy and French Catholics, and finally even the Italians themselves. In seeking to found an empire in Mexico, 1861-1867, he was threatened by the United States and suffered humiliation from the Mexicans. Having permitted Prussia to defeat Austria, he was duped by Bismarck's proposals of compensation and exposed as a bungler on the international scene. Every foreign failure encouraged criticism at home. A dictatorship was dismantled, but it was not clear that a coherent regime had replaced it. Aware that the Army was in bad repair, the Emperor had neither the ability nor the will to compel the generals to admit it or the politicians to provide monies for its modernization. Adolphe Thiers said in 1867 that there were no more mistakes to make, but Napoleon's final error was to let himself be maneuvered by Bismarck, an irresponsible court, and an outraged public opinion into declaring war in the summer of 1870. Thus, ill-prepared, plebiscitarian to the last, the Second Empire took the field and collapsed in a matter of weeks. Those who had profited most by it shed hardly a tear and set about making other arrangements conducive to their well-being.

War and Revolution

Europeans suspicious of France saw the declaration of war as another wild imperial adventure if not a belated attempt to resume the pursuit of a continental hegemony. This was a ludicrous misreading of events. Napoleon III had little in common with his illustrious uncle. If the decision for war was made at Saint-Cloud, the supposed threat and humiliation of the Hohenzollern candidacy for the vacant Spanish throne awakened an authentic national response. The court insisted upon a double and perpetual withdrawal of the candidacy by the King of Prussia, but it was the nation which, after so many foreign retreats, demanded the aggressive defense of national honor. The war had nothing to do with the pursuit of glory. It recalled neither the military extravagances of Louis XIV nor the profitable grandeur of the great Emperor. If the call to arms was not 1792 again, it was instinctive and it came from the heart. Catastrophe of course involved such a reorientation of things as made the recognition of this fact unsuitable. Once the debacle had set in, with Bazaine's army bottled up at Metz and Napoleon captured with MacMahon's force at Sedan, the revolutionary spirit of Paris flared. Everything was simplified: the crime of December 1851 was avenged, the plutocracy was discredited, the country was invaded, and the capital, aroused by the glorious memories of the Revolution (this now was certainly 1792 or 1793), would save France and redeem seventy years of error. Parliament was burst into, the Republic proclaimed at the Hôtel de Ville, and a provisional Government of National Defense formed by the capital's military governor and deputies of the Opposition. Animated by the Minister of the Interior, Léon Gambetta (an old foe of the Empire, who replaced the prefects and hoped to summon up a nation in arms to hurl the enemy out of the country), the Government adopted a Jacobin posture, while the more realistic Thiers vainly sought diplomatic support against the day of suing for terms.

Although France was willing, fate was against her. Paris held and the provinces rallied, but Bazaine capitulated, the new armies that Gambetta (who escaped from the capital by balloon) tried to raise in Tours could not halt the Germans, and an armistice had to be sought. Not the least of the Government's concerns were repeated left-wing attempts at insurrection in the capital and the establishment briefly of revolutionary governments in other cities. The decision for peace was therefore a decision not only to halt the enemy tide and to end the suffering of the besieged capital in bitter winter weather, but also for order and preservation of the social fabric. Seventeen-ninety-two must not become 1794, or worse. The elections held for a National Assembly to consider the conditions of peace repudiated the republican radicals led by Gambetta, who wished to continue the struggle, and returned a massive conservative, largely monarchist, majority. Provincial France had rejected the would-be Jacobin dictatorship. The Assembly approved Germany's terms: surrender of Alsace-Lorraine, partial occupation until an indemnity was paid, and a victory parade through Paris, which had held out under bombardment and starvation. Particularly galling to the spirited capital, already seething with radicalism, this acceptance and a series of unmistakably hostile and conservative decisions by the Assembly (which had moved from Bordeaux to Versailles, thus refusing to be put in the position of the constituent assembly of 1789, under the watch of factious Paris) provoked establishment in March 1871 of a revolutionary municipal government. It was a declaration that Paris would not permit itself to be overwhelmed again by the provinces. Much of the city was of course supine; part of it was hostile to the Commune; and as the days passed the moderates left for Versailles or elsewhere. The Assembly and its Executive, headed by Thiers, determined to smash this ghost of militant Jacobinism tempered by nineteenth-century utopian socialism and insurrectionism. Without a coherent program, smitten by a kind of paralysis, the Commune went down before the Versailles troops that May in fire, massacre, and hatred. Falsely claimed for its own by Marxist socialism, the Commune expressed a tangle of facts: the heteroclite character of the revolutionary tradition; the unending hostility between town and country; the gulf between the varieties of republicanism; the organization of class hatreds. From all this, a legacy of fear and hatred was handed on.

Having made peace and established order, the Assembly created a new regime. What now would divide Frenchmen the least? Portents were the election of a republican as president of the Assembly, the lukewarm Orleanist propensities of Thiers (made President of the French Republic in August 1871), the rival claims of Bourbon and Orleans to the throne, the survival of Bonapartists despite Napoleon's exile, and, not least, an overwhelming republican upsurge in supplementary elections that summer. Clearly the original Assembly had been chosen to make peace, not to reestablish the monarchy. The deputies could confine Thiers and, in historic suspicion of the executive power, place a barrier between him and themselves (and thus lead him to resign), but they could not get the Bourbon contender to accept the Revolution. All hope of monarchical settlement in his lifetime therefore faded. By 1875 disenchanted monarchists and conservative republicans made possible an acceptance of republican institutions which, however temporary some deputies may have hoped they would turn out to be, were to survive as the Third Republic until 1940.

The Third Republic

A President was to be elected for seven years by the Chamber of Deputies and Senate sitting together; the Chamber was elected by universal male suffrage for four years and could be dissolved by the President with the consent of the Senate; the Senate was partly nominated and partly elected by indirect suffrage for nine years. The object of all this was, while respecting the principles of 1789, to put restraints on a lower house likely to reflect radicalism and socialism. But nothing turned out as the

Assembly majority intended. Though monarchists, Bonapartists, and conservative republicans now wanted a strong presidency for quite separate and contradictory reasons, they had already set the office on the road to impotence. By 1876 the Chamber had been captured by the republicans, and when the following year President MacMahon attempted to sustain a ministry not pleasing to it and appealed to the country, he received a stunning repudiation from the electorate. Thereafter the presidency declined in authority, its powers falling into disuse. Soon the Senate was made wholly elective; its composition was already republican. It now remained only to check the Chamber, and the Chamber became increasingly sovereign. Loosely divided into Opportunists and Radicals, the republican majority accepted and rejected ministries with impunity. Ministerial instability (tempered by constancy of political personnel) became the condition of political life.

Though monarchists and Bonapartists sniped at the regime, they had no power to bring it down. The police, the administration, and the Army were loyal. Political scandals involving the notables of the Republic occasioned demonstrations by the embittered Right and the frustrated Left. An extraordinary political adventurer, General Boulanger, could exploit popular dissatisfactions and the most contradictory political ambitions to threaten dictatorship in 1889—a fate from which France was saved less by the strength of the State than the confusion of this man's mind. A fundamental schism appeared to open up as a result of the Army's condemnation in 1894 of a Jewish captain, Alfred Dreyfus, on charges of espionage for the German Empire. Though eventually cleared, Dreyfus became a martyr. The Army had been trapped in an act of gross injustice out of concern for protecting its procedures and honor. The case became a national *Affaire*. Those who sought to prevent its investigation—generals, politicians, clerics, and royalists—were furiously beset by the republican Left. If the masses were indifferent, the upper and upper-middle classes were rent. A new militancy appeared on the Left, and a new hostility to the parliamentary republic on the Right. From that time on, the violence of the Republic's internal dialogue was more marked.

The scars of the Dreyfus Affair remained visible for half a century. The Army remembered its purging as long; the Church hardly suffered less. Whatever its discontents with the Second Empire, the Church had prospered generally under Napoleon III. If it watched the State grow more jealous of the interests of secular education and saw the spread of anticlericalism, it enjoyed a kind of protection to the end. But the intellectuals were deserting it, the rigidly antiliberal attitude of the Papacy (which unhappily divided it) encouraged the laic ideal, and the failure of the monarchists by 1873 announced a republican assault. It had had no hope of achieving the monopoly of education held before 1789, but after 1880 it was driven out of its position in all state educational institutions. As a consequence of the *Affaire*, the Napoleonic Concordat was abrogated, relations between France and the Papacy were broken off, and religious congregations were forbidden to teach even in private schools. Though practice did not always conform to the letter of this law, the secular ideal was the dogma of the Republic. And it was the primary schoolmaster, heir of the Enlightenment and the Revolution, not the priest, heir of the *ancien régime* and the Counterrevolution, who must raise the children of the Republic. In practice, of course, not all attended the state schools, despite the important education laws, which vastly improved the availability and quality of teacher training and made primary education compulsory and free. God-fearing bourgeois and the unrepentant aristocracy sent their children to private institutions. Patriots France's children might all grow up to be, but their views of the secular Republic would hardly be the same. Moreover, the failure at this time to make secondary education free in the state *lycées* undoubtedly reduced the impact of the laic ideal on the country. For the poor and the clever few there was state assistance all the way through the highly competitive École Normale Supérieure, radical and even socialist, which trained the professors of the Republic. But it was a difficult ascent. For the well-to-do, if no less clever, there was the Faculty of Law and the École Libres des Sciences Politiques, which trained the higher civil service, and where the outlook was far to the Right.

By the early years of the century the state of France could be judged good. Unity might lie always ahead, but enough of a consensus existed to permit the institutions of the country to function. If the memory of the June Days and the Commune had been crystallized in the creed of syndicalism or of the Socialist party, which finally gathered in all the extreme left political threads of the nineteenth century, amnesty and time had combined with social conscience and acceptance of the inevitable to transfer action from the street to the Palais Bourbon or the *syndicat* meeting. Though the revolutionary tradition had been revealed in all its contradictions and its quarreling heirs still further fractured by the Industrial Revolution and a century of social and political experiments, there were on the whole few who seriously pined for the *ancien régime*. Predominantly secular in spirit, timid and Malthusian in its economic conceptions, no stranger to industrial and agrarian strife, with a population that had not kept pace with the European increase over the previous hundred years, France was nevertheless passing through what would be called the *belle époque*. The world of letters, music, and art was brilliant. Paris had no rival in this regard. No French regime could boast a more splendid display than this Third Republic: Cézanne, Monet, Renoir, Rodin . . . Saint-Saëns, Gabriel Fauré, Debussy . . . Anatole France, Gide, Apollinaire. . . . It was an extravagant outpouring of talent. And afterward it would all seem to have belonged to a fragile moment in time. Once more the country was about to be declared in danger, and patriotism would be called on to unite those who had grown so accustomed to struggle against each other for their various conceptions of what France should be.

FOUR

The Gale of the Twentieth Century

1914-1958

"Nous pouvons paraître grands dans un emploi au-dessous de notre mérite, mais nous paraissons souvent petits dans un emploi plus grand que nous."

Time, which makes fools of most prophets, has a way of discrediting both Cassandra and Dr. Pangloss. Those who despaired of France in the twentieth century were as short-sighted as those who talked as if she were the center of the civilized world. For her the first half of this stormy century was an era of painful redefinition of status and role. It was neither so glorious as it at first seemed nor so catastrophic as it came to appear. The triumphs and sorrows of the French mirrored too the apogee and the decline of the European star in the world. And in this sense, of course, it seemed true that France, like Europe, would never again be the unrivaled source of light and strength that she had been that half century ago.

Before the Storm

On the eve of 1914 the Republic was a great power. It appeared stable. The Legitimist pretender was long since dead, the Orleanist in exile. Boulanger, political daredevil and muddled champion of discontent, had shot himself years before. Dreyfus, an honorable man but no hero, was fully reinstated. The Army had survived persecution and ideological meddling to win popular applause on weekend parades the Government staged for the middle classes—if not for the workers against whose strikes troops were deployed. The disestablished Church had retained use of its churches by tacit agreement with the public authorities (despite the fury of Pius X) and the allegiance of the faithful. The Republic had been tested by almost every vicissitude but a major war.

The people numbered not quite 40 million. Forty-four per cent were still farm dwellers (it had been 52 per cent in 1870, 75 per cent in 1815). A quarter century of consolidation had halted the post-Revolution trend of subdivision of the land. Yet 40 per cent of the farms were smaller than 2.5 acres, and agricultural efficiency was well below that of France's neighbors. Protected by tariffs, however, with the number of farms now beginning to decline, and with a population drift to the town, agriculture

41

seemed healthy enough. The wheat farmer was secure against foreign competition; the winegrowers had survived the late nineteenth-century destruction of half their vineyards by disease to relocate and flourish again. Rural illiteracy had almost been stamped out. Peasant conservatism was reflected in both Chamber and Senate. Overproduction and bad marketing of wine led in 1907 to violent demonstrations in the countryside and resulted in Premier Clemenceau's calling out troops. Blood was spilt along with the wine. But this was exceptional. Life was laborious and orderly, comforts were few, in many areas the *curé* was still close, and parsimony was a cult.

Social strains were more evident in the city. Though industry prospered behind the tariff, and wages and consumption were up, by comparison with her neighbors France was falling behind. The world's second industrial power in 1870, she had now slipped to fourth place. Apart from iron ore and bauxite, raw materials were lacking; coal—and coke to process the ore—was insufficient. Few then sounded the alarm, for absolute increases hid relative decline and the unhealthy fact that light manufacturing predominated. But the increasing working-class population had not greatly improved its lot. Some elementary reform legislation had been passed and the labor movement been organized. The right to strike had existed since 1864. Tolerated earlier, trade unions had been legalized in 1884. Women and children enjoyed some protection; the six-day week and social insurance had been acquired. Yet the worker had no fully developed sense of his corporate interest (only one in six belonged to a union). Wages rose slowly; more than 80 per cent went for food and lodging. In 1906 a great labor congress had rejected collaboration with parliamentary Socialism, seeking to avoid the divisions of Socialism by embracing pure revolutionary syndicalism. With mounting unemployment in the next few years, violent strikes occurred. Here too the Government sent in troops and made arrests. In 1914 syndicalist leaders were only beginning to turn from the doctrine of independent direct action to cooperation with socialism. The myth of the General Strike, whose poet was Georges Sorel, remained ("To any declaration of war," the largest union, the *Confédération générale du travail*, taught, "the workers must immediately reply with the revolutionary strike"). Still, absolute wage increases helped disguise the proletariat's relative decline. Temporarily the war was to mute class concerns. Like the peasant, the worker would do his duty and the full development of his sense of alienation and distress was postponed.

Based upon the peasantry, not seriously challenged by the working class, this was the Republic of the middle classes and was rapidly becoming the regime of the *petite bourgeoisie*. Hard-working and orderly, with a varying range of education, the middle classes had a firm grip on the State. The 1914 elections were a success for moderate Socialism and the very moderate Radical Socialism; the Right was set back; the Center held the balance. This was to be the general pattern of politics for the next quarter century, with power flowing to the provincial and urban notables and drawn increasingly from the lesser bourgeoisie. The style of politics in 1914 was conservative. No alliance existed between the Socialists of Jean Jaurès and the Radicals behind Joseph Caillaux. Prepared in the circumstances to accept three years of military service, the country was reluctant to pay for it ("I crushed the income tax," Caillaux had boasted in 1901, "while seeming to defend it").

France was aware of her vulnerability. Forty years before, her population had been about equal to that of Germany; it was now more than a third smaller. She had never practiced a *politique de revanche* for 1870-1871. But if she had friends and allies, she had no important control of international politics. That had been lost under the Second Empire. Before 1890 only the cool friendliness of Great Britain and the modest patronage of the German Chancellor had qualified her isolation. By 1894, however, the Emperor Wilhelm's neglect of Russia, the Tsar's need for western capital, and a mutual French and Russian desire for an ally against the Austro-German alliance brought about the Franco-Russian alliance. It both bolstered France and rendered her less independent. Relations with Italy were by 1914 at once cordial and reserved, limited by Italian commitment to a Triple Alliance with Habsburg and Hohenzollern. After 1904 France's African rivalry with Great Britain gave way before an Entente Cordiale involving consultation on mutual interests, secret staff talks, and finally a moral undertaking by the British to defend the French Channel coast.

All this represented a striking alteration in the country's international situation: the isolation that had characterized it during much of the nineteenth century was over. Reassured, the makers of policy had not hesitated to pursue a French hegemony over Morocco. Twice, in 1905 and 1911, German challenges to this policy had threatened war. Retreating before the first, the Republic found its friendships dependable; negotiating away the second, it achieved its strategic and colonial goal. A slice of French Equatorial Africa to Germany was, for all the nationalist outcry, a small sacrifice. But if a direct Franco-German crisis was passed off, a worsening Austro-Russian rivalry in the Balkans and an Anglo-German naval race rendered France's role the more peripheral. Though the nation voted in 1914 as if war would not happen, the alarms had sounded in 1905. Those who led the nation believed the peace to be doomed. "War can break out from one day to the next," the Foreign Minister said in January 1914. "Our allies must rush to our aid. The safety of France will depend on the energy and promptness with which we shall be able to push them into the fight."

War and Peace

The assassination of Archduke Franz Ferdinand at Sarajevo on June 28 was the implacable fatality. Vienna believed they had to risk general war in order to strike down Serbia. Having encouraged them, the German Emperor drew back too late. The Russian mobilization resulted in ultimatums to St. Petersburg and Paris and war came to Europe. It bore no resemblance to the war of 1870. The German invasion of Belgium made good the Entente of 1904. Italy would join the Allies next year, the United States would do so in 1917. And when the worst was known, the words came easily: "*Il faut en finir!*" But in 1914 the French knew no more than any other people what was to come. Prevailing doctrine was that wars must be short, to be won by rapid mobilization, superior morale, and sudden assault. The French plan was made on such assumptions and in the confidence that a mass attack would catch the Germans with much of their strength in the east. But the Germans also had counted on a swift and deadly blow against France. Thus the French eruption toward the Rhine turned to disaster. Driven back and with the enemy approaching Paris, the Army was saved by cool heads, rapid transportation of men to stem the assault, and German retreat from the Marne. Everyone's plans had gone awry. The war in the west bogged down. There would be no debacle, but a heaving struggle of artillery, machine guns, barbed wire, and bayonets—and, later, tanks and aircraft—moving sluggishly back and forth in winter mud and summer heat.

There followed a four-year nightmare of heroism and criminal idiocies; the slaughter was unparalleled. Like everyone else, the French improvised the massive industrialized effort demanded by this insatiable war. Generals came and went; the monstrous offensives brought no decision. Rapidly parliament and the Government recovered the powers initially surrendered to the Army, and, with the bloodletting far gone and mutinies scarcely overcome, suffered the dictatorship of Georges Clemenceau in 1917 under the spartan slogan, "*Je fais la guerre.*" Faint-hearts and traitors were disposed of. Through all the carnage and disasters, from Serbia to Russia, the Republic held to its task. Exhausted, frightfully bled, and devastated, France had the satisfaction—such as it was—of dictating the armistice terms to the enemy. On November 11, 1918, the ordeal was over.

Of the major participants, France suffered the greatest losses proportionately: 7.9 million had been mobilized; 1.3 million were dead. The mortality figures could be put many ways: 27 per cent of French youth (18 to 27 years of age); 10 per cent of the active male population (compared with 9.8 per cent for Germany, 9.5 per cent for Austria-Hungary, 5.1 per cent for Great Britain, 0.2 per cent for the United States). The peasantry had been sacrificed; the intellectuals were decimated. Three million acres of land were torn up, 289,000 houses ruined. Industrial productivity had dropped by 40 per cent; ruinous inflation threatened. Supported by her allies, France had endured. But serious cracks had opened up within the nation. As early as 1915 the initial *Union sacrée* was menaced and socialist pacifism stirred. Front-line soldiers grumbled about young men held in industrial jobs, about profiteering farmers and businessmen. The holocausts of Verdun or the Somme encouraged clandestine "peace" contacts with the enemy. Even the last commander-in-chief of the French Army, General Pétain, was considered somewhat uncertain in a critical moment. But somehow the Republic had sustained its unity, and among the victors it held its place proudly. With the German Empire defeated, the Habsburg Monarchy in ruins, and Russia the theatre of revolution, it was the greatest military power in the world—strange destiny for a people in relative decline. Yet so it seemed as the allied forces paraded beneath the Arc de Triomphe and Paris was host to the peace conference.

The Peace of Paris disappointed everyone, above all the French. Their insecurity was extreme and their mood ungenerous. "We have been attacked; we want security," said the Foreign Minister. "We have been despoiled; we demand restitution. We have been devastated; we want reparation." Seeking permanent occupation of the Rhine bridgeheads, they wanted separation of the Rhineland from Germany. Instead they had to accept a fifteen-year occupation of this area, exploitation of the Saar mines, occupation and a plebiscite to determine in 1935 the Saar's political fate, and permanent demilitarization of the Rhineland and a 50-km.-wide area running east from the river. Of a League of Nations without an armed force they were wholly skeptical. The Anglo-American guarantee of their frontiers vanished with the United States' refusal to ratify the Treaty of Versailles and a consequent British withdrawal from the obligation. If Clemenceau hoped for reconciliation with the new German Republic, he expected renewed antagonism. Believing that the Germans would not fulfil the Treaty terms, he could only hope that the Allies would retain their bridgeheads and say, "We are on the Rhine and we stay there." Already British fears of a new French hegemony in Europe were obvious, and the Entente declined rapidly after 1919.

This old Jacobin had no postwar role. As a man of the former Left, as the wartime "dictator," he was rejected in the presidential elections of 1920. Dominated by the nationalist Right, parliament showed its old hostility to a strong chief of state by electing a President who soon had to retire for reasons of mental disturbance; and when his successor showed some forthright independence, he was forced out of office. But if the Right profited from nationalist euphoria at the polls in 1919 (and again in 1928), the Left held its own. Socialism split in 1920, and a new Communist party directed from Moscow was born to permanent opposition. The Socialists themselves refused participation in bourgeois governments. Thus ministries were controlled by Radicals and right-of-center Moderates. In fifty years of the Republic no strong national parties (apart from the Communists and, to a lesser degree, the Socialists and the Radical Socialists) had come into being. Secure from the threat of dissolution, the Chamber of Deputies was a closed arena. Parliamentary groups formed and dissolved, combined and broke up, with little reference to the national parties and the local organizations; they were multiple, ambitious, ridden with faction, and cannibalistic. Ministries came and went, lasting usually less than a year; ministers returned and changed places time and again; and the permanent bureaucracy, of course, went on forever.

The country recovered slowly from the war. Financial troubles were severe, not least because bankers and industrialists on occasion chose to discipline the political Left. But no one, rich or poor, wished to pay for the war, and it was clear that the Germans could not or would not. The result was inflation and such a fall in the franc as could be halted only by a government of national union in 1926 armed with decree-law powers. An ominous warning that the parliamentary system could not overcome its divisions to act in a crisis until the eleventh hour, this series of events showed again that if France's heart remained on the Left, her wallet was still on the Right. Four-fifths of the franc's value was gone; those holding the national debt or having small savings were the real victims. But production levels climbed past the 1914 figures, despite marginal modernization and high protection. Yet labor-management relations were not good. Wages lagged, trade-union membership fell off, and most workers had no affiliation. Rents pegged at 1914 levels encouraged landlord neglect and growth of slums. The encouragement of immigrant labor was interpreted as an employers' plot against wage increases. Conscienceless employer and embittered employee had not recently been more deaf to each other's claims. The peasantry, like the bourgeoisie, hid their true means to cheat the tax-collector; the working-class bore more than its share of the burden. Instituted in 1916, the income tax was not seriously applied. Taxation remained generally indirect, punitive, and unfairly distributed. All the same, in retrospect these would seem like good years. Church-State relations were improving. Only the Communists and the extreme Right outside parliament violently opposed the regime. Tom Appleton had said that "Good Americans, when they die, go to Paris," but many flocked there to live in the twenties, and the Germans still spoke of being "happy as God in France."

The aura of victory faded. Probably there was no solution to the French dilemma in a world of sovereign states. Already weak, the demographic situation was worsening by comparison with Germany's. Hypnotized by the fear of isolation and insecurity, France was intransigent, insisting at first on the Treaty and the schedule of payments laid down by the Reparations Commission. By 1924 this policy had turned to ashes. Great Britain was fearful of French dominance and desirous of German recovery. Premier Poincaré's sending troops into the Ruhr to compel payment, a *politique d'isolement et de force*, according to his opponents, caused the German financial collapse of 1923-1924, the scaling down of German liability, and weakening of the German Republic. British and American disapproval was warning that a more positive policy must follow. Out of international negotiations came the Locarno Treaties guaranteeing the Franco-German boundary by Britain and Italy in 1925, and, in 1926, Germany's entry into the League—after the French Government accepted, as did others, the fraud of public recognition of Germany's having carried out the disarmament clauses of Versailles. Thus the gap between the French people's and their Government's expectations widened, and the work of preparing for a general disarmament conference was rendered more futile.

France never gave the League her trust. Alone as she had not been in 1914, she proceeded after 1919 to contract treaties with Poland, Belgium, Czechoslovakia, Yugoslavia, and Rumania. The Soviet Union was as suspect as Germany. But all this was no substitute for the alliance of 1894, and Locarno (implying an eventual revision of Germany's eastern frontiers) called the eastern undertakings into question. Gustav Stresemann, the Weimar Republic's longtime Foreign Minister, said plainly in private, "We obtained at Locarno 100 per cent of what we desired. It preserves the Rhineland for us and allows us to recuperate the German territories in the east." Small wonder that France insisted the world was not yet safe for disarmament. And when Stresemann died in 1929, the bankruptcy of Locarno's hopes seemed complete. What had been denied this moderate man could hardly be granted his successors amidst German nationalist clamor. Successive German failures to meet reparations had nonetheless brought reductions and concessions. The bridgeheads Clemenceau had counted on were evacuated five years early in 1930. France might still block the proposed Austro-German Customs Union, but her position was undercut by international loans to Germany. By 1931 even a sound currency and the lonely glory of remaining on the gold standard when others had gone off could not affect the course of events across the Rhine. Reparations collapsed and Adolf Hitler was in the wings.

Depression and Decline

As America, Britain, and Germany slipped deep into the Great Depression, then, France appeared for the last time in her guise as the great military and financial power of Europe. The moment passed. Weimar stumbled toward extinction, with French fears of the old enemy about to be justified for the first time since 1919. And at that time France also was struck by a marvelously delayed crisis. Growing internal distress was reflected in the Left's victory at the polls in 1932. The balanced economy, tariff protection, conservative banking system, substantial gold reserves, and lack of agricultural surpluses—all helped to ease the shock, delay recognition of the emergency, and so prolong the malady. The regime of the *petite bourgeoisie* had no policy save to preserve what was as it was: deflation at the top and belt-tightening at the bottom. Immigrant workers were deported; the unemployed returned to their villages; tariffs and quotas were brought into play. Until 1936, Governments practiced the policy of economic *immobilisme*, modified by protection of the inefficient, defense of the obsolete, and neglect of the poor. Cabinet instability prevailed at home; prestige drained away abroad.

The dictatorships in Italy and Germany threw the discontents of France into relief. Antiparliamentary groups had for long echoed the Counterrevolution and its unrelenting hostility to 1789. Charles Maurras and his literary friends of the Action Française were royalist, reactionary, and politically impotent, dreamers of an old and confused dream rather than builders of a city of the future. Followers of the so-called Fascist Leagues were few, save for those led by the renegade Communist, Jacques Doriot. Colonel François de la Rocque's Croix de Feu movement, basically an ex-servicemen's organization, was numerous but politically vague. This sort of group battened on public scandals involving parliament, ministers, and justice, notably that associated with the swindler Serge Stavisky. The extreme Right and Left press whipped up an outcry; the already spectacular provocations of the Hitler regime in 1933 added to the public nervousness and charges of negligence against the Deputies and the Ministry. The result was a right-wing assault on the Chamber, February 6, 1934, broken by the police at the cost of some dead. While the rioters howled "À bas les voleurs!" Maurras hardly paused in writing the next day's editorial. Yet this rightist outbreak provoked a left-wing counterdemonstration six days later. Confused as the riots might be, an emergency existed because extremists were loose, parliament was, as usual, quite paralyzed, and the weakness of the executive was pathetic. And as usual a Government of national union was put together including a symbol of greatness, Marshal Pétain, who had mastered the mutinies of 1917. But by now this Jacobin reflex was scarcely more than a parody of its old self.

The panic overcome, the scandals suitably buried, and the Premier trying to increase the executive authority, the Chamber brought this Government down that same autumn of 1934. Moderates and conservative Radicals governed until the 1936 elections. Although deflation brought a slight improvement, recovery was slower than elsewhere. But by 1935 a new phenomenon had made its appearance: a shaky, opportunist combination of Socialists, Communists, and left-wing Radicals—a Popular Front to combat fascism inside and outside the country. Moscow had reversed its antipatriotic course and was now committed to support of French rearmament and a Franco-Russian alliance. In France, this turn of events aroused great hope among the working class. And in the spring of 1936 the new Chamber brought forth a *Front populaire* Government of Socialists and Radicals supported by the Communists, led by the Socialist Jew, Léon Blum. But no such political and social experiment ever started out in less propitious circumstances.

Blum's domestic program had to be less far-reaching than he wished, and his political allies were far from reliable. The notion of this combination headed by such a man simply chilled the hearts of the respectable, God-fearing, well-to-do, and mildly anti-Semitic business bourgeoisie, fossilized aristocracy, and military establishment. For people who equated Communism with the Anti-Christ, Socialism with the Commune, Radicalism with the disestablishment of the Church, and Jews with the horrors of the *Affaire*, it was all too much. And though Blum's hand was strengthened by massive sit-down strikes which duly brought acceptance of the forty-hour week, collective bargaining, wage hikes, and paid vacations by panicky employers, his eventual downfall was the more certain. Moreover, he was trapped in a series of contradictory and false moves. Committed to defense of the gold standard, the Government embarked on a large-scale social policy; coming at last to devaluation, it acted too timidly and too late; bound to rebuild the long-neglected defenses of France, it cut work hours, raised wages, and watched costs soar. The hoped-for increase of purchasing power did not materialize, nor did production, nor exports. The Government lived beyond its means, capital was hoarded or exported, and in 1937 the loss of confidence, the reaction of the Senate, and the disintegration of the *Front populaire* itself brought Blum down. A reaction had set in against labor; class war smoldered afresh. What remained was the legacy of principles accepted, the historic memory of a government—the first France had known—*for* the working class. It was also the reminder that the bourgeoisie had never ceased fearing the principles they had announced and the hopes they raised so rashly 150 years before. Their fright and resentment ("I prefer death to surrender," as one industrialist put it) led some to conclude that France would be restored to order only—to quote the President of the Chamber Foreign Affairs Committee—"when the German cavalry parade under the Arc de Triomphe."

Not the least of Blum's trials was his unhappy decision to follow Great Britain's lead and refuse direct assistance to the Spanish government, which was beset by military revolt in 1936. In a swiftly darkening international situation, France was bound politically, financially, and militarily to those with whom she had so often quarreled since 1919. By 1937 few illusions remained. The Disarmament Conference of 1932 had been an exercise in futility. By their successful aggressions in Manchuria and Ethiopia, Japan and Italy had destroyed the idea of collective security through the League. Hitler's proclaimed rearmament in 1935 and remilitarization of the Rhineland zone in March 1936 confronted France with the choice of acting alone or submitting. Abandoned by the British, she submitted. Humiliated by a bilateral Anglo-German naval agreement in 1935, perhaps the most senseless piece of diplomacy of the time, she swallowed her anger. Committed to a wholly hypocritical application of sanctions against Italy by London, she simply harbored her resentment. The Republic accepted it all, as it accepted German armed forces on the Rhine frontier. "We may be more easily beaten in two years time," a deputy remarked, "but after all, it means two extra years of life, and something may turn up in the meantime." The policy of intransigence disintegrated between 1934 and 1936; that of abandonment and appeasement was announced.

After Blum the game of musical ministerial chairs was resumed until the spring of 1938. If working-class resentment went underground and trade-union membership fell off, the nation accepted the strong financial direction given by the moderate Paul Reynaud in Édouard Daladier's cabinet. Confidence was restored, money came out of hiding, the working week was lengthened again, and strikes were discouraged. The brief leftist euphoria had vanished; the appalling reality of impending disaster in Europe loomed over the country. France was profoundly divided. But there was no longer any question of identifying Left and Right with a forward or a defensive policy. The relative militancy of the Right under the Republic had not entirely disappeared by 1936; it had been cut through and a substantial part of the Right was now in the camp of appeasement and accommodation. The relatively pacifist nature of the Left had not changed as a whole; it had been divided and part of it (Communists taking their orders from abroad and perhaps fewer than half the Socialists, those who followed Blum) was in the camp of resistance to aggression. In every party and class were those who believed that French interests could be served only by withdrawal behind the Maginot Line. If Great Britain would not act, how could it be in the interest of France to court adventure on behalf of small eastern states and in alliance with Bolshevik Russia? The *années creuses*, with their terribly reduced military classes, had arrived. With any luck and some display of strength by the western democracies, Hitler would leave the west in peace and dissipate his ambition in the east. There were others, of course, who did not accept such an argument. Rearming slowly, in this ambivalent state of mind, the nation watched the storm approaching out of central Europe.

As before 1914, but in a more bewildering way, France had lost control of events. Hitler's brutality strained appeasement to the point of collapse; Great Britain suddenly condemned it in 1939. *Anschluss* with Austria could be rationalized, and the abandonment of Czechoslovakia covered with arguments that the Sudetenland should never have been Czech in the first place. But Munich was the end of illusion, and the German entry into Prague was the prologue either to total eclipse as a power or to a military gamble. If the French nation was not at all united on the guarantees Great Britain offered to Poland and Rumania in March 1939, there was a consensus that France had to go along with them. And thus, having alliances with two states and military conventions with neither, trying *in extremis* to reconcile their mutual hostilities, France was deserted by the one—Russia—and went to war, led by Great Britain, for the other—Poland, which was beyond salvation. The whipcrack of 1931, the triumph of 1918, even the resolute defiance of 1914, let alone the impatience of 1870, had quite gone. "It is war," the defeatist Foreign Minister, Georges Bonnet, said in September, "and all we can do now is to be prudent and not bring in against us more enemies than necessary."

Defeat and Liberation

The war was unpopular. Just below the surface was twenty years of reflection on the bloodletting, and of bitterness with the British for wrecking the peace and provoking a new war. To the rich, war threatened disorder and Bolshevism; to the workers, the loss of such gains as survived from 1936. Driven underground after the Nazi-Soviet Pact in August 1939, the Communists defined the war as an insane British adventure. Premier Daladier pathetically argued that there would be no resumption of the murderous offenses of 1914-1918. Poland received no help, fought, and died. France's great conscript Army, from the Channel to Switzerland, dug in on the neutral Belgian frontier and sheltered behind the Maginot

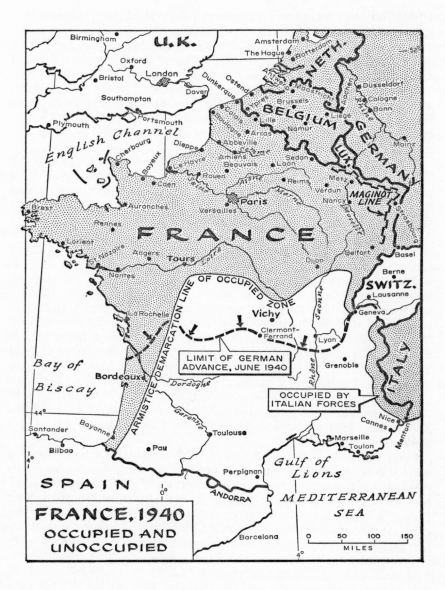

FRANCE, 1940
OCCUPIED AND
UNOCCUPIED

Line. "You can't get out of the concrete," General Maurice Gamelin said. "There isn't enough artillery in the world to get out of the concrete." That summer of 1939 no one had a plan of campaign, but the Germans made one and the allies talked of one. The two air forces were weaker than the Luftwaffe, the two navies far stronger than Hitler's fleet, but their military doctrine was less imaginative, less understanding of the roles of armor and air power. Bad weather postponed the German assault in the west; France and her ally had no thought of taking the offensive for years. Everyone hoped something would turn up. The allied war rotted in the rain or snow of eastern France.

The French mood was resigned. If Finland in her struggle with the Soviet Union beckoned as the field on which to strike a blow for liberty and against Communism and the German iron-ore supplies coming from Sweden, the idea appealed less to French Communists and the Swedes than to the commanders who glibly talked of wild expeditionary forces to Arctic ports or Balkan countries. As diversion from war on the western front, such schemes had everything but common sense. They barely camouflaged the lurking conviction that the country would not support the sacrifices a serious struggle must demand. Left, Right, and Center, antiwar, anti-British, anti-Government talk made the rounds. Beneath routine patriotism, political quarrels continued in a parliament which had surrendered all legislative authority and responsibility to the Government. Intrigues were universal, personal rivalry acute between Daladier and Reynaud. Gamelin, lethargic and complacent, became the center of their dispute after Reynaud replaced Daladier as Premier in March 1940. Confusion reigned in the planning of a descent on Scandinavia when the Finns capitulated that month. Still arguing about sending this unwanted force to Norway, the Allies were confronted suddenly in April with a German strike. About to be fired by Reynaud, Gamelin was reprieved, only to suffer a harder fate.

Caught wholly off balance, the Allies watched Denmark fall in a day and most of Norway be overrun in three weeks. Their expeditionary force, dispatched at last, was flung out of central Norway. More than ever, then, all eyes were on the Rhine frontier and the Belgian border, within which King Leopold's stance, like that of every neutral, was petrified expectancy. And the great German machine at last rolled on May 10. Misjudging its direction and distribution, incapable of reorganizing his own dispositions, Gamelin sustained a fatal reverse. Holland lasted four days, Belgium eighteen. The substitution of Maxime Weygand for Gamelin worked no miracle as the German armor split the French Armies in two, driving the powerful northern group (including the British Army) back on the Channel. Even though a colossal German error permitted a great evacuation from around Dunkirk, those armies were destroyed and the situation became irretrievable. Striking west and southwest, the Wehrmacht harried fleeing civilians and troops. All France seemed to be on the move, and by early June the military chiefs had concluded that the Government must shortly sue for terms. Though Reynaud talked of fighting on from the Empire, the Army would not have it. The exhortations of the British, led by Prime Minister Winston Churchill, could not prevail. Divided and helpless, the cabinet fell in Bordeaux, June 16, and the aged Marshal Pétain replaced Reynaud.

An armistice was requested and granted, but the terms were severe: most of France, in the west and north, was occupied; a free zone with its capital at Vichy accounted for the remaining third. Life slowly returned, like the refugees to their homes, but about 1.5 million prisoners of war did not. If there had been hard and terrible combats, there had also been total dislocation of the military machine. France was smashed but somehow terribly untouched—like the capital where the administration, the German authorities, and the citizenry were to live through four extraordinary years when, as it seemed afterward, time stood still.

Rejecting French assurances, fearing to see the French Fleet be one day used by Hilter, Great Britain seized some ships, immobilized others and launched a devastating attack on units at Mers el Kébin after the Admiral there refused to accept the various alternatives of a sudden ultimatum. Only partially successful, this melancholy action crushed the sailors ordered to carry it out and brought the Entente down in ruins. Apart from a few rebels who fought on from the Empire or England, all France expected the war to end quickly. But it did not, and Vichy remained the creature of the armistice. This Government was legitimate, contrary to the view of the British and the rebel *général de brigade* Charles de Gaulle, who led the French resistance in exile. On July 10, 1940, parliament completed its abdication by granting full powers to Pétain to promulgate a new constitution and submit it to the nation. Once more, this was an act of political suicide on behalf of order and authority. The constitution never materialized because the war did not end in the expected German victory. Instead, this vaguely authoritarian regime, a political, military, and technocratic confusion, passing through a number of phases, lived on at Hitler's mercy. Crowned by the vague yet strangely cunning Marshal, manipulated by the embittered former premier Pierre Laval, who believed that he alone could save something from the catastrophe, it concentrated increasingly on mere survival. Its controllers varied widely and changed as time progressed.

In this strange interlude, reactionaries and counterrevolutionaries, constructive technocrats and agrarian dreamers played roles. Undemocratic, anti-Semitic and vindictive, Vichy sought the basis for a reconstruction of a long-fractured society. The war swept away the foundation of a German hegemony on which it had tried to build. Thus it was doomed to have its popular support slip away. If it eventually passed on a constructive legacy of social and economic achievement, it collapsed in internecine strife, amid the blows of the Resistance it could not stamp out and the ruin of Hitler's empire which had made it possible. The Marshal was its increasingly inappropriate symbol, the technicians were its mainspring, and Laval was its political genius. He had his reasons for informing Hitler that he desired British defeat "with all my heart." To avoid the fate of Poland, he and his collaborators did much that was dishonorable. No one ever played a worse hand more tirelessly. It was a pathetic spectacle, but not quite tragedy. Laval seemed never to understand the immensity of the forces in collision and the impossibility of his self-appointed task. His was a virtuoso performance which, like Vichy itself, could have no happy ending.

Thus Frenchmen were divided—by the defeat, by the Resistance, by the Germans, by the British, and by the increasing hope of liberation. The bitterness of 1940 against the British and the ministers who had led France to war gave way to bitterness against those who had staked all on collaboration. Hitler's invasion of Russia in 1941 had unleashed the Communist Resistance. With the allied victories around the globe, the politicians who had shunned responsibility in peace and war began to pose as *résistants*. The genuine fascists, like Jacques Doriot, never turned back from the enemy camp. Within France, therefore, a savage civil war mounted in fury as the invasion of Normandy approached. Trapped once again by ideologies as well as by the terrible decisions forced upon them by the Occupation, Frenchmen butchered and tortured each other, while France held her breath and wondered what her fate was to be.

From London and Algiers, overcoming many challenges and really against all odds, General de Gaulle had by 1944 become the sole authority the country would recognize. His agents had succeeded in uniting rival resistance movements inside France. The Allied advance into France that summer showed that his claims were supported. The Anglo-American plans for a military government were abandoned. Laval's last effort to win recognition of the legitimacy of Vichy and achieve a kind of hand-over was rejected by de Gaulle. By the August day when the General, his soldiers, and the resistance leaders paraded from the Arc to Notre Dame, even the suspicious and reluctant Americans had recognized him *de facto*. Four years had passed since he flew out of Bordeaux to England, a rebel defying the Army, the State, and the enemy, soon thereafter condemned to death by a military court. Supported by Churchill, driven on by ambition and faith, he had won back part of the French Empire, and now the land that had scarcely heard of him before the war. On this great occasion, as he moved down the Avenue among the cheering crowds, he saluted Clemenceau, leaning forward there on his pedestal. Fortune's wheel had turned—and many times. Only four months had passed since the ancient Marshal had been received by cheering throngs at the Hôtel de Ville. But now at that moment the old man's attempt to dissociate himself from Laval and achieve reconciliation with his former disciple was spurned. A prisoner of the enemy, en route to Sigmaringen in southwest Germany, Pétain would soon return to stand trial.

Nineteen-forty-five brought no repetition of the weary glory of 1918. Though France had contributed to the victory—in Africa, in Italy, in western Europe, and at sea and in the air—the principal effort had been made by others. The deepest memories the nation held were of 1940, of the war that was lost, and of the Occupation. Whoever had been responsible for the course of events leading to that abyss, the Liberation only underlined how catastrophic the fall had been. The Republic had paid for its own divisions and irresponsibilities, and for those of some others too. Yet even as it started back toward reconstruction, it clung to the old symbols of prestige. Ahead lay some eighteen years of colonial warfare and an internal convulsion threatening civil strife.

The final recognition de Gaulle had demanded from the great powers was tardily accorded in October 1944. The Provisional Government of the French Republic he headed was established in Paris, and a month later the National Consultative Assembly was similarly transferred from Algiers to the capital. For more than a year then the General reigned uncontested with his Government drawn from the old Committee of National Liberation and the Resistance. The parties reorganized or confirmed their demise: the Right was compromised by its attitude toward Vichy; the Radicals were tarred with the brush of the Third Republic; the Communists basked in the glow of Soviet victories, claimed the Resistance for their own, affected amnesia about their 1939-1941 treason, and profited by de Gaulle's conclusion of a Franco-Soviet pact; the Socialists brandished their Resistance record and Léon Blum's stout defense of the Republic in the abortive Riom Trial staged by Vichy in 1942 and stopped by the Germans as too embarrassing; the new *Mouvement républicain populaire* (MRP) mushroomed out of the Resistance and the prewar Catholic center-Left. Though the General permitted the Communist leader, Maurice Thorez, to return from Moscow (whither he had deserted from the French Army during the war) and join the Government, he carefully excluded such people from key ministerial posts. Provisional dictator, he was faced with many tasks beyond the acquisition of rank, which, to the war's end, the allied powers refused France.

Despite a superficial unity, the scene was not immediately encouraging. The economy was dislocated, inflation and the black market flourished, transport was paralyzed. A measure of nationalization was effected, but no serious monetary reform. The General's mind dwelt naturally on other things. And a settling of accounts by assassination and by trial suggested the extent of the national fissures. A parade of prominent officers, businessmen, journalists, politicians, and administrators were charged with collaboration and treason; about 800 were executed, some 40,000 went to prison. Inevitably the symbol of four unhappy years was tried and sentenced to death. Almost 90 years old, trapped by vanity, duty, and history, Pétain had this savage sentence commuted to life imprisonment by his former protégé—a term cruelly to be served. But for Laval there was neither justice nor mercy. The scandalous trial, an exhibition of hatred and guilt on the part of prosecution and public, was another proof of the collapse of civic and moral values, a realm in which further lamentable departures from the Enlightenment and Revolutionary ideals were to be recorded in the years ahead. Refusing to defend himself or to be defended, this gambler in a game rigged against him from the start was condemned to death. His system of values collapsing as the hour for his death approached, he tried suicide, was snatched from death and, wracked by agony, was, on the General's orders, tied to a post and shot.

The Fourth Republic

The nation found its way back to the Republic. It voted in October 1945 not to revive the Third but to create a Fourth. When de Gaulle perceived that the Constituent Assembly, with a strong Communist, Socialist, and MRP majority, was bent upon establishing a parliamentary system, he contemplated a *coup d'état*, but decided instead to resign suddenly in January 1946. He expected a rapid recall on his own terms. It never came. After the Communists and Socialists had failed to get approval of a draft constitution providing for a unicameral legislature (and, therefore, for an executive completely subject to its control), a second Constituent Assembly restored the second chamber, wrote in stronger checks and balances, and, despite a Gaullist campaign against it, obtained approval of this second draft. The October 1946 referendum offered, however, only a minority decision: almost one-third of the electorate abstained, almost one-third voted against.

At best, the new Constitution was a compromise. It evoked the principles of 1789 and 1793, formulated the duty to work and right of employment and of strike, maintained the State's duty to provide social security and free, secular education, and in this way reached across 150 years from the Revolution to the Resistance. With the Council of the Republic less powerful than the old Senate, the National Assembly was even more sovereign than the Chamber of Deputies had been. Though the Assembly might not delegate its legislative function to the Government (as the Chamber had done under the Third Republic), the executive did not need decree-laws to take direct administrative action. The provision for dissolution of the Assembly was scarcely to be used by the Government, and was to prove useless in a multiparty situation. Proportional representation proved no panacea for cabinet instability. And as the months passed and the old faces reappeared, the ghost of the Third Republic seemed to have settled into the Palais Bourbon, despite the verdict of 1945 against it.

The record of this Fourth Republic was mixed. In the course of its twelve years the country swung away from the Tripartism of 1945 toward the center-Right and renewed political fragmentation. In 1947 the Communists went into opposition, and de Gaulle formed his *Rassemblement du peuple français* (RPF): both were dedicated to the destruction of the regime. A Third Force coalition of Socialists, Radicals, MRP, and Independents with a parliamentary majority struggled on forming cabinets. But it was rent by obvious religious, ideological, and class divisions. Moreover, the revived Radicals split into opposed groups, and the Gaullist RPF broke up when it seemed clear that the General's bid for power was unlikely to succeed by this means. Although there was some increase in the strength of national party organizations, bitter doctrinal quarrels did not make for governmental stability. The Assembly was still (despite the December 1955 dissolution) a closed arena, the presidency was as weak as it had been after MacMahon's defeat in 1877, and governments were perhaps even more subject to parliamentary control. The political influence of rural France, its farmers, shopkeepers, and lobbies, triumphed over the city. Since all governments were coalitions, though it was risky to do nothing it was probably fatal to do something that would result in withdrawal of some part of the cabinet's support. Few premiers were ready or able to play the delicate game of altering their government each time they tried to implement a policy requiring a slightly different variety of support. Instead they hung on until their fall could no longer be postponed, choosing to resign on an issue as close to principle as they could make it. The policy of *immobilisme* meant postponement of political decisions and a comparable increase of administrative powers. The consequence was an increasing divorce between the nation and its parliament, a mounting public contempt for the political system. After the better part of two centuries the problem of relating government to the people was far from solution.

But the record showed other facts. Although the Fourth Republic never mastered inflation, it achieved economic recovery. In spite of the specter of class struggle, its social-security system alleviated some of the injustices of industrial society. It made a beginning at least on the Republic's reconciliation to State aid to Catholic schools. It broke the Communist-inspired insurrectional strikes and faced down the attack from the RPF and the mindless rural reaction led by Pierre Poujade. From this Republic came many of the principal proposals for a sane reconstruction of Europe. The Anglo-French Treaty of Dunkirk in 1947 suggested revival of the Entente and a formal obliteration of the memories of 1940. Though the European Defense Community, which emerged from a French idea, was killed by France, the European Coal and Steel Community (also an attempt to control the reemergence of Germany) was a French conception leading to the 1957 Treaties of Rome, which set Europe on the road to a Common Market and perhaps to federation. The irony was that while year by year the national economic and demographic condition improved, the international stock of France diminished. De Gaulle had labored heroically between 1940 and 1946 to resurrect the prestige of France. But cabinet instability and imperial war steadily sapped the country's position among the powers. It was this appalling bloodletting in the Empire—known now as the French Union, a legalistic sleight of hand which became history before it was a fact—that prevented the nation from seeing clearly the interests of France as a whole.

By the spring of 1958 the Fourth Republic had survived numerous ordeals and much humiliation. In many ways it seemed healthy and even prosperous. What condemned it was the problem of imperial retreat, the fatal legacy, in particular, of Charles X's expedition, on the eve of his fall from power, to Algiers. After many warnings and much procrastination and timidity, the Republic was confronted by civil and military disobedience on a major scale. The nation was divided, if not simply paralyzed. Between the alternatives of a military *coup d'état* and possible parliamentary leadership in civil war on one hand, and the return of de Gaulle as mediator on the other, the notables of the regime chose de Gaulle. Parliament capitulated and, after certain assurances, invested him as the last Premier of the Fourth Republic. The search for consensus had not yet ended.

FIVE

The French:

A Group Portrait

*"Nous sommes si accoutumés à nous déguiser aux autres
qu'enfin nous nous déguisons à nous-mêmes."*

The game of analyzing the French character is one of the most popular. Frenchmen do it very well; foreigners often think they do it still better. Since there are no rules, no referee, and no terminal period of play, there can be no definitive judgment. Thus the game will go on, presumably forever, simply because the French are, on any evaluation, one of the most gifted and fascinating peoples, occupying one of the most important positions on the globe, having contributed as much as, if not more than, any other nation to western civilization. France, Charles Morazé maintained, is the world's microcosm. If this was an exaggerated claim, it was sufficiently justified to permit repeated reflection on her people and their way of life.

The State of Mind

As a breed, the French are mongrel and proud of it. Caste and class they have known, but not race. The efforts of their occupants after 1940 to distinguish racially among them were ludicrous, possible only in a regime becoming more irrational as its spectacular course came to an end. The French showed little receptivity to their German neighbors' delusions. Prejudice against Jews and foreigners has been observed often enough, but nothing approaching the Nazi hocus-pocus. The Comte Arthur de Gobineau, as much sinned against as sinning, found his most attentive audience across the Rhine. The French occasionally talk as if they were something apart, but that something is the product of history. In fact, they are a mixture of men of the north, of the continental center, and of the Mediterranean. Put very simply, some are tall and fair, descendants of Scandinavia, scattered along the shores and stretching back onto the farmlands from the Belgian border to the Breton Peninsula and south to the Pyrenees. Some are Celts, shorter and darker, from across the uplands of eastern France, the Massif Central, and over to the Pyrenees, round-headed Alpines. A third group, longer-headed, olive-skinned, dark-haired Mediterraneans, are characteristic of the south. France is thus populated by a mixture of the principal types found in western Europe.

Frenchmen sometimes dismiss this physical basis as the explanation of their talents and multiplicity of interests. And narcissistic as they may be, they do not embody the more aggressive qualities of genealogical self-concern. There have been times of course when they sought to impose themselves: the crusaders went forward with *"Dieu le veult!"* in their ears; the Revolution in arms became infected with a messianic contagion. But characteristically such expeditions were in the name less of a *people* than of a *cause* of which they, the French, simply happened to consider themselves the repositories. The Frenchman has always demonstrated attachment to his home, his soil, to the wonderful variety of his native land. He has been content with himself and with what nature gave him in the way of mountain and valley, lake and river, forest and field. This closeness to the land has made the diverse strains one. In a profoundly rural society, Paris was an almost unique metropolitan phenomenon. Having suffered the Industrial Revolution and the growth of urban problems, France reluctantly faced up to what had happened. Even when they inhabit the city, Frenchmen try to maintain contact with the land. They continued trying to live in a kind of rural idyll long after its physical basis ebbed away in the nineteenth and twentieth centuries.

But the insufficiency of rural France in the age of steam, iron, electricity, and mechanization had to be accepted. Acceptance was a painful, protracted experience. France's happy agrarian situation has not been paralleled by as fortunate an industrial bounty. Or is it that the mentality of "the French peasant" has not led to the rational exploitation of natural industrial resources which simply seem less rich than the land itself? The British turned an improbably poor and crowded island home into a vast workshop built on coal and iron; the Germans created an empire of steel and chemistry out of a relatively sleepy tract of rural lands in Central Europe. Both went out to capture world markets. The Frenchman, however, did not think he had the resources; above all, he had little wish to do so. Behind tariff walls he sought to preserve his independence, admit only the minimum Industrial Revolution, and let other peoples go their way.

In the first half of the twentieth century it became clear that this was impossible. The strain of trying to preserve the rural idyll opened up political, economic, and psychic cracks in the nation. The relative harmony between town and countryside, which had survived into the nineteenth century (not without numerous rough passages), broke down. The rebellious worker of 1848 had not really felt a fundamental hostility directed against him by the conservative farmer, but he was more aware of it in 1871; he could hardly ignore it by 1936. The urban manufacturer resented the political dominance of the provincial notables. The intelligentsia divided as between those who celebrated traditional France, and those, looking at America or Germany, who grew bitter with the failure to exploit the inventive genius of France which other peoples appropriated to their own profit. The eighteenth-century synthesis broke down. Not until the second half of the twentieth century did Frenchmen begin to reconcile once more their attachment to the land, their astonishing inventiveness, their industrial skills, and their ability to trade with the outside world. They came finally to recognize the full range of their diversities and to fuse them, as they long ago fused their principal strains in "a nation of patriots."

What the common denominator may be is hard to say. It is not economic interest, intellectual attitude, or "way of life." It may be that elusive thing, a way of *looking* at life, more accurately, a way of looking at oneself. Many of the clichés here are true. The Frenchman *is* an individualist, independent, *against* rather than *for*. Nothing is so necessary to him as a stance of ironic detachment; nothing so pleasurable as the analysis of other people's foibles, dogmas, procedures. Delighted to know about them, he is enchanted not to be captured by them. Perhaps the Duc de la Rochefoucauld was right to withdraw his maxim that goes, "We enjoy seeing through others, but not being seen through." If this be truth, it must of course apply to all men. Just the same, the foreigner may feel in some rather special way that he detects a peculiar propensity here on the part of Frenchmen he happens to know. For how many of them bring to mind that other maxim La Rochefoucauld did not withdraw, "If we had no faults we should not find so much enjoyment in seeing faults in others"?

The Frenchman prides himself on his intellect, the ability to see something whole. He is capable of pursuing his vaunted Cartesianism to total absurdity; he cares less for the conclusion than for the intellectual activity that produced it. This constant preoccupation with self and mind has made him dazzling to the outsider, a trial to his rulers, and a puzzle to his neighbors. It has led him into the most rigid inability to yield, to compromise, to choose between the attainable "less good" and the unattainable "best." All his brilliance has not saved him from being sometimes the first victim of his high standards, his relentless logic, and his atomistic independence. So penetrating about others, he has occasionally failed to see that if his intellectualism is a bright beacon to others, it may serve only as a cruel torchlight over his own self-induced misfortunes.

Family

But such a sketch is no more than a partial outline of the more obvious characteristics of the articulate urban classes. A national common denominator might be found in the style of, and the attitude toward family life. This, as every foreigner who has been privileged to catch a glimpse of it knows, is close. Penetration by the outsider is still rare. The repeated offer of a dinner *en famille* has been known to entrance a North American visitor over a period of a year, only to fail to be realized. Yet even the offer to so casual an acquaintance is the mark of change. Family life is loosening up, though the process may be slow. The orderly, hierarchical, rather sheltered family structure survives as the core of society, the one almost unquestioned source of authority. "The family in France," Salvador de Madariaga said more than a generation ago, "may be considered as the

field in which social and individual tendencies come to terms and compensate each other. It does not, as in England, yield before the pressure
of the national group. Yet, through it, the individual perceives the pressure
of the group and, thanks to it, a sufficient standard of collective behaviour
is maintained in the nation."

The judgment may be questionable. But the structure of the family remains clear, defined in the *Code civil*, consolidated by the *Code de la
famille* introduced in 1939, with a nice balance of authority established
between the mother and the father. Laurence Wylie, however, considers
that as the mother is principally responsible for raising the children, and
as the government *allocutions familiales* are greater if she does not seek an
outside job, her income and authority may exceed her husband's. If this
is so, the structure of family life is certainly altered, although not necessarily weakened. And families are much larger than they were before 1939.
Whether owing to tax allowances, family allotments, the old Marshal's
appeal in the hour of defeat, the influence of the Christian Democrats
(*Mouvement républicain populaire* after the war), or some undefinable
instinct to protect the nation—for whatever reason or combination of
reasons, the French began to have more children.

Strains have been imposed from without. The twentieth century has
dramatized the conflict of generations. The *mariage de raison* has yielded
to romantic love. No doubt arranged alliances take place, but in a world
where landed property is of slight significance the *situation* of each partner
is not what it was in the assessment of the match; the father of the bride
is more interested in his prospective son-in-law's education and professional prospects. If wives have still to reckon with a mistress, their
position has been enhanced by the degree to which the manufacturing
world competes fiercely for the expenditures which, as wives, they control:
many a husband receives instructions from his wife about the color of
their automobile. The industrialization of life has also widened the gap
between generations. The aging farmer, bourgeois, or worker finds the
spectacle of roaring scooters in a whirl of flying dust difficult to accept. In
many provincial towns one may see the startling contrast of quietly
promenading older citizens, in their Sunday-best, set beside the noisy
hangouts of the young with the incessant arrival and departure of
squealing tires and raucous exhausts. The conflict of generations is both
fostered by and reflected in the mass media. Whether by Billy Wilder,
Federico Fellini, or François Truffaut, the celluloid expression of the
dreams, disenchantment, and sadness of the young invades almost every
family to create an abyss between those who respond and those who do not.
It is not that French youth is especially rebellious. On the contrary, it is
rather conformist, set upon comfort and security, prepared to harbor even
fewer illusions than previous generations. Though youth may not be in
revolt, it no longer believes in quite such an orderly society as its families
took for granted. Already these shifting attitudes have worked their way

into a second generation. The real gulf lies between youth and its grand-parents.

External forces have not dramatically shaken the family, not even the American impact. The French family discovered the refrigerator and did not succumb. The slogan "Yankee Go Home" and the crackpot campaign to suggest that Coca Cola caused cancer were politically orchestrated. Even the rage for the automobile has not destroyed the unity and isolation of the family unit. A French family at dinner in the countryside some Sunday, its Renault or 2-CV parked outside the restaurant, is as circumspect and exquisitely observant of its neighbors' privacy as its North American counterpart is likely to be cheery, noisy, garrulous, and apparently starved for wider association. Children are brought up carefully and lovingly, but firmly, as little savages of nature who have to be civilized by discipline, reason, and love before it will be safe to let them loose upon the world. A hard school of authority and understanding, the family observes an elaborate etiquette. If it inculcates unprogressive habits, it produces an unusually mature product. And although it does what it can to preserve what it thinks best, it yields to the present where it must.

Class

The rigidities of class structure are also giving way. Society was never so neatly compartmentalized as the usual terminology suggested, but it is still convenient to use the labels of a more innocent time. The conception of class, and even caste, has not entirely disappeared in France. A proletariat, the *class ouvrière*, numbers about six million. Concentrated in the northeast, much of it in the heavily industrialized Paris region, it represents somewhat less than half of all wage earners. Despite periods of militancy, it has not been highly organized. Possibly not more than one-quarter of French workers belong to unions, a fact partly explained by the large number of very small enterprises, partly by extension to non-union industries of collective agreements reached elsewhere, partly by the low rate of unemployment since the war. The Communists were able to raise street demonstrations against the Algerian war and President de Gaulle; the unions defied the Fifth Republic's threat of requisition and imprisonment. But proletarian militancy is not great. Nineteenth-century socialist utopianism is dead, the lure of the Soviet system has faded; the workers' goal is to raise their standard of living and see their children acquire skills and enter well-paid occupations. The French *patronat* have become slightly more enlightened since the Great Fear of 1936 and the revenge they took after the *Front populaire* collapsed in 1937. A minority of progressive employers and skilled workers have set the pace for more harmonious labor-management relations, directing the proletariat away from social myth to social security. With better wages, family allowances, slightly improved housing (30 per cent of urban apartments still have no private water closet), the possibility of owning a car and having three weeks paid vacation, the worker may remain as contemptuous of the bourgeoisie as before, apathetic toward civic responsibility, skeptical, and generally resentful, but, willy-nilly, he is becoming *embourgeoisé* himself. In 1945 the Communist organ *L'Humanité* had a circulation of about 600,000; by 1960 it had fallen to 192,000.

Classification of the artisan depends upon the aspect of his life under consideration. A case may be made for calling him *petit bourgeois*. His skills at least equal those of the advanced worker; his ownership of the means of production may be as outright as that of the small shopkeeper. Numbered in the low millions, he is as resistant to change as any Frenchman. Threatened by industry, he pursues craftmanship in a world of mass production; enriched by an expanding complex of mechanical, electrical, and electronic appliances constantly in danger of breakdown, he is guaranteed survival and prosperity in some areas and threatened with extinction in others. Yet in general it may be true that the *artisanat* alters its skills but does not die. A link between the industrial proletariat and the lower-middle class, it illustrates again the difficulty of trying boldly to define classes in France. And, like the industrial worker and the *petit bourgeois*, it belongs in many cases to that darker area of the French economy which the nation as a whole has been so reluctant to recognize and to determine to eliminate.

Beyond the *classe ouvrière* and the *artisanat* lies the uncertain mass of the *classes moyennes*—the *petite bourgeoisie* and those separated from them by superior education. Here are found the shopkeepers and café owners, inefficient, independent, enemies of bigness, defenders of the little man in an age when mass production and the tentacles of the State threaten to destroy his marginal living, his tax evasion, and his undoubted right to run his own show as he damn well pleases. Here too are the primary and secondary school teachers, the typists and clerks, bus drivers, waiters, street-sweepers and *concierges*, post-office workers, policemen and others employed by that soulless employer which is the State. Thus some are self-employed, some salaried. All live modestly, few have wide horizons. Their goals are bourgeois, socially conformist, and respectable. They have been capable of so substantial a resistance as the short-lived anti-tax movement led by Pierre Poujade after 1953. Rightly or wrongly, they have been pilloried in literature as penny-pinching, grasping, and mean. Yet they have also epitomized the egalitarian tradition stemming from the Revolution, and when the country has been in danger they have not failed to offer themselves in its defense.

Rising higher, one meets the *moyenne bourgeoisie*, or *bonne bourgeoisie*, the upper-middle class of businessmen, professional men, successful writers and artists, and higher functionaries. As thrifty as the *classes moyennes*, they are generally better educated, housed, clothed, and fed. In town they may still have a servant; in the country, a small retreat. Ties with the university and the armed forces are often more than casual, though commerce and the civil service have largely given them their place, and, despite periodic economic and political catastrophe, their savings and their brains have kept them there. More than the *classes moyennes*, they have responded to, have been divided by, and have suffered from the century's ideological conflicts. Since 1945 they have shown adaptability. Fundamentally, the *moyenne bourgeoisie* inherited the earth in 1789, and it has weathered more or less successfully every kind of crisis since that time. Neither war and revolution, invasion and occupation, American civilization, nor literary ridicule has caused it to abandon the pursuit of comfort, order, service, and money.

The *haute bourgeoisie* is a vaguely determined province of the wealthiest manufacturers, professional men, bankers, and soldiers. Scattered over the nation, centered in Paris, it peoples the great clubs, racetracks, and celebrated watering places of France and Europe. Drawing from the *moyenne bourgeoisie*, shading off into the aristocracy, it is to be found in the Quai d'Orsay and the Académie Française and the ranks of the *grand patronat*. It too has not escaped the great controversies of the age, but it has weathered them better than those more directly *engagés*. The *haut bourgeois* has been both collaborator and resistance-fighter, though probably more Pétainist than Gaullist. Adaptable and indispensable, he asserted his own interests against the State under the Fourth Republic and continued as successfully under the Fifth—somewhat apart from the authoritarian regime, but always felt. For him also, 1789 represented a class triumph in the guise of "the revolution of the lawyers," though it served his purposes in the nineteenth century to deny the continuity of the revolutionary tradition. Socially cramped before 1789, socially at ease ever since, he has remained *bien pensant* through it all. His children and grandchildren, if not himself and his wife, may "twist" in chic casinos, but by wealth, family, or career his station is unquestioned.

The nature and extent of the aristocracy is less sure. How many North American students, searching Paris for a temporary home, have encountered some unsuspected *comtesse* living and renting rooms far from the imagined château? There have been so many aristocracies in France: the feudal *noblesse*, the *arriviste* aristocracy of the robe, the Napoleonic nobility of the Empire, and that of the Orleanist regime of Louis Philippe. Even before the Revolution aristocrats lived in diverse conditions of wealth and poverty. Under the Republics, titles came to be prized no less, and, precisely because they enjoyed no legal recognition, were both flaunted and invented. Genuine nobles of substance are of course known and, like the *haute bourgeoisie*, are securely located in the Académie or even the University, the great banking houses, and the armed forces. They too have their estates, their yachts riding at anchor in Cannes, and their winter sports at Kitzbühel or Megève. Of the lesser aristocracy, in Paris or the provinces, it may be guessed that their life is almost undistinguishable from that of the bourgeoisie.

Throughout the whole upper class a simplification of customs and style has been apparent since 1945. Servants are fewer, conveniences more numerous. The rites and ritual of the table have yielded to other pleasures or lengthier hours at the office. Dress is less formal, if no less elegant. The discussion of sex is more open. To hunting and horse racing have been added golf, tennis, and water-skiing. Scotch whisky is not only palatable but chic. If cocktail parties disturb the older generation, the small or family reception is coming to be considered a tiresome bore to those hopelessly subverted by (if still rather contemptuous of) *la vie américaine*. The upper class retains its style; its distinctiveness, in a broader sense, is on the way out.

Even the peasantry has not remained untouched by aspects of what Edward R. Tannenbaum called the "Euro-American civilization." The familiar portrait of the *fermier* as grasping, suspicious, and untrustworthy needs retouching—there is of course another literature which depicts him as the stalwart support of eternal France. If his frugality has not changed, the level of his education has improved. He still has no running water in about 75 per cent of his dwellings (Raymond Cartier wrote of "Asiatic conditions" in the smaller villages), but the radio and the television have broken into his insularity. A "rural revolution" has been in progress. Independence may still be carried to the point of running into debt by purchasing a tractor rather than participating in a cooperative, but farmers *are* using tractors. Membership in the *Jeunesse agricole catholique* (JAC) and a more positive attitude toward the state characterize the new generation. The pattern is not, as Gordon Wright showed, everywhere the same. If the Communist appeal remains, although communism has achieved little, the tendency is more instinctive than doctrinal. Vestiges of neo-feudal attitudes remain in the west, but the revolt against landlordism and state neglect has become spectacular.

The countryside is not unchanging. Less apposite now seems David Schoenbrun's remark that, if the French economy were one day found dead, it would be likely to have a pitchfork through the heart. The post-1945 decline has ended. Though differences exist between regions, in general the farmer is less exclusively village-centered: he sells in the larger market towns, goes to city hospitals, exports his children to industry. Social gradations still remain. Small landowners predominate, although the tenant farmer may be more prosperous because of compact holdings (the old inheritance laws left a legacy of scattered strips which forbade modern methods of cultivation). Beneath these *fermiers* proper is the *métayer*, a share-tenant or sharecropper, who may also be better off than the land-owning farmer. Then comes the *ouvrier agricole*, a permanent hired man, and finally the *journalier*, the itinerant day laborer. Even crops may suggest social distinction. "Wine people," as Wylie put it, consider themselves superior to "cow people," just as those close to the *routes nationales* consider themselves more in touch than the denizens of forgotten hamlets. Differences exist between the young men, drawn to the JAC, and the older generation. But although the small family farm remains the norm, the pattern of rural life is changing. Village shopkeepers and artisans (a disappearing group) and *fonctionnaires*, farmers, and gentry are, in spite of the past, being touched by the modernization of France.

In sum, French society remains conservative but not unchanging. It is class conscious but accepts social mobility. It has not forgotten the land, but its values are bourgeois. It accepts trans-Atlantic innovations and retains the assurance of its own superiority. It has access to a kind of generalized culture. Brigitte Bardot's heroines make little class appeal, Jean Gabin's heroes are in tuxedos or denims. *Colonies de vacances* for children of less well-to-do families often use the same beaches as those in more prosperous conditions. Behind the next pair of sun-glasses from Brittany to the Riviera, or on the slopes of the Jura, may be a *duchesse* or a typist. The glossy pages of *Elle* are read in cottages and country houses. No doubt the Auteuil crowd is not identical to the one in the Vélodrome d'hiver; those who play at *boules* in the dusty summer evenings are not seen on the golf courses of the Ile de France. Class phenomena, though present, have tended to fade: the Tour de France and water-skiing have different social connotations, but the trend is toward a leveling of interests and activity. At the lowest level, the young toughs of the *blousons noirs*, lower class and motorcycle riding, have been joined by the resort rowdies of the *blousons dorés*, middle class and equally hostile. At the highest, still unhappily rare, youth of all classes meet in the lecture hall, on the track, and at the theater. Less circumscribed by the past, society remains structured and orderly, and it is by no means certain that that will all pass away.

Society vs. the State

What is even less likely to pass away is the ambivalent French attitude toward the State. The Fifth Republic was articulate in this matter. " 'Gaullism,' in its essence, is France; and the movement toward restoring her to greatness," President de Gaulle once said. ". . . Of course we need help to do this, but the mainspring must come from within France herself. . . . Her own people must do it. . . . But never forget that the French people are not France. For a thousand years it has been like this. France is the State. And the State leads the people to greatness." Was any regime ever so frank, or so confusingly self-contradictory? Yet this notion of "we" and "they" haunts the French past. The hostility toward *fonctionnaires* is familiar to everyone who has waited at some postoffice or *préfecture de police* window, seeking to extract some paper without which life will become impossible, and witnessed native exchanges with these victims of popular opprobrium. None are so despised (unless it be taxcollectors in provincial towns of the southwest) as civil servants not on view but reported as playing cards all day at the public expense. "They" are the interfering, wasteful, inefficient, all-devouring State. Hence it is quite normal that everyone should play the game by running as much opposition as possible.

This ingrained habit and social philosophy had its philosopher in Émile

Chartier, who, as "Alain," was a kind of self-appointed theoretician for the Radical Socialists ("the greatest of modern philosophers," a party official called him before his death in 1951). Though he addressed himself to the little man, his words seemed golden to almost all. The message was one of perpetual resistance to the State, to *le contrôleur*, by constructing daily "a little barricade." That so primitive a notion, even on the merely symbolic level, should have passed as a philosophy remains mysterious for some outsiders. It would be interesting but irrelevant to speculate on the damage it did to, or the approval it conferred upon negative attitudes inherent in, the Third and Fourth Republics. The suspicion with which Frenchmen view the State may be more than the expression of anarchism in their souls. André Siegfried argued that since the family is prior to and more enduring than the State, it is preservation of the family against the State which motivates them. But not all instances of *incivisme*, or lack of *esprit civique*, fit neatly into that pigeonhole.

Only indirectly could the case of Pierre Poujade, stationer in the village of St. Ceré (Lot), and his sometime two-and-a-half million supporters be rationalized thus, unless every "descending group" in the nation is really protecting the family against the State. The Poujadist movement was sparked by a cabinet-maker appealing to his fellow municipal councillor for assistance against the tax inspector coming to check his books in July 1953. It was in fact an attempt to defend the inefficient activity of the provincial *artisanat* and *petite bourgeoisie*. The tax inspector was represented by the tough little stationer as the old symbol of State oppression. And yet Poujadism suggested that although hostility to the State may provide the basis for a political movement, it cannot sustain it. As it happened, Poujade shifted his ground to collect a wider following on the troubled issue of Algeria. Inevitably he lost both early and late supporters because he had no constructive program on any matter.

A cocky provincial shopkeeper with a band of angry disciples may momentarily embody the principle of resistance to the State, but clearly the principle is anarchic and thus antipathetic to organization. Moreover, the Frenchman both resists the State and considers it fair game. The Republic has been many times rocked by major financial scandals, but closer inspection suggests that only a small political opposition stood back of demonstrations of "national outrage." The Frenchman does not judge too severely those in office who succumb to temptation (though there was at least one exception under the Fourth Republic); he expects it of them as he expects the bureaucracy to be wasteful, just as he expects himself to resist *le Fisc*. "Unspoken disapproval is the lot of anyone in France who pays taxes or customs duties without first having tried to dodge payment," Siegfried remarked. "It is not so much that we consider him a simpleton as that we regard him as not having done all he ought to have done." This constant contest is known elsewhere, but the French have carried it to a certain refinement. The fact that this game results in the unequal distribution of taxation, the heaviest burden falling on those wage earners least able to pay, does not trouble the collective conscience. The whole object is to protect oneself, to avoid being taken for a *poire* ("sucker"). It does, however, make for social protest.

In France less than 30 per cent of taxes are directly imposed. More than 75 per cent of businessmen, shopkeepers, and artisans let the State estimate their income and decide how much they should pay on it. They supply such figures as they think suitable; the Ministry of Finance presents the bill, which may be appealed. Tax evasions in the recent past have by this system been estimated at 30 per cent in commerce and the professions, and 70 per cent in agriculture. The situation is denounced but tolerated. The system of judging income by the *signes extérieures de la richesse*, introduced in 1947, presupposes that an honest report from the tax payer is not to be expected. Thus maids, dogs, country houses, yachts, horses, and so on, are taken into account. The whole trick then becomes one of disguising everything from the tax inspector. "Everyone is a conspirator," Prime Minister Georges Pompidou remarked in the spring of 1963, when lauching a general investigation, which seemed called for since in 1961 alone 36 of France's 46 million paid no income tax, and scarcely more than a thousand admitted having an income over $12,800. Tax reform plans were many under the Republics, but the ancient opposition to the State always triumphed over *le Fisc*.

Alain's philosophy of a daily quota of "little barricades" is reflected in the network of pressure groups. Some are as large as the Church, the *Confédération générale du travail*, or the *Conseil national du patronat français*; some as minor as every ephemeral association for the defense of some obscure local cause. Each organization defends its interests and acquired rights (*droits acquis*) against the State or whatever else threatens them. In a nation with a long historical memory and a fiercely legalist spirit, this kind of activity can paralyze progress or, at all events, impede change. A 1959 government inquiry reported that the civil service could not deal with the problem since the bureaucracy had come to consider protection of such rights part of its work. And the variety of such rights is bewildering. Some are as undisputed as the seats in the Paris Métro set aside in rush hours for crippled veterans, then pregnant women, and so forth. More colorful is the sort of activity that led Paris butchers in 1963 to resist Government control of beefsteak prices; they closed their stores and resorted to at least one plasticine bombing. "We are no longer under the Occupation," the syndicate chairman proclaimed. "The Germans have left. Butchers, I am proud of you!" This might seem comic-opera to the profane, but in France it is taken as perfectly natural. There are times when the outsider imagines France as a vast battlefield covered by an infinite number of little fortresses behind which the furious défense of something is proceeding amidst cries of outraged patriotism and vengeance.

It is easy to conjure up this picture of nearly fifty million Frenchmen daily confronting each other with their legal rights. They brandish cards of *priorité*, cards permitting reduction of ticket prices, cards permitting them to stand in this line rather than that. When they have no such card, they still pursue their rights to the point of leaning slightly on each other in queues, attempting to slip ahead all-unaware (and, naturally, resisting such encroachments). At demonstrations, they threaten each other within an inch of violence; they dare the police to act one millimeter over the limit of the law, and, when this occurs, as it does all the time, enter the fray with cries of rage and joy in the combat for their desecrated rights. The walls of their towns and cities are painted with fading but precise reminders of what the law forbids, and placarded with the somber record of penalties inflicted for transgressions. The French contemplate the stones of their railroad stations or public monuments with equal satisfaction, it must be, whether the black lettering forbids them to post bills or to urinate, and, quite naturally, they seek to push forward the frontiers of their liberties by occasionally doing both. It is both startling and warming, this incessant national confrontation, a militant spectacle of perpetual *en-gardisme* by a free people, suspicious of each other, hostile to the State, locked in struggle to perpetuate their special advantages *vis-à-vis* each other, with (especially in the old days) their parliamentary representatives daily working to extract more. Periodically some great national issue has arisen to cause them to relax their stance and take up arms against a common foe; they then have formed *unions-sacrées*, a *bloc-national*, a *Société pour la défense de . . .* , or some other group to symbolize their complete or partial truce and their recognition of the interest of the larger whole. The year 1914 brought forth the most celebrated of these. Not even the perils of 1939 could make them repeat that miracle; the residual instinct for national consensus faltered and finally failed.

In view of so much militancy, the mood of political acquiescence under the Fifth Republic came as a shock. And yet from time to time in the past the French have evidently found the burden of struggling on the political level for acquired rights too heavy. After a decade of skirmishing during the Revolution, they laid down their political arms in return for a guarantee of rights already acquired. After 1815 they remained politically quiescent again, rising only when it appeared that the basic principles of 1789 were likely to be eliminated by a reactionary monarch. The defense of their political privileges in the revolution of 1848 was brief and feeble, collapsing long before Louis Napoleon imposed a dictatorship. It may well be, then, that outsiders have too long identified as a political characteristic what is more exactly a propensity for social strife and opposition to the State. Possibly the Third and Fourth Republics condemned the French to express themselves politically; de Gaulle relieved them of this burden. Hence the apparently paradoxical sight of this most political of peoples calmly accepting the chloroforming of parliament. Their instincts have been social from the first; they may have never been so content as under an enlightened despotism. This does not, of course, mean that they may not again sacrifice their tranquility to the excitements of political strife.

The French and the Outside World

A people so concerned with itself may not unnaturally have little regard for affairs beyond its own borders. Ambivalent is the single word best describing the Frenchman's attitude to the world beyond. The eighteenth-century epigrammatist Antoine de Rivarol noted that "The Frenchman, visited by people of every nation, feels himself relieved of having to travel in their countries as of having to learn their tongues, since he meets with his own everywhere he goes." In more recent times, Paul Morand put it another way: "France is a closed vessel, a complete existence, in which Europe is interested but which does not interest itself in Europe." If this was ever true, it would require some modification now. And yet the French view still persists that there are few problems and conditions, attitudes and movements in the world that do not find a reflection in France itself. "As in a microcosm," Charles Morazé said, "France reproduces humanity's problems." True or false, the self-consciousness is interesting, the way of projecting onto the international screen the domestic dichotomy of "we" and "they." With Rivarol and even Morand there is the sense of exclusiveness; with Morazé, a desire to encompass without sacrificing identity, to explain the difficulties of obtaining a French consensus by proposing that France is this extraordinary construction, "a juxtaposition of diverse societies opposed yet united within one nation." What emerges from such statements is the conviction of France's knowing in herself all that the rest of the world has to teach, certainly all that is worth knowing, and the suggestion of a certain superiority in addition. "*On est bien en France, hein?*" is the charming way in which the tourist or sojourner is invited to express his appreciation of what must surely be one of the most pleasant lands in the world.

The Frenchman knows of course that other places exist. He is admiring of Vienna, suitably impressed by London, prepared to be moderately overwhelmed by New York. These are cities to see; it would never occur to him that anyone in his right mind would wish to leave France to live in them. One sees them as one does galleries and museums, dutifully, appreciatively, but without passion and with the security of knowing that the visit cannot be interminably prolonged. What the Frenchman also sees abroad is not so much foreign lands as the reflection of France's stature. Moreover, he really assumes that it is possible to know nearly everything about the outside world without ever leaving France. He has a superb ability to reduce everything to epigram, to classify, and to catalog. Approaching no closer than Paris or Brest, with no knowledge of the language, and having an acquaintance with the people limited to observation of the throng at American Express or Thos. Cook & Son, he will be ready to discourse on American civilization, not least its faults. He long ago formed an estimate of his standoffish island neighbors, and the now famous judgment of de Gaulle in January 1963, say, was really as stock as anything could be —which may be only to say that the estimate was exact. The French listened with considerable skepticism to their President's praises of their German neighbors, remembering that it was he who had wished to break up the German state in 1944-1945, and concluding that the expediency of friendship with the Bonn Republic did not invalidate the basic evaluation of Germany previous generations had made. The redoubtable Madame de Staël, put it gently but with that incisive frankness the French lavish on others: "In leaving France, it is very difficult to get used to the slowness and dullness of the German people." After you have said that, there is little point to the various qualifications and shadings with which you may follow.

When they are worried or beset, the French may say "Il y a trop d'étrangers en France." Occasionally they wish, as Édouard Herriot once said, "to withdraw into their own grief." More often it is otherwise. To visiting foreigners they are normally generous, usually welcoming, invariably accommodating. The Anglo-American caricature of a people ready to take advantage of the helpless foreigner may well be perpetuated in Rue de Rivoli boutiques or expensive restaurants, but generations of growling taxicab drivers and surly hotel-keepers have still not made it universally applicable. The French may not be enchanted by the non-French world, and they may feel envious of American wealth and superior to German or British materialism. They may feel unappreciated, badly treated, and unduly put upon for having had (as they see it) to bear the brunt of defending the civilized world against barbarism. In the first half of the twentieth century they certainly passed through appalling experiences of loss, humiliation, and misery. But a more forthright determination to collaborate with the outside world has evolved. Contacts have increased steadily, and France may yet realize the ambition to show the way between the "extremes" of the Soviet and American camps. In that way, as de Gaulle suggested in 1964, "human souls, wherever they are on earth, will meet each other a little sooner at that rendezvous which France gave the universe 175 years ago, the rendezvous of liberty, equality, and fraternity." The world has certainly known less attractive statements of national purpose. It has also, alas, known some less remote from the discouraging realities of the twentieth century.

SIX

CULTURE AND THE NATION

*"Nous pardonnons souvent à ceux qui nous ennuient,
mais nous ne pouvons pardonner à ceux que nous
ennuyons."*

In the days of the great colonial empires, every "master" nation proclaimed its mission. Now, when the empires have mostly gone, only France retains something of her *mission civilisatrice* in conceiving herself as the center of a world culture. From time to time the Fifth Republic emphasized this role, above all in the areas, such as Latin America, where the urban bourgeoisie has long looked to France. The appeal of French culture is as wide and spontaneous as ever; the paradox of its universality and its intense parochialism as baffling. In this sense, nothing has changed since the age of Louis XIV and the Enlightenment. Articulate and intellectualized, it is accessible to the rational mind and unmuddied by the stirrings of folk culture. It celebrates no hoary past and is not overly deferential to past epochs of greatness. As a national phenomenon, for instance, it has had the good fortune to escape much of the romanticized medievalism which came to characterize German culture in the nineteenth century. Though it purports to concern itself with the nature and achievement of man, Frenchmen scarcely reflect that its definitions and approaches are often peculiarly French. Or it may be that they consider it only proper that the rest of the western world, at least, should hunger after what France is, what she has, and what she is ready to share.

The Literary Intelligentsia

Above all, French culture is literary. What other people expresses itself so well and communicates so convincingly the impression that the last word has been said? What other people so naturally reaches for its pen? The forms of its literature are diverse, of course, from the truly classical to the pretentious and tawdry. They are also voluminous: France is the birthplace of Balzac, Proust, and Romains. The publishing house of Hachette turns out 55 million volumes annually. The number, size, variety, and quality of literary periodicals is astounding. This is not to suggest that all Frenchmen read great literature. The classics find themselves reduced to serialized comic strips in France too. Newsstands are replete with the literary refuse found all over the world. Métro riders may well be reading not Simone de Beauvoir but the sort of evanescent romance entitled *Passion orageuse*. Nonetheless, despite television and other distractions, France reads and writes with an intensity and quality other nations may admire. Her men of letters are honored and have a national role in a way unknown in the English-speaking world.

This has been so since the Enlightenment at least. The intellectuals, and primarily the literary intellectuals, occupy a place in French society quite out of proportion to their numbers. Every part of the political spectrum can boast its literary ornaments, and all regimes have honored these men. Moreover, the links between politics and the intelligentsia have been close. Often the writer has played the role of critic only, but, like Voltaire, he has not hesitated to risk his own well-being on behalf of fundamental reform. Hugo's exile in Guernsey as a consequence of his bitter feud with the Second Empire, or Zola's flight to England following his condemnation for accusations against the Government and Army in the Dreyfus Affair, suggest that the eighteenth century had no monopoly on literary *engagement*; and though Jean Giono suffered for his opposition to the war of 1939, the denunciation of the war in Algeria by Jean-Paul Sartre showed that in France even a strong government might not dare to prosecute a celebrated intellectual whose criticisms were as embarrassing as they were partial. Moreover, French intellectuals have not merely chosen sides in national debates, they have assumed direct responsibilities. The suitability of this role might be doubtful in such cases as, say, Benjamin Constant in 1815 or Lamartine in 1848, where the results were discrediting and the decision to participate seemed ultimately mistaken, but the success of Thiers or Guizot, if not of Léon Blum, seems unquestionable. Yet the progress of Jacques Soustelle, from a precocious assistant directorship of the Musée de l'Homme through a ministerial career under the Fifth Republic to dissidence and exile, underlined the dangers the intellectual in politics must court.

Other kinds of intellectuals have known this political activity—the chemist Marcellin Berthelot, with portfolios of education and foreign affairs, in the nineteenth century; the physicist Frédéric Joliot-Curie as a militant leftist in the twentieth—but while an artist such as Picasso may achieve some political notoriety and even importance in France for his views, it is the men of letters who have dominated controversy. And they have been divided Left and Right, though perhaps on the whole the most distinguished group has inclined to progressive causes. The Enlightenment had its intellectual opponents, and the Counterrevolution in the next century was upheld by De Maistre, and in the twentieth by Maurras. The *Affaire* indeed seemed to show that the best known of the literary intelligentsia were anti-Dreyfusard: against Zola were Barrès, Paul Bourget, Jules Lemaître. It revealed also a split ideologically between letters and the university, with the Sorbonne and the École Normale inclining to the Left and the Académie Française to the Right, an orientation which has in a general manner persisted; it is also true that the Académie has never been representative of the Republic of Letters and in the twentieth century has pursued a conservative course in its elections, bringing it criticism and ridicule.

The twentieth century has been so stormy, so filled with war and revolution, so rent by ideology, and France's situation has been so exposed to the winds of change, that it is not surprising to find literature responding sensitively to her troubled experience. In the nineteenth century—hardly less turbulent—it had done as much, of course. The responses were varied then also. If neoclassicism was condemned by the romantics, and the ideal of realism set up as the goal, the forms realism took were as different as the poetry of Alfred de Vigny was from that of Théophile Gautier or the novels of Alexandre Dumas from those of Balzac. The striving for realism and naturalism comparable to the exactness of science found technicians in Flaubert and Zola; for expression of inaccessible realities of the mind, in Baudelaire, Verlaine, or Mallarmé. But it was inevitable that young writers should turn back toward the facts of that external reality rejected by the symbolists, and about 1890 some at least began to insist upon the social and historical context within which alone the individual could find meaning and fulfillment. So the ties between literature and society and politics, evident in Stendhal or Balzac or Hugo, were reaffirmed by the nationalists Paul Bourget and Maurice Barrès. The *Affaire* intensified the commitment and deepened the divisions, separating the fiercely right-wing polemicists around Charles Maurras and the Action Française, from the Dreyfusard humanitarians and socialists such as Anatole France and Romain Rolland.

The pre-1914 years were filled with this literary strife, shifting its ground from the *Affaire* to the debate on a darkening European situation. At the same time, however, younger men turned away from the political scene to concern themselves, as writers or artists, with their social responsibilities to the collectivity. Still others, like André Gide, renounced all politics and ideology for "pure" literary values. In literature, as elsewhere, a mood of confidence seemed to have overtaken the uncertainties of the *fin de siècle*. Henri Bergson's celebration of free creativity in art, of anti-intellectualism, of the conception of *élan vital*, of the superiority of will to external reality infused letters as it did art and military thought. A certain satisfaction characterized this bourgeois society and its literature, punctured perhaps by the shafts of Alfred Jarry and a faintly perceived concept of the absurd, but largely unaware of the extent to which the political and ideological facts of the new century were soon to weigh.

The impact of the war was somewhat delayed. It killed the novelist Alain Fournier, the poet Paul Drouot, and that peculiar and saintly figure, the Catholic socialist and burning patriot, Charles Péguy, yet it did not constitute a notable landmark in literature. Rolland withdrew almost at once to exile and a refusal to commit himself to so criminal a European civil war, Henri Barbusse and Georges Duhamel sought to communicate at the time what it was like, but Marcel Proust was not distracted from his great psychological enterprise launched so quietly and with such difficulty before 1914. Guillaume Apollinaire and Jean Cocteau mocked the solemnities of the conflict, and the postwar invasion of Dada and its coterie of poets such as André Breton and Paul Éluard assailed the warring camps represented by Barrès and Anatole France. Indeed, the generation that survived the war now had no use for these symbols of former causes. The young writers invoked not the mystical national past, which had so preoccupied Ernest Psichari and his friends until the war killed them, but rather the lure of the exotic, which drew André Malraux to the Far East. Or with Breton they upheld the new freedom of surrealism, anticonformist and antinational, seeking to liberate man, to bring him to see himself whole and to understand his real relationship to the physical world. The postwar decade was perhaps singularly free of commitment. With Proust and Jacques Lacretelle, novelists became introspective; with Jean Giraudoux, they alternated between *exotisme* and *politique*; with François Mauriac, they explored the desiccated lives of a provincial bourgeoisie trapped between the commands of religion and nature.

Literature and Ideology

The era of militant ideologies had begun in the second decade of the century, and increasingly the world of letters was to reflect its strife. Maurras had long since made war upon the bourgeois liberalism of the Republic in the name of a vague counterrevolutionary royalist myth; how hopelessly anachronistic this was, the events of February 6, 1934, were to reveal and the Vichy regime was to underline. But the polarization of antiliberal thought in the years between the wars found expression on the French literary scene among his disciples, on the one hand, and the adherents of Moscow, on the other. The Russian Revolution attracted some of the most distinguished men in French letters. To the disapproval of Julien Benda, intellectuals such as Gide, Barbusse, and Rolland "betrayed" their calling to engage in more or less minor flirtings with the extreme Left, proof, if proof were needed, that the literary establishment had shifted away from the Right. More lasting was the translation of Louis Aragon from surrealism to communism, a commitment Breton could not make. Aragon's epic of the working class was only one of a number of attempts to record in the manner of the multivolumed nineteenth-century novel the tendency of the twentieth century, the conflict of ideas within a class or between classes in a society undergoing profound technological change: thus Roger Martin du Gard's chronicle of the well-to-do bourgeoisie, and Jules Romains's enormous canvas of his own times.

On a smaller scale than the works of these writers or those of Duhamel or Lacretelle, some, like Georges Bernanos, railed against the sickness of the age, some, like Henry de Montherlant, declared an anticonformism and a hostility to the vulgarities of the mass civilization, and some, like Jean Giono, took refuge in a rustic idyll. Perhaps the most devastating protest against the century, against the State, war, persecution, the bloody ideologies and unlimited cant of politicians, came from Louis-Ferdinand Céline in a number of violent, extravagant tracts on behalf of the individual threatened by every kind of modern horror and incapable of anything but enduring a life without purpose or meaning. In all this anguish and cynicism prompted by the futility of international politics, the misery of peoples, and the supposed enslavement of man to an oppressive conformist society, Antoine de Saint-Exupéry held up the ideal of service on behalf of humanity and of the conquest of nature with the aid of the machine (in his case, the airplane) in a lyrical prose-poetry of heroic action unmarked by ideological or patriotic concern. So too, in another way, and in a committed sense, did Malraux exalt man for himself and his values, and preach an ethic of service at the risk of life itself, a principle that he made good in fighting for the Spanish government.

The last tormented years of the peace, with the betrayals of the League and the successive submissions to Italo-German blackmail and force, saw the Republic of Letters considerably divided. In the name of anti-communism or Catholicism, Henri Massis or Robert Brasillach supported the Spanish insurgents against André Chamson or Jean Guéhenno, who backed the legitimate government in the name of liberty. For Catholics like Bernanos the spectacle of the Church supporting the violence of the insurgents was heart-rending. Few French writers went all the way toward fascism: Montherlant was tempted, Abel Bonnard spoke up for the gang around Jacques Doriot, Pierre Drieu la Rochelle pursued a tortured course which finally brought him to suicide, but the young men around Maurras, e.g., Brasillach and Lucien Rebatet, held nothing back. As for the Left, it was doomed to successive disenchantments with the obvious bad faith of communism and the break-up of the *Front populaire*, the Moscow trials and purges, and the final blow of the Nazi-Soviet Pact. The last months of peace witnessed a not very heroic stance on the part of most, tempered by wholesale subscription to appeasement by such as Montherlant and the most violent tantrums against the Jews, the British, or whoever, on the part of Céline. Then all was swallowed up in the conventionalities of wartime patriotism. Or so, on the surface, it seemed.

In the immediate aftermath of defeat there could be no doubt that the preponderance of French letters supported the Vichy Government. Giraudoux might retain a sardonic detachment from this incredible administration headed by an almost senile Marshal, glorified by Maurras, and served by such Academicians as René Benjamin. But most simply adopted an attitude of watching and waiting. Saint-Exupéry took the road to exile that Bernanos had taken before the war; Malraux joined de Gaulle in dissidence. Drieu la Rochelle and Brasillach committed themselves fully to the impossible hope of a rebirth of Europe and humanist values through the German hegemony. Small wonder, therefore, that alongside the awakened Resistance of the Communist poets Aragon and Paul Éluard, should have come into being a youthful new literary elite attracted to existentialism and committed to the remaking of a liberated France. The older generation of Gide and Giraudoux was nearing its end; the voices of Duhamel or Romains were low and uncertain. If Mauriac went over to the Resistance, most of those who joined it were to the Left. And in the collapse of Vichy the credit of the literary Right was at least temporarily destroyed.

Thus the decade following the Liberation was dominated by the existentialism of Jean-Paul Sartre and Albert Camus, with its dogma of *engagement* and the ineluctable necessity of having to choose freely and thus assume responsibility for what one is. Literature, therefore, like every act, like man himself, is socially committed, and since man is his freedom, the commitment is to the cause of liberty. And for Camus the problem to be resolved was to discover how man could live in dignity and freedom in an absurd world to which he alone could give the values he sought in it. It was an heroic doctrine, suitable to the hopeful but bleak aftermath of the Occupation, suspended between the instinct to rebel and the taste for order, caught between the claims of society and the desire for solidarity, on the one hand, and the overwhelming conviction of isolation, on the other. The Sartre-Camus nucleus broke on the issue of Marxism, the claims of which Camus could not accept, and the initial spell they had both exercised seemed broken. A young movement arose to oppose the literature of *engagement*; the Right revived; the Left disintegrated. Older writers such as Giono, Romains, and Duhamel returned. Aragon pursued his Marxist chronicle, but Mauriac turned his attention mostly to politics. The old *Action Française* group sustained the loss of Maurras, doomed to life imprisonment for his wartime role, and continued its polemics on the Right, but its brilliance and its message were dead. The anti-novel and the non-poem appeared to express a rejection of everything in the literary past, and then, inevitably came a New Wave of writers seeking to reconstruct literary forms long neglected because of a commitment to ideology or psychic self-probings. Well into the second half of the century, then, the quarrels of the previous seventy or eighty years seemed often far distant. There were still some echoes from the more recent past, and some reflections of a present condition of tension in the world, but the most serious objective seemed to be a probing of the human condition and of the possibilities it entails.

Literary Arbiters, the Press, and the Language

The literary pyramid is crowned (at least theoretically) by the Académie Française, founded by Richelieu in 1635 and composed of forty elected "Immortals" whose task it is to revise the dictionary, purify and preserve the language, and award some seventy prizes. Too small to include all candidates for immortality, too conservative to admit Molière, Flaubert, or Gide, it has sustained endless ridicule but preserved its luster. It has elected Marshals not notable for their literary distinction, has known political interference in its elections, and has heard many *tours de force* in the traditional acceptance speeches praising deceased members—those on Pétain and Maurras in particular. In the world of the *bien pensant* upper classes, no prize is more fiercely coveted than a chair, and even the aged *enfant terrible* Jean Cocteau was content to finish his days beneath the golden cupola of the Institut de France.

There are other arbiters of taste. The Académie Goncourt (founded in 1896 to protest the Académie Française) had the honor of launching Proust's fame seven years after the appearance of *Du côté de chez Swann* and has been discerning since; other juries less so. Publishers have assailed them, for a major prize (though in all some seven hundred now exist) means a certain fame and financial success. Cynicism about the trade hardly lessens the annual pre-award tensions. The French care about letters, even though they appear not to mind that *Le Figaro Littéraire* or *Les Nouvelles Littéraires* publish sense and nonsense rather indiscriminately. Indeed, they devour books, articles, and articles about books avidly, asking only that they not be boring. Nearly 20,000 book titles appear every year, and in so large-scale and flourishing a business, values are necessarily uneven. But if fashions seem often ephemeral, the serious and important river of literature flows on. Time will doubtless make the essential judgment on, say, Saint-John Perse's luxuriant evocation of the vast rhythms of man and nature and Raymond Queneau's experimental sonnets with each line set on a separate strip of the page; and will distinguish between the works of Pierre Emmanuel and five-year-old poetesses like Minou Drouet who once turned literary Paris upside down. The compelling violences of Jean Genet's tortured world may, for all their insight and lyricism, seem one day little more than footnotes in the cause of a larger understanding of the human predicament. But the literary cognoscenti have always followed every development as if some final revelation were imminent. The many follow at a distance and savor a varied tradition from which present ferments stem.

Frenchmen read books without shame and with less huckstering than do North Americans; they read reviews and newspapers in superior quantity. Circulations are often small, as with the somewhat dusty, right-wing *Revue des Deux Mondes*, so recently full of solemn pieces on the Empire. The bias is clearcut in, say, the Marxist *Pensée*, the liberal Catholic *Esprit*, or the forlornly counterrevolutionary *Écrits de Paris*. Weekly journals of news and opinion, such as *L'Express*, offer the same general recipe as their Anglo-American prototypes, as does the spectrum of slick middlebrow, picture and women's magazines, which retail the literary wares on sale from Sydney to Stockholm. The daily press has fallen off since the years between the two wars, although some 123 dailies exist still and about 66 per cent of the population is said to read at least one paper. Of the important Paris press (accounting for more than a third of the country's total circulation) *Le Monde* is far and away the most serious and respected organ, its content and point of view lifting it much above the old *Temps* of the Third Republic. Communist papers have fallen off badly since the Liberation, with only *L'Humanité*, a shadow of its pre-1914 greatness under the editorship of Jean Jaurès, surviving on the national scale. The decline of Socialist fortunes may be read in *Le Populaire*, the ghost of its former self, when Léon Blum guided it before the Second World War. In *L'Aurore* the republican Right has had its defender of *Algérie Française* and assorted lost causes in a rather shrill manner not noticeable in the quietly conservative, right-thinking *Figaro*. Since the Liberation, papers have come and gone. Some remaining are the lineal descendants of the press of the Third Republic, bearing the same name or another where the title disappeared in the catastrophe of 1940 or was suppressed for collaboration. If the press under the Fourth and Fifth Republics has been less venal than under the Third, it has also been less influential. Some of its malicious verve has gone (*Aspects de la France* is a pale reflection of *L'Action Française*), and it may be that the editorials of *Le Monde* exert less influence than those of *Le Temps*. But this is a lively press in an age when few great newspapers exist anywhere and all are threatened by the economics of the profession.

Restrictions on publishing are few. The laws of libel have always been loose, and pens sharp. French publishers have been prosecuted, but they have been able to distribute titles banned in the English-speaking world. The State has protected itself with censorship during the century's wars, as it did at various periods in the nineteenth century, but even then France's journalists proved themselves as adept at circumventing the law as did their ancestors under the *ancien régime*. Revelations of the tortures practiced by Army units in the Algerian war brought not just the protests from generals, which not wholly dissimilar stories had occasioned a century earlier, but police seizures and prosecutions. And if the Chiefs of State of the Third and Fourth Republics had to endure attacks almost as fierce as those borne by Charles X or Louis Philippe, the law after 1958 was more protective of the office, resorting not only to fines but to the futility of ordering destruction of offending books, a solution that had seemed unsatisfactory 200 years before and had unhappy associations in the recent past.

The presidency might be protected in this way from the shafts of, say, Alfred Fabre-Luce, but the language of France was less well defended. Despite the best efforts of the Académie, the responsible press, and the literary establishment in general, the inroads of foreign barbarisms multiplied in an age of mass culture. Asking whether almost everyone would end by speaking *"Franglais,"* René Étiemble found the national tongue seriously corrupted since the Liberation. French youth was thought to use American words as 25 per cent of its vocabulary and to be likely in adulthood not to be capable of reading Molière, let alone Proust. Evidently Frenchmen were beginning life as *"babys,"* engaging in *"le sport"* during their *"teens,"* growing up to be great *"supportères"* of *"football"* and racetrack *"trottings,"* reading *"cover-stories"* in magazines with *"cover-girls,"* holding *"réunions de briefing"* in office *"buildings de grand standing,"* and gobbling their *"snacks"* in cafeterias monstrously known as *"le quick"* before retiring at day's end to order *"un baby Scotch sur les rocks."* Undeniably repulsive, the jargon had certainly made headway. But how to prevent its progress in a western world that had come to share so much film and literature in common, no one could say. It seemed, at all events, a sad return for all that France had exported to the English-speaking world since the Enlightenment.

Art, Architecture, and Music

Rightly concerned for the national language, France was also beginning to take better care of her monuments and art treasures. The July Monarchy had taken some interest in this work, owing to the promptings of Victor Hugo and others, but the resultant restorations by the romantic medievalists, of whom Viollet-le-Duc was the most notorious, had by no means pleased all. The Revolution, which had effected not a little damage itself, had proposed an inventory of the national storehouse, but it was André Malraux, Minister of Cultural Affairs, who undertook the work in the 1960s. Although this task would require a generation to complete, the State began to show a livelier concern to protect, encourage, and preserve art and architecture. Symptomatic was the splendid funeral for Georges Braque with torchlights flickering over the vast crowd in the Cour Carée of the Louvre while the rain descended one September evening in 1963. "Never before has a modern country rendered such homage to one of its dead painters," Malraux said. And thus art's "long history of disdain, misery, and despair" and "the impoverished obsequies of Modigliani and the sinister burial of Van Gogh are revenged." Doubtless France's artists had suffered indifferent earthly fortunes; but though the nation may well have let too many of its treasures slip out of its hands into those of foreigners, still it had for long respected its artistic past, even though its shabby museums too often suggested the limits of its affection. What was new under the Fifth Republic was the degree of State concern, the intent to set an example and establish a style.

The past seemed assured of preservation; the present assured itself. Despite a strong current of regional decentralization in the twentieth century, Paris remained the artistic center. Impressionism and post-impressionism, cubism and surrealism had long ago ceased to surprise or scandalize. Although there was neo-cubism and neo-surrealism, contemporary movements were not easily defined and generations were mixed up. With some 40,000 painters, the capital seemed free of revolt under the Fifth Republic. Experimentation had not died out, but prosperity and a widening market encouraged the prolongation of established movements, objective or nonobjective. Jean Dubuffet once said that the function of art was "to dance and yell like a madman," but a quieter search for unity could be discerned. "The sole issue for painting is its power to suggest," noted Michel Carrade. "Hence there is no question of abstraction or of figuration, but of a true organic contact between man and the world."

Much the same might be said of sculpture and architecture. The past weighed heavily. It remained true of France as of the rest of the western world that sculpture awakened only a fraction of the interest aroused by graphic art. The influence and patronage of the Church continued to be significant. But the market was small and products were derivative. As always, the public followed at a distance. If Rodin and Maillol or Brancusi had become objects of veneration and of imitation, the attempt of Nicholas Schöffer, for instance, to construct cities of the future around moving or stationary sculpture and to synthesize sound and vision was known only to the avant-garde. Movements toward a spatio-dynamic sculpture, however, involving Pierre Henry's music or the dancing of Maurice Béjart, demonstrated again that even without revolutionary portents the creativity of France had not slackened.

The French have been properly admiring of their architectural past, whether the glass and stone of Chartres, the rococo harmony and elegance of the Place Stanislas in Nancy, or the romanesque churches of the Midi. The spectacles of *son et lumière* at Carcassonne, Versailles, or Chenonceaux won their place not merely for the theatricality of the lighting and the *petite histoire* dispensed, but for the silent stone's historical presence. But the architectural record after the eighteenth century was slim. Spared much of the Gothic horrors of the Victorian age, French architecture passed rapidly through the iron age to the era of reinforced concrete, of which the brothers Perret were the high priests. Tony Garnier's daring vision of an Industrial City remained as an ideal; Auguste Perret's career passed from the rue Franklin apartment house through the Church at Le Raincy to the rebuilding of Le Havre after 1945, freeing walls of structural burden and creating lightness and space. That other foreigner by birth, Le Corbusier was less traditionalist. Like Garnier, he used strikingly new materials and conceptions, and in his own lifetime such a former "joke" as the Marseille Block of apartments became a national monument. But architecture in France, as elsewhere, remained uneven and the century was still seeking its style. Whatever it was, some part of it seemed to show in the cantilevered *tour de force* Guillaume Gillet designed for the French pavilion at Brussels in 1958, in Henri Chomette's opera house at Addis Ababa, or Le Corbusier's city at Chandigarh.

Perhaps both architecture and music were arts conservatively practiced in France, at least in the twentieth century, but whether more so than elsewhere only the bold or rash might say. It had become difficult to imagine the initial impact of Berlioz or Debussy, and the scandal of pre-1914 Stravinsky was as hard to evoke. Realism and post-impressionism had been accepted, but, despite the work of René Leibowitz and Pierre Boulez, French composers showed little affinity for the atonalities of Schönberg and his disciples. Both electronic and concrete music sought to express objectively the condition of modern man, but the following was uncertain and, not unnaturally, the musical public preferred the familiar idioms of older generations. Jazz in all its forms achieved a secure place among the young and the intellectual, but the public here, as everywhere, gave its heart to those who touched its emotions more obviously—above all, to Édith Piaf and her ballads of love and loss among the urban poor. When she died, thousands surged to Père Lachaise in nostalgia for an experience she had seemed to share and they thought they understood. In its way, the response was a kind of counterpart to the flickering torches offered to Braque in the Cour Carée.

Theatre, Film, and Television

Even as late as 1964 an imaginative, if rather bizarre, production of *The Damnation of Faust* could produce the kind of eruptions *Hernani* occasioned in 1830 and *Le Sacre du Printemps* in 1913. That the theatre could still do as much by then was less certain. The capital's sixty theatres offered everything down to imported "musicals" improbably translated and sometimes unbelievably performed. The range from Corneille and Marivaux to Paul Claudel and Camus was immense and wealthy, as witty as Giraudoux and as comically numbing as Samuel Beckett. The stage reflected the state of letters, restating timeless problems and the dilemmas of conscience, both affirming life and stripping it of all illusion, both classical and experimental in form. Inevitably, the message was not clear and playwrights seemed to be living on the capital of an earlier time. Moreover, the theatre in France could not escape the universal fact in the twentieth century of competition from newer media which, if they did not necessarily draw off creative talent, did at least reduce the theatre-going public which might have encouraged that talent.

Far happier, then, was the condition of the French film, with its pioneer tradition going back to Louis Lumière and Charles Pathé and its internationally acclaimed successes under the Third, Fourth, and Fifth Republics. Though great movies were made by Marcel Carné and Jean Renoir before the war of 1939, the industry matured and secured its serious audience during the Occupation. The theatre, too, had paradoxically achieved a brilliance in such somber conditions, but it was the film that retained its wartime impetus and audience. It had, too, a more obvious focus than the theatre and its most direct appeal was to the young. Film art came to be debated as passionately as politics once had been. The new film makers after the Liberation became the center of something like a cult, and the names of Alain Resnais, François Truffaut, or Louis Malle were more familiar than Carl Dreyer's had been between the wars, if not as prestigious as that of Cocteau. What they had to say was possibly less cynical and less dreamy, though no less satirical, than the message of the pre-1939 generation. Poetry was less conscious and mannered, despair less resentful. Knowing neither the poverty nor the social tensions of the Third Republic, the Fourth and Fifth were content to be shown the abyss not of the class system but of the human condition.

The other modern media, radio and television, continued to speak, as radio alone had spoken before the Second World War, with a babel of tongues. Millions of receivers diffused the varied wares dispensed by the

State monopoly, ranging from informative lectures and serious forms of music through tiresome costume plays and, especially under the Fifth Republic, a dreary round of official efforts to "enlighten" public opinion, which led mostly to indifference and apathy. If the discriminating preferred, where possible, to pick up the sights and sounds emanating from foreign transmitters, there was no doubt that the *Service public de la radiodiffusion télévision française* (reorganized in 1964 as a more clearly autonomous public enterprise, the *Office de la R.T.F.*) constituted an important instrument of unification, which the leaders of the Fifth Republic had learned to use more effectively than, say, premier Gaston Doumergue (proposing governmental reforms in 1934) had been able to do a generation before. And, a certain authoritarian bias notwithstanding, the quality of the programs emitted from the splendid circular glass and marble structure on the Quai Kennedy bore comparison with that of other nations.

Education, Scholarship, and Religion

No aspect of French culture has been more praised and criticized than the educational system. Marked by severe overcrowding and a labyrinthine system, it was doubtless more democratic than it had been thirty or sixty years ago. A series of streams carried children through nearly a decade of compulsory education in either private or free public institutions. If the over-all structure remained monolithic, stretching down from the Ministry of Education through the twenty-one *académies*, each with its university, France had progressed from the militantly laic attitudes of the Third Republic at the turn of the century. Public funds were available to Catholic schools. While some of the post-Liberation state commission's recommendations were rejected as politically motivated (both the chief commissioners were Communists), other proposed reforms went into effect. A wholly free tuition modified slightly the virtual caste system prevailing before 1941. Yet access to all levels for all classes was still not assured. Despite the fact that the Grandes Écoles (Normale Supérieure, Polytechnique, and Nationale d'Administration—all outside the university system) had always drawn from the less affluent families, higher education remained largely an impossibility for most. Only one in eight children continued beyond elementary school. The Grandes Écoles could accept only one applicant in ten. The whole educational system remained hierarchic, rigidly centralized, fiercely competitive, inclined toward the literary, and lagging in science. Under the Fourth and Fifth Republics, the shortage of teachers at every level, the failure to provide the necessary facilities to meet the population explosion, from *écoles maternelles* to university lecture halls, had attained crisis proportions. Libraries were antedeluvian, laboratories overwhelmed, and if the Paris area was the most hard hit, only some of the provincial centers were better off. Students (and teachers) who a century before, and even a generation before, had demonstrated on behalf of politics, seemed now to be at least as troubled by the crisis of education.

In a Republic so sensitive to its cultural mission, the plight of education, dramatized by strikes and collisions with the police, was almost incomprehensible, and contemplated reforms seemed unhappily delayed.

Apart from this critical school and university problem, the world of scholarship remained as distinguished as it had been under previous regimes. It was a fact, however, that in the twentieth century French science had fallen behind the achievements of at least the more populous nations of the West. Distinguished names such as those of Frédéric Joliot-Curie and Paul Sabatier marked the continuation of a great tradition. The Fifth Republic committed itself to research in State and private institutions. But the scientific lag was unlikely to be closed in competition with the vast resources of the United States and the Soviet Union at least. On the other hand, the Centre National de la Recherche Scientifique, the Collège de France, and the five Académies grouped in the Institut de France sponsored and encouraged work in every field from microbiology to the fine arts, and the standards of humanist scholarship remained as high as ever. A nation so evidently gifted with imagination and insight required only the assurance of material support to continue to shine brightly.

As late as the 1950s parliamentary debate on State assistance to Catholic schools suggested that if the militant anticlericalism had not entirely disappeared, the quarrel endured under the Third Republic belonged to the past. And yet though the Catholic Church had altered its image in the previous generation, no religious renaissance seemed imminent. The struggle leading to separation in 1905 had been decently laid to rest, partly because of the Church's loyalty in two wars and a largely correct attitude under the Occupation. Regional characteristics of piety or abstention held roughly true as they had 50 or 150 years earlier. A majority continued to participate in the rituals of baptism, marriage, and death, but that was all. If the hierarchy had ceased to be narrowly identified with the anti-republican Right, it had evidently not wished to channel the faithful into the liberal MRP. Struggling against communism, it had not hesitated to join Communists in opposing the Catholic Chief of State when it judged its social conscience to be involved. In the forefront of such successful movements as the *Jeunesse ouvrière chrétienne*, it nevertheless ended the worker-priest movement (begun in 1944 to make contact with the alienated working class) when convinced that the dangers of a counterproselytization were grave. Without wealth or establishment, the Catholic Church in France remained a spiritual and social force; its action groups interested themselves in housing, education, and the realization of "the European idea"; some of its priests, however, were sorely troubled by the winds of reform coming from Rome.

Protestant, Jewish, and Moslem minorities were mostly descendants or remnants of persecuted communities. Scattered east, south, and west, the Protestants numbered less than one million. Perhaps one-third that size, the Jewish community was preponderantly urban. After Vichy's shameful discrimination against Jews, and surrender to the enemy, the virulent anti-

Semitism of the interwar years—an indicator of France's unhappiness with herself—seemed almost to have departed. After 1944 the expression of such bourgeois or working-class prejudice was of course hardly fashionable, although Pierre Mendès-France felt its sting and extreme Rightists like Jean-Louis Tixier-Vignancour and Jean-Marie Le Pen occasionally recalled the less attractive moments of the Third Republic. As for the Moslems, their numbers were uncertain. Most were either beneficiaries of the Empire or refugee victims of its North African collapse. Of the three minorities, only this third group's social situation appeared distinct and troubled. What its position within the nation might become was impossible to predict. But the conditions in which it and a black African minority lived in France were so squalid and so out of keeping with a prosperous society that the continued toleration by the State of *bidonvilles* and other urban ghettoes of misery seemed difficult to explain.

Taken all in all, the nation's cultural life remained varied and attractive. Following the Liberation, Frenchmen—and more particularly French "mandarins"—dwelt upon the twin dangers of *la peste américaine* and *la choléra russe*. To the outsider it would appear that really they had escaped both horrors. Yet as late as 1964 Maurice Duverger insisted upon the continuing threat of at least one of the contagions: "There is only one immediate danger for Europe, and that is the American civilization. There will be no Stalinism or communism in France. They are scarecrows that now frighten only sparrows. Today all that belongs to the past." Certain that France would not, happily, reach the stage of socialization until the present phase of the Soviet dictatorship was finished, he was much less sure that the stage of abundance would be delayed in French society until the American hegemony had receded. And he feared that the nation's culture and "scale of aristocratic values" might not be sufficient to resist the American assault.

A foreigner could only note that such an alarm awakened many responses in France. Perhaps it was well justified, perhaps not; but millions of Frenchmen would think that it was. No doubt a nation that succumbed to the lure of the Wild West, approved of *My Fair Lady*, or committed the linguistic crime of adopting "*le coffee-break*" was in danger of losing some part of its cultural heritage. But it seemed difficult to imagine that such errors—however grievous they might be reckoned—were harbingers of a coming cultural debacle. Indeed, this sort of reaction against them might provide the stimulus essential to throw off the alien encroachment. Time alone would tell.

SEVEN

IMPERIAL TWILIGHT AND DARKNESS

"On ne se peut consoler d'être trompé par ses ennemis et trahi par ses amis, et l'on est souvent satisfait de l'être par soi-même."

Every European empire was the work of a minority. The French experience was in no way unique. The colonialist minority became articulate in press and parliament, but whether it was more influential than similar groups elsewhere would be difficult to say. The peculiarity of the French experience, perhaps, was that the second French Empire of the nineteenth century was collected in the aftermaths of military defeat and came to have, above all in the twentieth century, symbolic value as the reflection of a European and world authority at the precise moment when that authority was falling away. Empire was increasingly and falsely identified with national independence and the national title to respect in the international arena. Thereby was to hang the blood-spattered last tale of the struggle in North Africa which destroyed the Fourth Republic.

Before the First World War

The first French Empire never quite disappeared, but in ceding control of India and Canada to Great Britain in the eighteenth century, France lost her major claim to imperial greatness. This was to become more evident at a later date. The retention of San Domingo, Martinique, Guadeloupe, the slave-trade stations on the West African littoral, and commercial outposts on the Indian coast resulted in the doubling of French trade with the Americas and India before 1789. But with the ending of the slave trade in the nineteenth century and the declining importance of the West Indian sugar islands, France's bargain at the Peace of Paris, 1763, seemed less favorable. Despite, if not because of, the loss of the Thirteen Colonies, Canada was to become perhaps the most important element of the British overseas Empire; India, brought under political control, the very touchstone of Victorian imperial prestige. Though Jacques Cartier had penetrated to Montreal, La Salle to Louisiana, Francis Xavier to Goa and Japan, and others as far south as Rio, France had failed to make good her imperial footholds or was being compelled to relinquish them. Napoleon's vision of a renewed empire on the American continental mass expired in

87

the Louisiana sale and the Latin American refusal to recognize his brother
Joseph as King of Spain. By the peace treaties of 1814-1815, France ceded
Mauritius in the Indian Ocean, Malta, Tobago, and St. Lucia to England.
A remnant of West Indian islands, St. Pierre and Miquelon in the Gulf of
St. Lawrence, and West African and Indian trading stations were all that
remained.

From that base, monarchs and republicans constructed a new Empire.
Alleging the insult to the French consul Pierre Deval at Algiers three years
earlier ("You are a wicked, faithless, idol-worshipping rascal," the Dey
said, striking him one April day in 1827 with a flywhisk, after failing to
obtain monies owed him by France), Charles X sought popularity by
defeating the quarrelsome Dey and seizing his treasure in the summer of
1830. Thus a swat in the face, though it did not save the Bourbon monarchy, provided the occasion for creating a North African empire. Louis
Philippe went on from this success against Algerian pirates to spite Great
Britain and subdue the rest of the vaguely defined country, to collect Nossi
Bé, Tahiti, the Ivory Coast, and the Comoro Islands. The Algerian campaign itself was long and savage, with brutalities on both sides which were
to last for 130 years. "We have burned everything, destroyed everything,"
wrote the young Jacques de Saint Arnaud, future Marshal of France. "How
many women and children have died of cold and fatigue!" Though the
generals failed to establish the military colony they wished, camp followers and land speculators brought in the French, Italian, Spanish, and
other settlers who, with the Army, were to make this territory one day
the last stronghold of the imperial impulse. The republicans of 1848, uncertain imperialists, proclaimed the policy of assimilation: Algeria was
henceforth but three departments of France, and all who lived in the
Empire (slaves were freed) became French citizens with representation in
parliament.

Napoleon III pushed on, despatching troops to Syria to protect French
Christians (1860-1861), sending an expedition to Saigon in 1859 to protect
missionaries, seize the naval base, and open up the China market to the
north. The Church, the armed forces, and the mercantile interests thus
combined with the Government to lay the foundations of empire in the
Middle and Far East. A more direct assault upon China came in the
Second Opium War, when another French force combined with the
British to extract concessions from the Emperor. Both fought their way
to Peking; the British burned down the Summer Palace (1859-1860). It
was a rough age, and nothing was so useful to imperial purpose as dead
missionaries. Less unhappily, and less by design of those in France, a West
African domain was carved out by General Faidherbe, Governor of the
tiny colony of Senegal around the town of St. Louis. Dreaming of empire
from the Atlantic to the Red Sea, he made at least a strong beginning in
the decade before 1865.

Under the Second Empire, Algerian conquest was completed. But the
short-lived new segregationist theory of its being an Arab Kingdom, with

Napoleon cast as Emperor and Sultan, only retarded European colonization and Algerian economic development. Momentarily the policy of assimilation was abandoned. Once more the whole Empire was ruled directly as a series of dependencies and protectorates, presumably on the road to self-government in accord with Napoleon's enthusiasm for the principle of nationality.

The great imperial effort came in Mexico, and ended in defeat. A three-power plan to collect debts from President Juarez's turbulent republic collapsed. Under the influence of the Court, Napoleon launched a French expeditionary force. "France goes to war for ideas," he had claimed somewhat improbably. The Mexican capital was occupied, and Maximilian of Habsburg proclaimed emperor. A Catholic, diplomatic, military, and economic success for France, as it seemed, the adventure rapidly turned to disaster. Juarez's supporters harassed the French Army; the United States compelled withdrawal in 1867; with Maximilian's execution the last vestige of the Second Empire's prestige disappeared.

If there was moderate popular approval of empire, it did not survive Napoleon III. Empire was costly (revolt occurred in Algeria in 1871), commercial intercourse with the colonies was small-volumed. The nation was indifferent to its explorers in Africa. The Left objected on principle, the Right on grounds of expediency. But as the defeat of 1870-1871 receded, a new imperialist wind blowing through Europe caught France. Adventurers, financial speculators, missionaries, publicists, administrators in search of careers, and officers in search of glory all provided the permanent substructure for colonial rebuilding when the political ban should be lifted. As late as 1874 the Duc de Broglie halted the gradual conquest of Indo-China and evacuated Tonkin. Four years later, however, Great Britain and Germany encouraged France to "protect" Tunisia, to forestall Italy there, and to shift her interest from the loss of Alsace-Lorraine to empire. On a flimsy pretext, this was done in 1881 and the country was subdued. The policy was made by the Ministry of Foreign Affairs, supported by commerce and finance, tolerated by parliament, and paid for by the enthusiastic Premier, Jules Ferry, whose position it finally undermined.

Tunisia was an important beginning. Though others failed to share in the protectorate Great Britain effected in Egypt in 1882, in his second ministry Ferry showed fresh colonial zeal. Madagascar was subdued; out of various explorations came a French Congo. The proconsuls in Indo-China were permitted to retake Tonkin, make war on China, establish a protectorate over Annam. Substantial losses and military reverse permitted Ferry's enemies to pull him down in 1885, but anticolonial cries were unavailing. By 1899 a great Indo-Chinese empire existed; Madagascar was annexed; vast West and Equatorial African holdings were consolidated. Partly imperialist, partly anti-imperialist, largely indifferent, the Republic accepted its growing Empire and gave its soldiers and administrators free rein. In their minds, empire and prestige were inextricably entwined. And not even a provincial *commerçant* could be wholly indifferent to the task of diffusing French civilization.

Well before 1914 the European rush for the spoil was over. France's Empire, second largest in the world, had its following in the civil service, the universities, the Church, the armed forces, the geographical societies, and banking and manufacturing groups. But investment was small (about 10 per cent of French capital exports), imperial commerce hardly larger. There was no symbol to focus public enthusiasm, as the imperial crown focused it in the United Kingdom. Although Algeria's European population was then over the half-million mark, Frenchmen were not populating the lands collected in their name. They bristled over the collision at Fashoda in 1898, when the French west-east drive collided with the British north-south push in Africa, but they did not make war. Surprisingly swiftly the confrontation was followed by the Entente Cordiale. The quarrel with Italy was buried by diplomacy. The two Moroccan clashes with Germany were settled short of violence, although public passion was such that the minor concession made in French Equatorial Africa was proclaimed a serious loss. An insignificant price to pay for the establishment of a Protectorate over Morocco in 1912, the bargain revealed irrational attitudes which would grow monstrously.

From Victory Through Peace to Defeat and Liberation: First Losses

From defeated Germany after 1918 came Togoland and the Cameroons; from Turkey came Syria (to be administered under League of Nations mandate, a qualification more theoretical than effectual). The heterogeneity of the Empire was great. With their small European minorities, Morocco, Tunisia, and Indo-China depended on the Ministry of Foreign Affairs. Algeria, legally and fictionally part of metropolitan France, depended on the Ministry of the Interior. The rest depended on the Ministry of Colonies. It was a centralized and paternalistic empire—one of merchants and proconsuls, multinational European settlers, and multicolored subjects. It had its injustices. Algerian Moslems were readily rendered landless (by purchase or confiscation) and, though not French citizens unless they renounced Islam, conscripted into the Army. Conditions varied greatly: Senegalese natives made excellent troops, the Congolese were unfit. Of the old policy of assimilation, there remained exploitation tempered by road and hospital building, and the education of an elite—first in native schools, then in French universities. The newer policy of association (theoretically more tolerant of native cultures) led thus far and no farther down the road to self-government. France talked loosely of one hundred million Frenchmen but practiced racial segregation in fact. Her rule could be as hard but worthy as Marshal Lyautey's in Morocco, or as ill-starred as General Sarrail's in Syria. In Casablanca, Dakar, Djibouti, and Hanoi, the same flag flew, and even critics felt a surge of pride. It was a neomercantilist empire, though Syria, Equatorial Africa, Togo, the Cameroons, Morocco, and Indo-China, by international agreement or by sheer distance, were open to broader development. Costly to administer, it was also, inevitably, a prey to emergent nationalist stirrings, and thus, like all colonial empires, doomed.

The years between the two wars foreshadowed this fate. Nearly two million troops had come from the Empire in 1914-1918, and promises had been made which were painful to contemplate afterward. Arab nationalism, sectionalism, and French administrative arrangements brought revolt in Syria in 1925-1926. Military suppression, and weary efforts to satisfy native demands short of granting independence, followed. The treaties of 1936 promising a three-year transition to independence were never ratified; the discontent was swallowed up in war. The Riffian revolt of Abd el Krim in Morocco, 1925-1926, ended Lyautey's era and was pacified by Marshal Pétain, but nationalist demonstrations and French suppressions followed through the '30s. It was the same in Tunisia. And in Algeria inequalities remained flagrant. Serious reforms were rejected by the European *colons* and by parliament. Revolution in China and Communist propaganda encouraged the claims of a rising native elite in Indo-China too. But France had no policy save vague promises and ruthless repressions before 1939. When the *Front populaire* warned that reform was necessary, it was denounced as antipatriotic. No one in those days was giving away empires. The publicity mills ground out endless dithyrambs on the French colonial achievement. Ordinary Frenchmen could hardly assess the claims. What they saw was the Spahi cavalry, the Senegalese infantry, and the romantic Legionnaires on the Avenue every July 14. It was a brave display, but not the whole truth.

During the Second World War, the Empire remained loyal. But France was divided. Through the military disaster and the Armistice, the discipline of civilian and military administrators held. Nothing, however, could save Indo-China from Japan, and if General de Gaulle was rebuffed at Dakar in September 1940, the tide swung against Vichy. The Free French won over Equatorial Africa, the Cameroons, New Caledonia. With British aid, they obtained Syria and Lebanon. Defying the fury of Washington, Ottawa, and London, they seized St. Pierre and Miquelon. After the Anglo-American landings in Northwest Africa in late 1942, the whole vast French imperial domain abandoned the Armistice and rejoined the war. Following the defeat of Japan, Indo-China was restored. But something had been irretrievably lost: prestige. The eclipse of French power and the wartime declarations from the Atlantic Charter to the United Nations Charter encouraged native hopes of independence.

No such intention moved de Gaulle and his countrymen. A collision course was set. The Free French Brazzaville declaration of 1944 had promised autonomy within the Empire; the Preamble of the 1946 Constitution promised a future self-administration. In practice the instruments of the French Union (as the Empire was now renamed), parliamentary, representative, juridical, merely cloaked a return to the rule of the proconsuls, centralized in theory, often local and arbitrary in fact. The distinction between citizens and subjects was renounced in name, retained in practice. It was not enough that more than eighty Deputies sat in the National Assembly for Algeria and the Empire (the distinction would be retained to the last), or that France was more solicitous of her people's needs. She had set her face against the increasingly loud demands of the nationalists. From that tragic fact rivers of blood were to flow.

The first rivulets had already started when the Fourth Republic came into being. Algeria was to be the beginning and the end. A victory parade of Moslems in Sétif, May 8, 1945, turned into a demonstration for independence and for the liberation of imprisoned nationalists. It was market day, the town was crammed. Shots were fired, a wave of assassinations of Europeans by stones, axes, and knives followed in the area, and then an atrocious massacre by the Europeans and the Army, navy, and air force. About one hundred Europeans died violently; perhaps 15,000 Moslems were slaughtered. It was an incident only. More than nine years of underground activity followed before the final rebellion began. But young men like Mohammed Ben Bella, who had just served in the French Army in Italy, knew that day what eventually they must do. The ordeal at Sétif foretold the long agony to come. "For North Africa," the right-wing *Écho d'Alger* said, "it is the hour of the policeman."

The abandonment of Syria and Lebanon that same year was bitter but far less bloody. The time had come to make good the wartime promises, but during the political negotiations with the native leaders, fighting broke out. France moved in troop reinforcements and even shelled Damascus. What the ultimate French intention had been may be guessed. But Great Britain's hostility to the continued presence of France in the Middle East was flimsily covered by her assertion that she must intervene to protect her own communications to the East. London played a very tough game; de Gaulle's resentment was fully justified, but the French withdrawal was inevitable. The Levant was certainly lost. What was unforgivable was Great Britain's shabby performance in humiliating France and her Army.

Disaster in Indo-China

Syria was a mere sideshow compared with Indo-China. There the odds were overwhelmingly against France, who had ruled and exploited this large and diverse area of twenty-five million people with impunity before 1939. Some 20,000 Frenchmen, a few thousand Annamese *assimilés*, and a larger number of *intermédiaires* (natives with a degree of French education, but identified still with the local society) had been her instruments. The Annamese Emperor's authority (exercised through the mandarin class) had declined before 1939 while simultaneously the French sought to bring him directly under control. All this coincided with growing resentment of the French plantation economy that competed with native subsistence agriculture, and with the educated class's discovery of Marxism and nationalism. The war changed all.

Vichy had accepted the necessity of collaboration with Japan. Th of Vichy brought French Resistance opposition to both the collabor. and the Japanese into the open. The Japanese response in March 1945 was to attack this Resistance and simultaneously proclaim "independence" in Laos, Cambodia, and Vietnam. Nothing could save France from having to reconquer her colony. Though autonomy within the French Union was promised, the intention was colonialist. Moreover, British and Chinese forces were principally responsible for expelling the Japanese occupant. France had lost face repeatedly. And to compound the difficulties, a Vietnamese revolutionary government (Vietminh), led by the Marxist Ho Chi Minh, was established in Tonkin. The Emperor Bao Dai abdicated and a Republic was proclaimed. Fighting with the French occurred in Saigon. Thus General Jacques Leclerc reported to Paris that reconquest would require half a million men and many years of fighting.

The implication was that Paris must negotiate with Ho. But while Ho was in Paris in the summer of 1946, discussing Vietnamese independence and possible alliance with France, the French in Saigon prepared a coup. Ho returned empty-handed. Admiral Thierry d'Argenlieu (a carmelite monk) and the proconsuls at Saigon took matters into their own hands, "amazed" that the generals "should prefer to negotiate rather than fight." After failure of a French attempt to massacre the rebel garrison at Hanoi, war broke out in December 1946. The fantastic intrigues of the local French have never been fully unraveled, but enough is known to shed the cruelest light on the incapacity of Paris, constantly blackmailed, divided, paralyzed, and with no policy save to continue "the struggle against communism." The last chances to negotiate with Ho vanished, in 1947, frustrated by Vietnamese émigrés and the Saigon establishment. The ensuing desperate war was fought by the professional Army (no conscripts could be dispatched). It was costly, dirty, and destructive. The reluctant puppet Emperor Bao Dai was returned by the French in June 1949; a treaty granted the monarchical regime considerable independence. It did no good. France's weakness was to have to concede the nationalist demands of discredited Vietnamese reactionaries. And the war was unpopular. "The French public, I regret to say," Guy Mollet remarked, "doesn't give a damn about it."

Following the Communist victory in China in 1949, Ho was supplied by and doubtless subject to Mao Tse Tung. After the Korean War broke out in 1950, the fight in Vietnam intensified. Suddenly, therefore, the United States ceased to carp about continued colonialism. As suddenly, however, the Korean armistice of 1953 left the French stranded with "the war against communism," sustaining a now increased onslaught. Paris still refused compromise. Drained and embittered, the Army was committed to a final strategic blunder in making a stand at the exposed fortress of Dien Bien Phu on the Laotian border in the north. After some wild talk in Washington about possible intervention with nuclear weapons, the fortress fell in May 1954. The shock was acute; it ended the struggle. That July a new government, led by Pierre Mendès-France, concluded negotiations, which partitioned Vietnam around the 17th parallel.

Thus communism triumphed in the north. In the south, an independent Vietnam joined Cambodia and Laos, both granted independence in 1949, to form a kind of no-man's land between the Western and Communist camps. As a settlement, the 1954 agreements crumbled away steadily. The tragedy that had led to it was the product not merely of the Vietminh and its Chinese backers, but of an intractable colonialist reaction in Indo-China and a divided Fourth Republic in which power went to the boldest, loudest, most selfish interests, and the people dimly followed the bewildering intrigues, for which the professional soldiers paid in blood. Stunned by the heartrending Dien Bien Phu debacle, the nation approved the initiative to halt the senseless struggle. Indo-China could not have been saved even by a French national mobilization. It had set the scene for a still worse trial and defeat.

North African Retreat: Morocco, Tunisia, and Suez

By then North Africa was smoldering or aflame. The causes of the 1945 Algerian revolt had not been eliminated. The British and Dutch devolutions of empire after 1945 had continual repercussions for France. An example was the sudden native rising in Madagascar in March 1947. Withdrawal of British forces there (after wartime occupation), the small French police force, economic hardship, new native political awareness, and old tribal primitivism—all this produced the explosion. Leaderless and confused, rebellion became mindless massacre of French settlers. It was put down in a military blood bath, used by the colonialists to condemn education of native elites, and condemned by the Communists as another western hypocrisy. Though the Republic sought to hush up the details of the punitive expedition sent out and the disgraceful perversions of justice that followed, the affair made bad publicity. The North African revolt would be better led, supported, and reported, and no less violent. At Sétif the whirlwind which was to tear the North African empire to shreds had been announced.

The principal distinctions to be made among the fates of Morocco, Tunisia, and Algeria follow from history and demography. The two Protectorates won their independence with relative ease. Once the fiction of the Bey's and the Sultan's "sovereignty" broke down, France's position became untenable. Once these native rulers identified themselves with the Neo-Destour or Istiqlal demands, condominium gave way to political and social strife, the settler minority (5 per cent in Morocco, 7.5 per cent in Tunisia) appealed to force, and France had to make a choice. Measured in roads, schools, hospitals, ports, factories, investment, and subsidies, the French contribution had been great. But in neither country had the masses shared in the benefits of the modernized sector. Rapidly increasing population outran economic growth, especially in Tunisia. Squalor lived on in the shadow of colonial showpieces. Discontent bred fear and intransigence. Nationalist leaders apparently refused to accept arguments that the Protectorates were not viable without French personnel and subsidy; in fact they believed they could have independence *and* aid. The Europeans refused to contemplate loss of privilege, let alone Moslem independence. The result was native terrorism in both lands, repression by the authorities, and an increasingly embarrassing defiance of France by Bey and Sultan.

In Morocco such Residents General as General Juin cultivated Mohammed ben Youssef's opponents among the rebellious tribal caids, the most backward traditionalists, and tried vainly to obtain Paris support for a deposition in 1951. Juin was removed and made Marshal of France, but the intrigue continued in the circle of the Residency and the aged, corrupt Berber Pasha of Marrakesh, El Glaoui. At length, in August 1953 the functionaries connived at a Berber march on Rabat and brought about the Sultan's deposition. Paris accepted the *fait accompli*. Mohammed was exiled to Corsica and then to Madagascar. His aged, weak-minded uncle, Moulay ben Arafa, El Glaoui's creature, succeeded. Public disturbances, assassinations, and terror followed. Not even Mendès-France, taking office in June 1954, promised more than reform. Atrocities increased on every side. The Afro-Asian bloc in the UN pressed for intervention. Worried about its Moroccan bases, the United States hectored Paris. Finally, after complex negotiations in 1955, France announced a policy of "independence within interdependence," and amid the scandal of conflicts with Juin and others, Edgar Faure's Government ousted Ben Arafa and restored Mohammed that November. The Protectorate was abolished in March 1956, and later that year the Sultan took the title King Mohammed V. Lyautey's domain was gone, though France remained on by treaty right to garrison bases, train the royal army, and provide assistance. Henceforth Morocco was face to face with her tremendous political, social, and economic problems.

The Tunisian crisis evolved and found its solution in much the same way. By 1950 Habib Bourguiba's Neo-Destour party had the public support of the Bey in its demands for virtual independence. The *colons* were a motley breed of Europeans, many no more than entrenched time-servers. They and their supporters in parliament, the ministries, and the armed forces forbade serious concessions through the next years. The French Resident Jean de Hautecloque from January 1952 to September 1953 conducted himself like Caesar. Bourguiba (who had been loyal to France during the war) and other ministers were arrested and exiled in 1952. Native terrorism followed, and the usual French reprisals. This guerilla warfare lasted until Mendès-France flew to Tunis in July 1954 to promise internal sovereignty, and thus make good his dictum that, since France's ills resulted from "the multiplicity and weight" of her self-imposed tasks, "To govern is to choose, however difficult the choice may be." Surprisingly, Juin supported the Government, and thus both reassured the *colons* and spiked their opposition. By June 1955, with the support of the Arab leaders in Cairo and of the growing rebellion in Algeria, Tunisia obtained the promise of home rule. Bourguiba approved the ensuing agreements, but more extreme nationalists had their discontent increased by the approaching independence of Morocco. As they saw it, by means of resistance, backward Morocco was about to win even more than Tunisia. The Bey, fearing republicanism, was hesitant. But equivalent demands were made in Paris, and faced with the threat of unilateral Tunisian declaration of independence, the French Government acceded in March 1956. As it happened, the Bey's fears were justified: he was deposed in July 1957. Dependent upon French assistance, as was Morocco, Tunisia became a republic.

In each case the French had capitulated in the face of the threat of full-scale guerilla war. After the Indo-Chinese defeat, they dared not try to fight a massive campaign throughout the Maghreb, having neither the military strength nor the world support for it. France's situation in Tunisia and Morocco was limited by the treaties of 1882 and 1912. But she had, or thought she had, title and resources to put down the rebellion in Algeria. The legalism of Algeria's being part of metropolitan France was a claim not to be discussed. Yet the risk France took in granting Tunisian and Moroccan independence in 1956 was that both states would provide bases for the Algerian rebels. Such was to be the case. But having surrendered so much, having sustained so many retreats and defeats, the determination of civilians and military men was the more grim. Neither Moslems nor Europeans could foresee how desperate it was all to be.

In 1956 the Fourth Republic was still unbowed. When President Nasser seized the Suez Canal in July, French anger was intense. It was, after all, Ferdinand de Lesseps who had obtained authorization from Said Pasha to dig the Canal, aroused France to subscribe more than half its capital, and struck the first pickaxe into the earth almost a century before. Moreover, Nasser, who had promised to recognize the Canal's international status, was the primary outside source of assistance to the Algerian rebels. Successful action against him could not only recover the Canal and the prestige lost in Europe and the Middle East, but also sever rebel supply lines. France, however, could not act alone. Great Britain, hardly less outraged by Nasser, was divided. Anthony Eden's government was aware of the uselessness of appealing to the UN and fearful of alienating the United States. As the months passed, the possibility of successful direct action in Egypt faded. Yet action was plotted in secrecy with the government of Israel. And suddenly, on October 31, once the Egyptian army was being flung back pell-mell across the Sinai desert by the Israelis, the British and French struck at airfields and installations in the Canal Zone. It was "a 40-hour war," and the international uproar was intense. Both the United States and the Soviet Union condemned the action as French and British paratroops seized parts of the Canal on November 5. For the French Army, however, after so many humiliations, this was welcome revenge. Bidding fair to sweep to Cairo and overthrow Nasser, the raid was popular in France. But British opinion was more sharply divided, and in the face of U.S. opposition and Russian threats, Eden backed away. Deserted and under pressure, Guy Mollet's government also withdrew. The adventure had become humiliation, deepening the Algerian crisis, lowering the Republic's stock, bewildering the public. Undertaken by a Socialist premier, Suez was a last, bungled demonstration of the imperialist reflex, a momentary rallying of a humiliated people to the policy of the big stick in which they had never before shown a serious interest.

Algeria under the Fourth Republic: Rebellion and War

The Algerian war differed from the skirmishes and raids in Morocco and Tunisia. The French commitment was far greater, economically sanctified by the great promise of Saharan oil. The Europeans numbered more than one million, living largely in modern cities (20,000 were on the land) with a high standard of living, providing between 80 per cent and 90 per cent of the country's managerial personnel and 90 per cent of its capital investment. Unlike Frenchmen in Morocco, they were not divided about negotiating with Moslem nationalists, and, as in Indo-China, they appeared to have Army support. Perhaps one to two million Moslems participated in the modernized sector of the economy; the rest were hopelessly poor, illiterate, excluded from any share in urban prosperity. Two or three million were dependent on the wages of about 400,000 Algerian workers in France itself. These vast disparities in ways of life were the result of European privileges, natural and acquired, politically and socially guaranteed by France, and of a high population growth (2.5 per cent annually) among a primitive population in a land where agriculture can support properly only two to three million. Arab nationalism naturally condemned not only the imposed rule of an alien people, but also the civilization that was evidently so little prepared to share its wealth.

Before 1939, there were small-scale nationalist organizations dedicated to independence, such as L'Étoile nord-africaine (1926), dissolved by decree and then reformed by the extremist mystic Messali Hadj in 1937 as the Parti du peuple algérien, dissolved in turn in 1939. The more moderate L'Union populaire algérien of Ferhat Abbas and Ahmed Francis (1938) sought full rights for Moslems without separation from France. Though Messali was jailed in 1939, the course of the war compelled the Free French by 1942 to seek his cooperation. Asked for a new political, social and economic deal, they hedged and stalled. Minor concessions proffered by de Gaulle in 1944 were unsatisfactory to Abbas and Messali, for by then Abbas had become a nationalist also. Shortly before the Sétif uprising, Messali was exiled; after it, Abbas was imprisoned for ten months. But Abbas and colleagues were elected to the Constituent Assembly in 1946. There they found little sympathy for their cause. The Organic Statute of 1947 provided for direct rule from Paris—an Algerian Assembly to be elected in two wholly unequal colleges (one for Europeans; one for Moslems), perpetuating the old "citizen" and "subject" distinctions. Moreover, to prevent extreme nationalists' being elected, the French authorities packed the Moslem college with puppets. The regime was a scandal.

The struggle grew more bitter. Ferhat Abbas, pharmacist and writer, who in 1931 had declared, "I would not die for an Algerian fatherland because such a fatherland does not exist," was now fully committed to bringing it into existence. If there was no love lost between him (in 1946 he regrouped his followers into L'Union démocratique du manifeste algérien) and Messali (who had regrouped his in 1946 in the Mouvement pour le triomphe des libertés démocratiques), to Europeans their aims seemed identical. Some 80 per cent of the colons had been born in Algeria. How could they contemplate living in a Moslem state? Faced with a challenge that would destroy their world, they could not believe France would not stand by them. But Abbas and Messali were by no means the sole leaders of dissidence. Younger men, like Ben Bella and Belkacem Krim, were at work, and, encouraged by promises from Cairo after 1952 and by Tunisian and Moroccan successes, they formed a Comité révolutionnaire d'unité et d'action. Out of a maze of plotting, of squabbles and jockeying for position among the rebels, came the outbreak at 1:00 A.M. on November 1, 1954, in the Aurès mountain region and elsewhere. Armed bands struck with rifles and bombs all over the country, against individuals and installations. The Comité changed its name to Front de la libération national (FLN). Its army was tiny (about 300 men). But it grew rapidly, spread its network of operations, ruthlessly terrorized all who refused to cooperate with it against the French, and shortly committed France to a massive guerilla war of terror, mass reprisals, and nameless atrocity.

The Mendès-France Government rushed reinforcements by air and refused to talk with the rebels. Other governments would strike the same pose. The FLN tried incessantly to have the matter aired at the UN, and though the French delegation walked out of the General Assembly in October 1955, France could not prevent the war from becoming an international issue. On the one hand, she promised reforms (local autonomy, land redistribution, etc.), on the other, she tried to destroy the rebels. The Algiers colons refused any fundamental changes. In February 1956 they greeted Guy Mollet at the war memorial with shouts of death and a barrage of cabbages, tomatoes, and filth. The police just watched. Mollet at once broadcast his comprehension, arranged for the resignation of the moderate Resident Minister designate, General Georges Catroux, and replaced him with Robert Lacoste, who soon adopted the policy of pacification. It was a critical moment, marking the surrender of Paris to Algiers. The Moslem moderates drew the obvious conclusion: Paris dared not negotiate. Accordingly the FLN grew in size and respectability. Ferhat Abbas and his UDMA saw that they must go all the way. The rebellion became a mass movement that year, and it was all-out war.

In Paris the National Assembly granted the Government extraordinary powers. In Algiers the new Resident Minister (as the Governor was now called) proclaimed a state of siege, martial law, and censorship. Four-hundred thousand soldiers (professionals and conscripts) were committed to the campaign. From Egypt, Morocco, and Tunisia came arms and other supplies. The violence increased reciprocally. In 1956 European counterterrorists first used the plasticine bombs which were to become notorious there and in France. It was "a dirty war," characterized by assassinations, the massacring of village populations by both sides (for aiding the enemy), the enforced migration of Moslems to internment camps away from the Tunisian and Moroccan borders, by mutilation, and torture (French paratroops were the experts here, using water, electricity, bottles, and other ancient and modern refinements). For the great mass of the Moslem people it was unmitigated misery; for the *colons*, much suffering and the pervading fear that France might abandon them.

Increasingly, policy came to be made in Algiers. Lacoste was under pressure from the local notables, and early surrendered authority to the military command. Contemptuous of the *gros colons* and the *petit bourgeois pieds noirs* (small farmers), the Army was hardly less so of Paris. It was determined not to lose *this* war. Algeria offered the professionals a kind of permanent mission, and they had long considered that they represented all that was best in the nation. They were shocked by the incapacities of the Republic, sickened by its intrigues, resentful of popular apathy and the reluctance of French youth to serve in North Africa. Still disciplined, they were moving toward the state of mind that contemplates a *coup d'état*. In October 1956, Algiers arranged for the highjacking of five FLN leaders, who were flying as guests of the King of Morocco from Rabat to Tunis; the pilot of the chartered Air Atlas plane was ordered into Algiers. Mollet hesitated and then accepted and defended this kidnapping of Ben Bella and four other rebels. Local commanders also took action against Tunisian territory, from which rebel raids were launched, and Paris acquiesced. The bombing and strafing of Sakiet Sidi Youssef in February 1958 was the most flagrant such reprisal; and, despite the international furore, Paris was helpless. But the incident heralded the beginning of a new phase. Tunisia demanded that French troops leave, and that the war in Algeria be mediated. In Paris, governments that proposed internal political reforms in Algeria were pulled down in the Assembly. With the fall of Félix Gaillard's caretaker Government on this issue in April 1958, the last political crisis of the Fourth Republic had opened up.

The protracted interregnum ended when a *Mouvement républicain populaire* liberal, Pierre Pflimlin, formed a cabinet and called for negotiations at some favorable time. Parliament appeared to be coming round to the view that France could not withstand outside pressure and support the continued drain of the war. In Algeria, among the *colons* and the Army, the alarm was up. Lacoste, opportunist, tough and outspoken, the archetype of insubordinate official, disloyal to his political superiors, told everyone that a "diplomatic Dien Bien Phu" was imminent. General Raoul

Salan, commander-in chief in Algeria, warned President René Coty against "a sell-out government," and was supported by the Chief of Staff, General Paul Ely. As always, the United States was accused of working to displace France and seize the Sahara oilfields. A whole series of plots against the Government mushroomed and was now triggered in a bewildering interplay. On May 13, civilian activists seized the government buildings in Algiers and formed a Committee of Public Safety, partly civilian, partly military. Salan "acquiesced" and the Army was thus openly catapulted to power.

De Gaulle and Algeria: War, Rebellion, and Peace

In France and in Algeria, the supporters of Charles de Gaulle were in action. Twelve years on the sidelines, inveighing against the sins of the Republic, traveling around the world, writing his memoirs, keeping close touch with political leaders even after the disruption of his *Rassemblement du peuple français,* de Gaulle stood ready to "assume the power of the Republic" in the extremity he had believed must come. As Gaston Defferre was to say, "He has the taste for drama, the taste for calamity." The offensive on his behalf was more easily realized in Algiers than in Paris. Salan pronounced his blessing, but the National Assembly voted in the Pflimlin Government on May 14. Though some were for capitulation at once, a majority appeared ready to defy both Algiers and de Gaulle. This position collapsed in the next days. To forestall a military coup and compel Pflimlin's withdrawal, de Gaulle suggested he was about to take over, May 15. Salan was induced to cry, *"Vive de Gaulle!"* But the situation was tense. Preparations were made for a military descent on Paris. Marshal Juin supported Algiers.

Everything pointed to a Gaullist solution. Mollet and the Independent Antoine Pinay communicated with him. Having talked with him, Pflimlin was convinced he must resign, and, as the Algiers commanders got ready to strike at France, President Coty threatened his own resignation if the Assembly did not invest de Gaulle as premier. After further negotiations, with the invasion threat poised, the politicians heard de Gaulle's declaration, reluctantly but probably thankfully, June 1. Always scornful of the political circus, he had to be prevailed upon to go through even that ceremony, the shortest of the Fourth Republic. His investiture was approved 329 to 224, and he was granted full powers for six months and the authority to draw up a new constitution. The Fourth Republic was sentenced to death, the specter of civil war banished. Without a reliable police force and army, or even the obvious mass support of the public, the regime may have had no alternative.

Three days later, de Gaulle appeared on a balcony at the Algiers Forum to tell the throng below, *"Je vous ai compris"* and thus open up one of the most fateful *équivoques* of modern times. Both Moslem and European hoped for the contradictory and the impossible from him. While he ruled absolutely, brought in a new constitution, and became President of a new

Republic, de Gaulle carried on an extraordinary activity. Simultaneously he supported and appeased a nervous, truculent Army, pacified the *colons*, avoided a UN vote of censure, and held out to the Moslems a more liberal policy if they would lay down their arms. At Constantine, October 1958, he announced a five-year plan to provide more education, better housing, rural improvements. But it was too late. His political pronouncements were vague, temporizing, incapable of clear analysis.

To the Provisional Government of the Algerian Republic, headed by Ferhat Abbas, he offered "the peace of the brave"; to the *colons*, assurance that France would never abandon them; to the Army, the certainty of ultimate victory. But the war raged on. His offer of self-determination within four years of the rebels' laying down their arms also came too late. Moreover, it deeply offended the soldiers, and in January 1960 the offer produced first a clash with the popular Algiers commander, General Jacques Massu ("At the right moment [the Army] can impose its will"), and then rebellion by the civilians. The Army remained divided but loyal. The President stubbornly reaffirmed his policy and the Revolt of the Barricades collapsed. With special powers granted to him, de Gaulle talked now of the necessity for "an Algerian Algeria" and the possibility of "cease-fire" negotiations. He alienated both the Algerian rebels (in the abortive talks with their representatives and his at Melun, in the summer of 1960) and the Army. Relieved of his command, Salan was returned to France. But he then fled to Spain, from where he defied the President. If a January 1961 referendum gave approval to de Gaulle's policy of self-determination for Algeria, the divisions this policy occasioned in French society—or at least *articulate* society—went deep.

In April 1961 his rule was suddenly and openly challenged. With the good offices of Bourguiba and Mohammed V's successor, King Hassan II, he was obviously about to initiate serious negotiations with the rebel government. Bombings and assassinations assailed both France and Algeria. The Army command had long since written off de Gaulle's October 1958 promise to Salan, "We must not give up Algeria," as a deliberately misleading lie. In Algiers, four generals (commander-in-chief Maurice Challe, André Zeller, Edmond Jouhaud—joined by Salan, arriving from Spain) declared a revolt on the night of April 24. Panic ensued in Paris. Airborne invasion was expected from North Africa. But the mass of the Army did not join the rebels, nor did the air force and navy. De Gaulle held fast. Five days later the rebellion collapsed. Challe surrendered at once, Zeller a few days later. Both were tried and condemned to 15-year prison terms. Jouhaud and Salan went underground, the latter heading the *Organisation de l'armée secrète* (OAS), dedicated to destroy de Gaulle and his policy of self-determination; tried in absentia, both were condemned to death.

Wearily the war smoldered on. Negotiations with the FLN delegation that summer of 1961 were unsuccessful, each side testing the other, claiming the Sahara, accusing the other of bad faith. Replacement of Abbas by Benyoussef ben Khedda seemed to indicate a hardening of resolve. On both sides of the Mediterranean, frightful assassinations occurred. The brutality with which French armed forces retaliated against Bourguiba's sudden ultimatum to France to evacuate the Bizerte base suggested deteriorating prospects in North Africa. In fact, these were merely moves in a ruthless trial of strength. Neither clandestine calls for insurrection against de Gaulle, nor Algerian rebel firmness, halted progress toward a settlement. The OAS continued its outrages that winter of 1961-1962, but a settlement was achieved and signed at Évian-les-Bains, March 18. After referendums in France and Algeria, the President was free in July to announce formal recognition of the independence Algerians had overwhelmingly chosen. France had obtained guarantees of her interests, military installations, and citizens in Algeria; she would share the Saharan oil wealth with the new Algerian Republic. Almost unbelievably, the 132 years of rule had come to a close. "You are merely passing guests," Abd el Kader's men had told the French a century before. "You may stay three hundred years, like the Turks, but in the end you will leave."

In the summer of 1962 the OAS broke up, at least in Algeria, after a final orgy of inhuman atrocities against Moslems and those Europeans who had accepted negotiation and independence. Jouhaud and Salan were tracked down (they had certainly been protected by military men in high places), arrested, tried, and sentenced: the former to death, the latter, amazingly, to life imprisonment. More than three-quarters of the Europeans poured out of their homeland for exile in France, Canada, or elsewhere. Assisted by France, the wounds of each of them still gaping, Algeria embarked upon a long struggle to make a nation. Civil strife, dictatorship, and economic hardship would mark the way.

Algérie française had died badly. This war was the worst, as it was the last, of France's colonial struggles. It had been fought by the FLN in the name of a nation that never existed, and by the French in the name of a myth—a nation of Frenchmen stretching "from Dunkerque to Tamanrasset." The victims were more easily identified than the victors. Apart from the men, women, and children slaughtered by both sides during the struggle, primary victims were the Moslem *harkis* who had fought with the French, many of whom were now abandoned to the savage reprisals of this rough new regime. The fate of all who had collaborated with the French was to be tragic. For France, the brutal legacy was not only in the dead and wounded, the property lost and prestige reduced, but also in nearly eight years of exposure to, and apathetic acceptance of, frightful violence. Barbarism had bred barbarism; psychological warfare achieved a refinement of cruelty. The harassed Paris police had even murdered Algerian terrorist suspects (some in the presence of Maurice Papon, Prefect of Police, in October 1961) and thrown the bodies into the river as warning. Like the Ministers of the Fourth Republic before him, Prime Minister Michel Debré had publicly lied about the use of torture. By censorship and seizure his Government had tried to suppress unpleasant facts about the manner in which France had fought a savage foe. Those intellectuals, writers, teachers, and clergy who proclaimed these facts were branded as traitors, dismissed, tried, imprisoned, and fined. Some who fell into military hands were tortured; some disappeared forever, like Maurice Audin, a Communist professor at the University of Algiers, tortured and strangled to death by officers whom the State protected. The courts were lenient toward such military offenders as did appear before them, ruthless toward those who protested the war and the means used to prosecute it.

A very dirty war indeed, it was fought without pity, viewed with vast indifference and apathy by the man in the street, and hated by those whose sons were committed to its uncertain battlefields. France had been caught in the nightmare of the *colons's* tragedy and the Army's crisis of conscience. Unable to identify with people of whom only a portion were French and who were essentially North Africans, whatever their ancestry, the nation was painfully aware of its responsibility to them—if only because this had been shouted from the rooftops. How often had France been told that without Algeria she would be reduced to an insignificant European hexagonal? She had preferred not to know the truth, to proclaim a routine patriotism, to listen to absurd stories about a war to save North Africa from communism and about American imperialist machinations. If de Gaulle's tortuous, machiavellian policy, with all its contradictions and all the injustices it involved for many men, had done nothing more, it had at least brought the Republic out of its destructive hypnotic trance. But it was almost disturbing to witness the rapidity with which the bloodstained episode was consigned to oblivion and the ash heap of history.

Community: The Devolution of Empire

That summer of 1962, little remained of the great Empire. The French Union of 1946 had given way to the Community of the Fifth Republic. Even under the Fourth Republic, in June 1956, a *loi-cadre* (drawn up by Gaston Defferre) had offered representative institutions and domestic autonomy to the West and Central African Territories and to Madagascar. Demands for independence were being heard in Ivory Coast and Senegal. The 1958 Constitution created an elaborate Community executive, a Senate, and a Court of Arbitration. The working of this apparatus was to depend upon organic laws. In August 1958 de Gaulle visited the African colonies and there decided he must offer, at the forthcoming referendum on the Constitution, either acceptance of the Community or rejection and independence. The latter alternative would mean an end to French aid and preference within the tariff system. As it happened, only Guinea chose independence; a severe application of the penalties followed. Some Territories chose to remain as they were. In fact, the Community, like the French Union before it, was destined to be less a reality than an historical project.

Decolonization was moving rapidly everywhere, as de Gaulle recognized; and the mood of Brazzaville 1944 had quite disappeared. Led by Senegal and Soudan, the African colonies took the road to independence in 1959 and 1960, and the Constitution was revised to permit membership in the Community just the same. The defenders of a black African empire went down to defeat. De Gaulle's prestige and the concerns of the Algerian war ensured the smooth evolution of affairs. Six of the new states remained within the Community; six others remained outside. Contractual agreements with France provided for indispensable economic aid and cooperation in defense and foreign relations. By the end of 1961 little else was left of this "transformed" Community. With bolder visions of a multiracial empire gone, France still hoped for a strong cultural, economic, and military role in the new Republics. Proof of the usefulness of this cordial relationship was the turning back of Guinea in 1962 toward the Community she had rejected—when she was disenchanted with the Soviet camp, and independence was no longer a bar to association with the Community.

The Community would never be comparable to the British Commonwealth. Although some of the African republics could boast statesmen as cultivated as the poet Léopold Senghor, President of Senegal, or as politically sophisticated as President Félix Houphouet-Boigny of Ivory Coast, most were hard pressed to find the necessary native cadres. Few were politically stable. Togo's President Sylvanus Olympio was assassinated in 1963. Riots in Chad and Senegal occurred that same year. In 1964 French paratroops and naval units were repeatedly dispatched to Gabon (rich in uranium, manganese, and iron ore) to rescue the recklessly authoritarian regime of President Léon Mba from its domestic opponents. Other states, like Dahomey, had known similar attempts at *coup d'état*, and if Ivory Coast's capital Abidjan was a showcase for French achievement, its politics were not free from witchcraft. Whatever France's responsibilities were for this native elite's preparation, her economic burden in the republics and her economic interest in some of them was great. Not surprisingly, she was concerned to have them associated with the Common Market, and this was effected in 1957 and 1963.

Overseas Territories such as the Comoro Islands or St. Pierre and Miquelon appeared quiet and content. Such Overseas Departments as crowded Martinique and Guadeloupe, with low standards of living and considerable slums, manifested unrest after 1945. But so dependent were they upon French aid that no serious independence movement appeared in the Carribbean area, not even among the local Communist groups. Moreover, under the Fifth Republic, France was somewhat more aware of these islands. On the occasion of de Gaulle's brief stopover in March 1964, Government House at Fort de France was given its first coat of paint in thirty years.

Once the Algerian war ended, France's relations with Morocco and Tunisia improved; until that time Army reprisals against rebel bases and supply lines in these states had led to counterreprisals against French citizens, businesses, and government installations in them. Moroccan bases were evacuated by the end of 1961. Nevertheless continued nationalist agitation for the Government to expropriate foreign holdings created periodic tension with France. Nationalization of French-owned lands in Tunisia in 1964, in violation of agreements for a gradual take-over of such foreign ownership, similarly had diplomatic and economic repercussions. France's nuclear tests in the Sahara had also brought strong protests from Tunisia and Morocco. Perhaps the worst event followed the rash ultimatum to withdraw from Bizerte presented by Bourguiba in 1961. The response was a devastating French assault on the town. However, negotiations brought a settlement one year later, and in October 1963 the great base was evacuated. For France it was retreat all along the line. More expropriations in Algeria and a tough attitude on the part of the Ben Bella dictatorship hardly deflected France from her costly assistance to the new republic and her determination to assert her influence through the Maghreb. By mid-1964 all French troops, save in such leased bases as the anchorage of Mers el Kébir, had been withdrawn. It seemed that the nationalists' hopes that they could enjoy both independence and support had been made good. And this was the case even as the revolution continued on its way (with the fall of Ben Bella in 1965) and devoured its own.

The old imperialism was dead. What had emerged was a kind of cultural imperialism, founded on economic aid, transmitted by French teachers, technicians, and administrators, guaranteed by language. The high cost of all this had its critics in France who argued that the funds might better be used to modernize the homeland. Lavish receptions for visiting African chiefs of state caused wry Parisian comments about *"les républiques cannibales."* But the profits and losses of imperialism have always been variously reckoned. For the moment, at least, the rulers of France insisted the expenditures were in the national interest. And though the symbols of that other Empire had gone, the symbols of a new world-wide French-speaking community might yet be found to catch the imagination of France.

EIGHT

PEOPLE, PARLIAMENT, AND POWER:

THE SHORE DIMLY SEEN

"On trouve des moyens pour guérir de la folie, mais on n'en trouve point pour redresser un esprit de travers."

Like the Third Republic, the Fourth fell because it was not able to grapple successfully with the crises its own weakness provoked. In each case an essentially external problem was permitted to develop to the point where it had either to be met head on by a divided nation or permitted to impose its will. The cases were vastly different, to be sure. And the second of them was solved short of catastrophe. But the Fourth Republic was as much a casualty as the Third had been. Both collapsed after they had overcome their worst period of economic and financial troubles. The final years of each were marked by profound rifts in national opinion, serious demoralization of large parts of the population, and a neglect of the issues of most immediate national concern for a cultivation of individual interest. If France was not bored, she was indifferent. No one would propose that after the Liberation the nation had been united. It was a matter of record that the Constitution of 1946 had been accepted by less than half the nation. Nevertheless there had been a fresh wind blowing through the land; there was hope, and there was even, from the Resistance, a kind of *mystique*. But there was to be no new beginning. The regime and its parties never solved the riddle that had confronted every regime since 1789: how to organize opinion and so structure it that a consensus might emerge in parliament and a government be formed to carry through a national policy. Almost the oldest of the great democracies, France had found no satisfactory resolution of democracy's political problems. For both foreign and domestic affairs it was a crippling limitation.

Failure of the Fourth Republic

Various electoral systems had been tried since the Revolution, but none discouraged the proliferation of parties and parliamentary groups. Religious, historical, economic, and ideological tendencies cut across them. Rigid discipline existed in none but the Communist party (and even there lapses were not unknown). A percentage of party members was liable to oppose the party majority on any issue and vote against "their" government. After 1947 the Fourth Republic's governmental majorities were the more precarious because of the Communist and RPF (Gaullist) opposition. In all, perhaps a third of the National Assembly would have been happy to overturn the regime. And as these Deputies represented a higher fraction of the electorate than that, the outlook for the Constitution was not brilliant. That it survived at all may have been owing to the electoral law of 1951, devised to reduce the opposition representation. By the law of 1946 these opposition parties would have been able to capture more than half the Assembly seats. Mutual foes though they were, they could have combined to bring the Republic down. The new law, however, gave the center parties a slight overrepresentation. In 1951 a kind of six-sided distribution of the parties characterized the new chamber. The permanent opposition remained: when the RPF was dissolved in 1953, the followers of Pierre Poujade were soon to appear on the extreme Right in the 1956 elections, and the Communists increased their strength that year also.

The chronicle of governments during the twelve years of the Fourth Republic was that of the increasing fragility of coalitions. The rather strained post-Resistance unity of *tripartisme* (Communists, Socialists, and MRP) was condemned by the ambitions of both Stalin and General de Gaulle. Having held up through two Constituent Assemblies to create the Fourth Republic, it broke down in the spring of 1947. For a would-be head of government there was nowhere to move in search of a majority but to the Right: hence the Third Force coalitions of Socialists, MRP, Radicals, and Independents before 1951. This migration away from the Left became more pronounced that year with MRP evolution toward the Right, trying to win back some of those opportunist conservatives who had made use of the party before the RPF existed and while the old conservative parties were still under a cloud. Before the December 1955 dissolution, governments came to have a right of Center character. But what that second Assembly of 1951-1955 seemed to show was that the pull from Left and Right (despite disintegration of the RPF in 1953) was fatal to the stability of the Center. Breakup of the Radical party into three rival groups demonstrated this fact, although personal rivalries also played some part in the process. The 1956 elections underlined the fragmented nature of the Center. Though the RPF was now gone (save for a small group of its heirs, the *Républicains sociaux*), much of its strength had flowed back to the old conservative parties. In short, the MRP, a contradictory mélange of Catholicism and progressivism, liberalism and colonial conservatism, was a permanent casualty. And with the Communists more powerful and the Poujadists established in some force, Socialist participation in the governmental coalitions became necessary once more. Those who had so recently denounced each other to the electorate were thrown together. United in opposition to the extreme Left and Right, the coalition groups made curious bedfellows where domestic issues were concerned. In the face of Army restiveness and the Algerian rebellion, their position became both ridiculous and tragic.

The apparent slight shift to left of Center, with the Government formed around the Socialist leader Guy Mollet in January 1956, was quickly revealed as meaningless. Thoroughly shaken by the opposition in Algiers to his proposed liberalization of policy there, Mollet embraced the tough line on Algeria, suspended any left-wing domestic program, and thus assured his coalition conservative support for sixteen months. Outdoing the Radical master of *immobilisme*, Henri Queuille, he finally fell in approved fashion for proposing measures to appease the working class. But whatever the relative success of his tenure, it was evident that the system was in danger of breaking down altogether. Such an obvious sacrifice of principle to expediency disgusted many who had looked hopefully for integrity at the Center, had been disenchanted by the failure of Mendès-France to reform and hold together the Radical party, and who now were convinced by the Mollet experience that parliamentarism was incapable of either integrity or reform. The fierce partisanship which produced protracted crises after Mollet's fall seemed to confirm this diagnosis. Three weeks were required to form the next cabinet; 35 days the one following; 27 that headed by the MRP leader Pierre Pflimlin, the last before de Gaulle took power. If the Socialists now showed a kind of discipline which French parties had so notoriously lacked, it was put to use for destructive purposes: to pull down ministries at the command of the party executive outside parliament. The fragmented Assembly seemed as unimpressed by the prospect of a cabinet collapse as it was incapable of putting together some new majority. The nation might be weary of the Palais Bourbon, but the Assembly was a mirror to the nation. However capricious, parliament reflected the fissures in the country. The last crisis came when Pflimlin suggested seeking a way out of the Algerian impasse. Then, momentarily, the events in Algiers on May 13, 1958, brought a closing of parliamentary ranks on behalf of the regime against what appeared to the parties as equally unacceptable alternatives. It was too late for equivocation. If rank and file struck intransigent poses, leaders like Mollet and Pflimlin were convinced that parliament could not deny de Gaulle's bid for power and embark on an adventure against Algiers.

The General Returns

Charles de Gaulle's career was a study in the triumph of will. Born in Lille in 1890, son of a retired Army officer and professor of philosophy, he had passed through St. Cyr, served with distinction in the First World War ("In all respects an officer without equal," read the citation signed by General Pétain) before being wounded and captured at Verdun, achieved distinction after the war by both lectures and writings on military affairs, and come to be the champion of a professsional mechanized, armored force. Thereafter the close relationship that had grown up between him and the Marshal dissolved. The Army was hostile to de Gaulle's views, the more so as he now sought another avenue for the advancement of his doctrine. Few read de Gaulle's writings, but in the Chamber of Deputies the conservative Paul Reynaud put forward a proposal for an armored striking force in 1935.

Their collaboration was to continue, de Gaulle urging Reynaud not to be discouraged by the rejection of the scheme, offering to be of any service he could. The Germans had already begun the construction of such armored divisions, and France too began to plan for them. But the basic Army doctrine was hostile to de Gaulle's conceptions, and the great chiefs, Pétain, Weygand, Gamelin, and others, disliked him as an arrogant and conceited military journalist.

When the war of 1939 was declared, nothing marked out Colonel de Gaulle for an extraordinary destiny. To the annoyance of his superiors, he continued to press for creation of a great independent armored force. In the battle that opened up in May 1940 he was given command of a still skeletal armored division, France's fourth and last. By then Reynaud was Premier, and after a brief command and some local success with his force, de Gaulle was summoned to the cabinet as Undersecretary of State for National Defense. In the tragic days thereafter he did all he could to bolster Reynaud's determination to resist the Army's demand that an armistice be sought, collided bitterly with Weygand, and, having failed to prevail in the governmental collapse at Bordeaux that June, left to raise the standard of rebellion in London. Supported by Churchill but much suspected by all, this extraordinary man rallied a small and sometimes strange band of Free French to him, prevailed by the most ruthless means over every challenge to his leadership, and emerged the unquestioned leader in Liberated France.

All that was an epic; his place in history was assured. What followed was anticlimax, miscalculation, and a long eclipse. Having abandoned office in January 1946 rather than participate in a political system he could not control, he considered but shunned the temptation of *coup d'état*. Six months after the Fourth Republic's Constitution was approved, the RPF came into being. Though de Gaulle insisted it was not a party, in fact it behaved like one and the frustration of its condition occasioned internal quarrels which, despite the strong showing in the 1951 elections, brought collapse within the year. Voters defected in by-elections; the revival of the old Right accelerated its disintegration, and in May 1953 the General abandoned his enterprise. If the *Républicains sociaux* remained faithful, many others readily merged with the older parties. Clearly it seemed to most that de Gaulle would not return. "It is my intention," he said with some bitterness in July 1955, "not to intervene in what is conventionally called 'the public affairs of this country.' . . . I say farewell to you and perhaps for a long time to come." Working on his memoirs, he came to Paris weekly to receive the undaunted, to speak his scathing evaluation of the pigmies who now occupied the seats of authority in the world, to predict the coming disaster. For he knew that, short of disaster, the politicians would not have him back.

Indeed, the road led downhill. The bombing of Sakiet in February 1958 and Premier Gaillard's acceptance of Anglo-American good offices in the resultant dispute with Tunisia announced the final crisis of the regime.

The Army was disobedient; in the Assembly Left and Right snarled at each other. How insecure the Government was could be seen when 7,000 police marched on the Palais Bourbon demanding bonuses for the very real danger they ran at the hands of Moslem terrorists in the capital. The United States Secretary of State, an obtuse and heavy-handed diplomat whom a lifetime of contact with foreign affairs had somehow monumentally unfitted for his present great responsibilities, threatened an "agonizing reappraisal" of the American position in Europe unless France settled the Algerian question that year. Paris grew tense. Opinion tended toward the polarities. But this was the very weather for de Gaulle. And with the formation of Pflimlin's Government, the rising in Algiers, and Marshal Juin's disloyal pronouncement that he had "no more confidence" in the regime (this was his second abandonment of a regime, for he had served Vichy before switching his allegiance after the 1942 landings in North Africa), de Gaulle stepped forward as arbiter and savior. Though he told representatives of the parties that he wished to solve the Algerian problem in a French way with equality for Europeans and Moslems and to stabilize the executive, everyone knew he would return only on his own terms. If he was prevailed upon to appear in the Palais Bourbon which he so despised, promising respect for universal suffrage, responsible government, separation of powers, and a distinction of office between President and Prime Minister, he was no Adolphe Thiers: he had written President Coty to say that should "an uncomprehensible factionalism" prevent his "once again saving the Republic," there would be "nothing left for me but to spend the rest of my days with my grief." The threat sufficed. The full powers were granted for six months.

After a slow start, the new Constitution was swiftly drafted. Approved by the Government, it was made public at the end of July and submitted to the Advisory Constitutional Committee and to the Council of State. A referendum held in France and the Empire at the end of September overwhelmingly approved the final text: 66.4 per cent of the registered voters in the metropolitan area (79.2 per cent of the actual votes cast). The comparison with the referendum of October 1946 or the piecemeal procedure of 1875 was striking. Since his speech at Bayeux in June 1946, the General's desire for a presidential system had been known: he wanted a Chief of State "placed above party feeling," choosing a Prime Minister acceptable to a parliament (the lower house elected by universal suffrage, the upper by general and municipal councils and including members of economic, social, and intellectual organizations), but himself ready to play the role of arbiter in the Council of Ministers (or by calling for national elections in time of serious trouble). Above all, the President must be the guarantor of France's independence and treaties. The 1958 document was largely ascribed to de Gaulle's young lawyer friend Senator Michel Debré, critic of the Fourth Republic and shortly to be the Fifth's first Prime Minister. And Debré was on record as desiring administrative reform, strengthening of the central authority, and establishment of a responsible parliamentary system in which the legislature would cease to be a closed arena and become the expression rather of a stable method of voting, which yields a clear majority as in Anglo-American systems.

The Constitution of 1958

Promulgated on October 4, 1958, the Constitution seemed to provide a cross between the parliamentary and the presidential systems. As the regime actually functioned, however, the presidential power dominated. The Prime Minister and his colleagues were apparently instruments of the presidency. Parliament was reduced to a minor role, which bore almost no comparison with that which it had had—and abused—under the Third and Fourth Republics; its one revolt, in 1962, was not supported by the nation. The regime was less political than administrative, plebiscitarian, and authoritarian in nature. If the experiment seemed to be the successful conclusion to the long search for a national consensus, it was nevertheless shaped by circumstances that were temporary: the Algerian drama and the unique figure of Charles de Gaulle. Yet it was by no means a purely personal regime. The rallying of the country to this man at least suggested an echo from the calamity of the sixteenth century which was resolved around the person of Henri IV; it was not wholly unrelated to the rough closing of ranks behind the Jacobin dictatorship; it awakened memories of the crumbling regimes out of whose ruins conservative saviors stepped forward in 1871, 1940, and 1944; it recalled the more radical instinct to fight to save the Republic: 1870, 1917, and again, but quite differently, 1940. The Fifth Republic embodied many of the aspirations of previous Republics. But, however strong this sense of the past, conscious or unconscious, may have been, the dominant fact was that in September 1958 a majority of the voters chose not a constitutional document but a man who promised to assume the responsibility for leading them out of the impasse into which parliament had either led them or permitted them to wander. And when in October 1962, after doing this, he asked them to approve alteration of the Constitution in a manner which every independent legal authority assured them was unconstitutional, they clarified their vote of 1958 again by doing what he asked.

The President was elected, for a seven-year, renewable term, by a college of some 80,000 notables (members of parliament, overseas representatives, and, principally, mayors and municipal councillors). According to the 1958 text he would be chosen by representatives of rural France, likely to pick a conservative. The 1962 amendment (approved by 46.66 per cent of the total electorate, but by 62.25 per cent of those actually casting votes) substituted direct popular election and was designed to give the office a prestige and authority which a lesser figure than de Gaulle would not himself possess if he were merely the choice of the notables. The General was haunted by the catastrophe of 1940, the total lack of authority then inhering in President Albert Lebrun, and the confusion amidst which the Republic went down (though it would be difficult to show that a strong President might have saved the situation). De Gaulle may have wished such direct election in 1958, but only the prestige acquired by ending the Algerian war permitted him to put it through in 1962 against the old parties. Doubtless it reduced the probability of his successors being mere figureheads, but the presidency would still be very much what the incumbent made of it.

Elected to the office in December 1958, de Gaulle was theoretically an arbiter, providing for "the regular functioning of the public authorities and the continuity of the State." He was also "protector of the independence of the nation, of the integrity of its territory, of respect for treaties and Community agreements." He presided over the Community. He was commander of the armed forces. He appointed the Prime Minister and, on the latter's recommendation, the other Ministers. He promulgated laws, but might first ask parliament to reconsider them. After consultation with the Prime Minister and the presidents of the two chambers, he might dissolve parliament (but not again for twelve months following the elections). Article 16 gave him the right to use emergency powers when regular functioning of the Government was interrupted by "a serious and immediate threat" to the nation, its institutions, territory, or fulfilment of its international obligations—all this after consulting the Prime Minister, the chamber presidents, and the Constitutional Council. He must inform the nation of the fact by message and was forbidden to dissolve parliament during the exercise of such "exceptional powers." On the Prime Minister's proposal, he shared with parliament the right to propose constitutional amendment. He negotiated and ratified treaties. Answerable for his actions only in the event of high treason, he could then be indicted on majority approval of an identical motion in the two chambers and tried by the High Court of Justice.

Even on paper, therefore, the presidential powers were potentially great. Those of the Government were less clear. In theory, the Government made and carried out national policy, directed the administration, and controlled the armed forces. Responsible to the National Assembly, it was free to propose legislation and (unlike the President) could appear to be heard in both chambers on request. The Prime Minister had "general charge of the work of the Government," was responsible for national defense and ensured execution of the laws. He might request a special session of parliament and might propose constitutional revision to the President. His acts were countersigned by the Minister(s) responsible. No Minister might be a member of parliament or any trade or professional organization, or be publicly or professionally employed.

Thus the separation of powers seemed distinct. Everything depended upon the smooth operation of the relationship between Prime Minister, Ministers, and the President, on the one hand, and Government and parliament on the other. If obligations and duties were manifest, the lines of authority and power were less certain.

Parliament consisted of two chambers. The National Assembly was elected by direct universal suffrage (an organic law set the term at five years) the Senate indirectly (by deputies and local councillors for nine years). The Senate's power was principally to put moral pressure on the Assembly in the interest of Government bills. Parliament met by right in two ordinary sessions (October to December, and in late April for not more than three months). Like the Prime Minister, an Assembly majority might request a special session with a specified agenda (subject to presidential veto) of not more than twelve days. Like the Government, it might amend bills. Should Assembly and Senate disagree (after two readings and a joint committee deadlock) on the final version of a bill, the Assembly might adopt its own, or the committee's, text. Government bills and private bills accepted by the Government had priority. The Assembly might challenge the Government by vote of censure 48 hours after introduction of the motion (signed by at least one-tenth of the Deputies), which must receive majority approval to carry. It might also challenge the Government pledging responsibility on passage of a bill by approving a motion of censure put forward within 24 hours. Following censure, the Prime Minister must resign.

Two Councils existed to support the Ministry against parliament. The Economic and Social Council (selected by the Government) now advised the executive branch (rather than the legislature, as under the Fourth Republic) on its proposals; thus a favorable opinion would bolster the Government morally. The Constitutional Council (nine members nominated for nine-year terms: three by the President, three by each of the chamber presidents—plus former Presidents of the Republic for life), which must approve organic laws and parliamentary procedures, would seem likely to support the Government against unwelcome bills or procedures.

De Gaulle as President: The "Elective Monarchy"

Clearly the constitutional texts constricted the activity and power of parliament. After 1958 both parliament and Ministers had their position drastically circumscribed in practice. By late 1959 the conception of the President as arbiter gave way to the reality of the President as ruler. The dialogue that Debré may have intended between parliament and Government never occurred. The Gaullist experience showed not how the Constitution must work out, but how it could work out in the presence of the massive authority of de Gaulle. It showed how constitutional texts could be interpreted by Government and President in a manner displeasing to parliament and constitutional lawyers, provided that popular approval was brought to bear on the executive branch's behalf. Challenging de Gaulle's declared intent to revise the Constitution by referendum, parliament overthrew the Government, October 5, 1962, and was dissolved. The President could of course have been repudiated in the referendum or at the polls; even without his threat to resign, his position would have been untenable. The point was that his enormous personal authority (strengthened no doubt by virtual monopoly of radio and television) permitted him to triumph over the old parties and the learned authorities who were clear that amendment by referendum was violation of the Constitution.

Moreover, the Constitution did not permit presidential initiation of the referendum at all. Yet from the date of his election, de Gaulle declared that he would "exercise supreme power to the full." As early as September 1959 he pledged himself ("provided God grants me life and the people listen to me") to a referendum in Algeria. In each case he insisted that the referendum was *his*, not the Government's, to "tell me if I can and should pursue my task in the service of France." On the eve of the January 1961 referendum concerning self-determination for Algeria, he said, "Women and men of France, it is to me that you are going to give your answer. I need—yes, I need—to know what is in your minds and hearts. In truth—who is unaware of it?—the matter is between each man and woman of France and myself." Thus the referendum became an instrument for measuring popular approval of the man who "for twenty years"— thereby he erased the legitimacy not only of Vichy but of the Fourth Republic—had been "the country's guide in the serious crises through which we have lived."

Less controversial than his use of the referendum, though not unchallenged, was the President's use of the emergency powers permitted by Article 16. Invoked during the April 1961 Generals' Revolt, they were used for five months and with moderation. But Article 16 provided that the occasion be marked by "an immediate and serious threat to Republican institutions" and interruption of "the regular functioning of the constitutional public authorities." The first condition had certainly existed, the second had not. Though the President might have been justified in taking action on that grave occasion, evidently there was no safeguard against a possible arbitrary interpretation of "immediate and serious threat" to the Republic. Moreover, his interpretation of what parliament might do in special session during the emergency was open to question. Out of much maneuvering and argument came the cloudy conclusion that it could not do much. The President could not dissolve parliament, but the Assembly could not censure the Government. At the same time, de Gaulle's claim to interpret the Constitution himself (citing Article 5, which provided that the President endeavor "to ensure respect for the Constitution") was dubious.

That the President's actual powers went beyond the letter of the constitutional law was made possible by a certain vagueness of the texts and the no-man's land in which executive authority lies. In fact a conflict could occur between President and Prime Minister, the former appealing to the nation, the latter to his parliamentary majority. Even if the President's national majority permitted him to stand firm, dissolution of the Assembly and return of a hostile majority there would place him in an untenable situation. That no open conflict had taken place during the early years of the Fifth Republic was doubtless owing to de Gaulle's ascendancy over his Prime Ministers, the disarray of the old parties, and the over-all success of his various policies. Indeed, de Gaulle appeared to have virtually absorbed the powers of the Prime Minister, despite the promise given in May 1958. Young, ambitious, a supporter of *Algérie française*, Michel Debré was said to have refused in January 1960 to carry out the President's wish to order the Army to attack the rebel barricades set up in Algiers. Yet he had remained on, sustaining more than one flat presidential contradiction of his public statements. Press and parliamentary opposition heaped criticism upon him. After conclusion of the Évian accords, he was immediately replaced by Georges Pompidou (who was later rumored to have successfully taken a strong line with the President against execution of the rebel General Jouhaud). Debré's defeat in the November 1962 elections and subsequent arduous, but successful, campaign to be elected from Réunion in the Indian Ocean in May 1963 seemed hard after so many proofs of loyalty to his master. "Debré is Saint Sébastien," the General was quoted as saying. "Each arrow he receives makes him suffer, but he loves it."

Other Ministers found that this President, who presided over the Council of Ministers, was the real master of the Government. Just as politicians like Georges Bidault, the former Resistance leader who was repeatedly Foreign Minister under the Fourth Republic, did not obtain ministerial post though they helped to bring de Gaulle to power in 1958, so others who had performed the same role, like Jacques Soustelle, were belatedly given a relatively minor portfolio—and Soustelle was sacked soon after the January 1960 Barricades Revolt, presumably for opposition to the President's Algerian policy. Both Soustelle and Bidault, irrevocably embittered by the Algerian settlement, joined the militant opposition against him and roamed from exile to exile. As the collaborators of gangsters and assassins, they suffered perhaps no more than justice. Others who had done less to bring de Gaulle to power, men such as Guy Mollet or Antoine Pinay, took office to serve with him and then came to the parting of the ways. Ministerial turnover was heavy. Politicians gave way to businessmen, lawyers, *fonctionnaires* (Pompidou had no parliamentary experience). All were treated as servants. Though four Independents refused their party's order to quit the cabinet after the President's public outburst against the views of European integrationists ("myths, fictions, and parades"), the five MRP Ministers sitting in the front row at this press conference, May 15, 1962, had no choice but to resign next day. The size of his Assembly majority—the *Union pour la nouvelle république* (UNR) (formed to ride his coattails to victory in the November 1958 elections) and those who had broken from the considerably shaken older parties—made him less than cautious about directly affronting his colleagues.

Superficially the President's position rested upon the loyalty of the Prime Minister and the vague Gaullist coalition in the Assembly (by the electoral law of 1958 vastly overrepresenting these who had cast their votes for the indeterminate UNR). In the Senate, however, as in municipal elections, the Gaullist UNR lost heavily. In short, serious parliamentary opposition existed, but the President's position was not shaken. Old political habits might be hard to eradicate in the electorate, but however it voted in municipal elections (on which the Senate was largely dependent, of course), it knew who it wanted in the Elysée. It showed a marked ability to reconcile its ambivalent attitude by blaming unpopular policies upon the President's Ministers. And it was clearly fascinated by the spectacle of this "somewhat fabulous personage" (de Gaulle's description of himself) acting out the role of the great man which he had described in Le Fil de l'épée more than thirty years earlier. Writing of this "jealous lover of authority" who scorns the epithets of "arrogant" and "undisciplined" flung at him by his "mediocre" superiors, he had laid it down that "there can be no prestige without mystery, for familiarity breeds contempt. All religions have their holy of holies, and no man is a hero to his valet." Much later, in 1940, he remarked that "the terrible thing is to feel myself alone. Always alone." But in fact he cultivated the isolation, which was natural to him. Though he claimed in his memoirs that it was "the fact of embodying . . . the image of a France indomitable in the midst of her trials" which dictated his bearing and imposed "upon my personality an attitude I could never change," the self-imposed task had merely deepened the characteristics he had always demonstrated and admired. "My own nature warned me and my experience had taught me," ran another passage, closer to the truth, "that, at the summit, one can preserve time and strength only by remaining on the remotest heights."

De Gaulle revealed himself publicly, choosing time and place, staging the performance carefully. The dramatic appearance in the Place de la République to make a televised plea for the draft Constitution, September 4, 1958, was against a theatrical backdrop on the eighty-eighth anniversary of the proclamation of the Republic in 1870. The biennial press conferences in the Salle des Fêtes of the Elysée, with his Ministers before him like dutiful pupils, were masterful memorized monologues, ranging over history and current problems, on which the world's capitals hung. The regular provincial progresses in a motor caravan, from Brittany to Burgundy, were quite another order of direct contact with villagers, mayors, local notables: "The man of character," ran another dictum in Le Fil de l'épée, "then draws to himself the hopes and the wills of everyone as the magnet draws iron. . . . The knowledge that lesser men have confidence in him exalts a man of character." Sometimes he chose to chat amiably with a selected group of Deputies in the Elysée, to flatter, reassure, and drop confidences in the certainty that they would be in print before many days passed. His television appearances, in dark days or bright, were both familiar and impressive, and always skilled. Usually he addressed himself to "Frenchwomen and Frenchmen," but in January 1960, with rebellion in Algiers, he said, "Well, my dear old country, here we are together once more, facing a harsh test." And that rang true, for he was a lonely lover of

France, as the first pages of his memoirs had told the world: "All my life I have thought of France in a certain way. . . ." It was France as historical phenomenon, "like the princess in the fairy stories or the Madonna in the frescoes," that he loved and spoke to and communed with. All the rest, the provincial crowds he plunged into, from which he drew strength, were what he had called "the multitude." He appealed to them directly, as in April 1961, crying out "help me!" But that had been a desperate moment perhaps. The fundamental style was more austere, paternal, remote, and France was obviously under his spell.

The Eclipse of Parliament

If the role of the presidency under the Fifth Republic, and especially following the 1962 constitutional revision, was spectacularly magnified, that of parliament was diminished infinitely more than might have been foreseen in September 1958. By increasing the authority of the Senate beyond that enjoyed by the Council of the Republic after 1946, the Constitution had appeared to put a conservative, largely rural check on universal suffrage and the Assembly. But far from lending moral support to the executive, the Senate had become the home of the old parties and of opposition to continuance of a strong presidential power. After the Algerian war ended, the Senate had wished to see presidential authority recede and parliamentary control of the Government reaffirmed. Instead it witnessed the presidency absorbing the office of the Prime Minister, total elimination of parliamentary role in the election of the President, and consequently drastic reduction of its own function to that of futile harassment of both the executive and the Assembly. As the expression of agrarian, backward France, refuge of the provincial notables, the Senate seemed marked out for elimination in its existing form. At Bayeux in 1946 de Gaulle had proposed a second chamber of notables and representatives of economic groups. Trade-union and new, dynamic political groups now spoke of a purely economic second chamber. It appeared likely that a fresh constitutional revision could not be put off much longer.

The regime of 1958, which Maurice Duverger characterized as Orleanist in character, had evolved away from its parliamentary nature. Though the Government was still responsible to the Assembly, the Assembly's power to overthrow it was drastically reduced, and the threat of dissolution constituted a serious restraint upon the impulse even to try. It quickly became clear that only matters of secondary interests were submitted to parliamentary debate. Restive and declamatory though it might be, the Assembly was largely impotent. The executive device of extracting *loi-programmes* (legislative delegation of authority to the executive to issue decrees on general matters without obtaining parliamentary approval for each particular) was used for everything from housing to the nuclear *force de frappe*. Before the summer of 1962 it had been assumed that authority would flow back into a Ministry responsive to the Assembly. "I am at the close of my life," the General had remarked in November 1961. "My task is to end the

Algerian war. . . . I am not eternal, and you will get along without de Gaulle." When it became evident that solution of the Algerian problem was only the first part of his task, and that he intended to revise the Constitution in such a way and by such means as would subordinate parliament entirely to a kind of presidential system, the struggle was on.

"I intend to maintain the prerogatives of parliament," the President told a group of Deputies in the summer of 1962, but in "a French style regime, taking account of the diversity of parties." The old parties had no faith in such confidences. Government refusal to permit a vote on conclusion of an Assembly foreign-affairs debate had already provoked a massive walkout by 293 Radicals, MRP, and Independents. This only convinced the country that parliament was up to its old tricks. A terrorist ambush that August, which almost killed de Gaulle, reminded the nation again that between it and possible chaos was this one man's life. The President's masterly pre-referendum address, an amalgam of flattery, self-congratulation, brilliant panoramas, and denigration of the opposition—a direct violation of his 1958 promise to the Consultative Constitutional Committee that he would never use a referendum to arouse opinion against parliament—and a by then familiar threat to retire unless supported finally drove the Assembly to pull down the Government, October 5. Next day the chamber was dissolved.

The old parties drove straight toward their Waterloo. Rent by the Algerian war and on whether or not to support the new regime, they had suffered greatly in the 1958 elections. Though the honeymoon period between de Gaulle and Pinay, Mollet, or Pflimlin was long since ended, the fractured character of the opposition still prevailed. The President of the Senate, Gaston Monnerville (in the event of de Gaulle's sudden death, his *pro tem* successor), denounced the forthcoming referendum on constitutional revision as an "outrageous violation of the Republic." The General's old friend, Paul Reynaud, turned to Pompidou in the Assembly and flung out a bitter farewell: "Mr Prime Minister, go tell the Elysée that our admiration for the past is intact, but that this Assembly is not degenerate enough to renounce the Republic." Monnerville accused the President of "at best, a sort of enlightened Bonapartism"; de Gaulle lashed out at "all the seditionists" with their "common professional passion," whose claims to represent France were "simply derisory." The referendum majority for the President was slim, but opposition election hopes proved wildly exaggerated and tactics disastrous. Mollet blundered badly by calling for a second-ballot switch of votes to a Communist candidate, if necessary, in order to defeat a front-running Gaullist. Such opportunism seemed to underline the President's charges. The nation saw no alternative to de Gaulle and did not believe he sought to destroy the Republic.

When the smoke cleared, the UNR and the Gaullist Left (*L'Union démocratique du travail*) had 234 of the 482 Assembly seats. With 43 Independents, Radicals, and MRP pledged to the President, they controlled the Assembly. Though the old parties continued to hold their own in Departmental General Council elections, they and the parliamentary regime had been defeated. "Foam," de Gaulle remarked of the opposition, "nothing but the foam of the wave. The depths of the masses are with me." He had set out to break the old parties and had found it "remarkably easy." Before this rout, former Premier Edouard Daladier had remarked, "Politics! But there *is* no politics. Between General de Gaulle and the bureaucracy there is nothing!" After November 1962, France seemed more nearly *dépolitisée*. The President claimed that he welcomed "free debate" and "ideas, proposals, and improvements" from "those who are not biased," but he continued to revile "the old hands at repining, disparagement, and bitterness," who continued "to vent their spleen, spit out their bile, and distil their vinegar." As it stood, he found parliament a useful safety valve and no threat to what he privately called his "elective monarchy." Rejecting both the old "Assembly system" and the American presidential system, he publicly defended the regime, in which parliament was eclipsed and the Prime Minister was no more than the President's delegate. "Rarely," commented *Le Monde* of de Gaulle's January 1964 analysis of this situation, "has the theory of absolute power been revealed more complacently, clearly, or rigorously. . . . If one admits that everything in a country may depend on one man only, a more or less totalitarian dictatorship is already present in germ." No doubt this was true in theory. During the Algerian war many illiberal acts had been committed by police, courts, Army, and administration. But nevertheless the regime was still liberal and the first President of the Republic was a benevolent elected dictator.

In retrospect, the evident desire of Debré and others to achieve some degree of parliamentarism on British lines seemed naive. The fundamental rift between nation and government had never been successfully closed since 1789, and, because of the lack of a two-party system in France, it could not be closed by the electorate virtually imposing a Government as it did in the British system. De Gaulle's evolution toward a presidential system after Debré's fall effectively ensured that the Fifth Republic would not realize the intention of its Constitution's principal drafter. Whatever the prospects for the political parties regrouping and reorganizing themselves had been before October 1962, and they had been systematically assailed and perhaps further weakened by the regime in its first three years, there was little hope for them to achieve parliamentary government thereafter without revision of the Constitution. It was true that parties struck down were sick and had been so long before the advent of the Fifth Republic. Charged with perpetuating old ideological quarrels, with failure to renew their leadership and ideas, with having lost contact with the nation, they had not seriously tackled the most pressing national problems; they had avoided taking an unequivocal stand on the colonial wars, which were tearing France apart. Their spineless opportunism in the assembly system of the Fourth Republic had prepared the way for their humiliation under the Fifth. Virtually paralyzed by the entry into politics of the Army and the proconsuls before 1958, they went down before the assault from the Elysée thereafter.

The Parties

The multiplicity of French parties was partly explicable in terms of the past. Though they might be thought of as belonging to two principal blocs, what François Goguel called the Party of Movement and the Party of Established Order, their essential attitudes and nuances made such a classification no more than approximate. The Right had become particularly fractured in the nineteenth century: Legitimists, Orleanists, and Bonapartists. They united against the Republicans after 1876 but the royalist cause had sunk very low by 1914. The survivors were joined during the Dreyfus Affair by a part of the moderate Republicans who were encouraged by the rallying of some of the royalists to the Republic; and then in 1914 by a group of Radicals who supported the Three Years military service law and opposed the income tax. Thus the Right came to include royalists and republicans, Catholics and anticlericals, the old landed interests, the newer Orleanist and Bonapartist bourgeoisie and the arriviste wealthy of the Republic. What they had in common was their social conservatism and their economic orthodoxy. But their attitude toward parliament varied and their lack of structure encouraged the development of both authoritarian (the Poujadists were one example) and democratic (for instance, the MRP) parties. In the same way, the Left came to have a multiple character. If some part of the moderate and radical Republicans gravitated toward the Right, various Socialist tendencies appeared at the end of the nineteenth century. They united in 1905 to form the Section française de l'internationale ouvrière, but the majority abandoned the SFIO in 1920 to form the Communist Party. And though Radicalism shifted through the twentieth century from Left to Center Right, and the fortunes of the Socialists declined under the Fourth Republic, a new Parti socialiste unifié (PSU) came into being in 1960. Thus the Left maintained its fractured nature also.

The most important new party of the Fifth Republic was the UNR, created in October 1958, heir of the non-Communist Resistance, of the tiny Gaullist Union of 1946, of the RPF, and the Républicains sociaux Its composition was almost as varied as the old RPF's; its original orientation was farther to the Right. The desertion or expulsion of the Algérie française group in 1960, acceptance of the General's Algerian solution, and fusion with the Union démocratique du travail (the Gaullist Left, which the President did not encourage) in 1962 turned it back toward the Center. With some 30 per cent of the popular vote, more conservative in its leadership than in its following, but with neither coherent doctrine nor assured structure, it was the largest party in the country and had possibly the most uncertain future. Its testing time would come when de Gaulle passed from the scene.

The old conservatives, parochial, undynamic, and even reactionary, were grouped after 1949 in the *Centre national des indépendents et paysans*, a loose association without unity of policy or organization. Having done well in 1958, it was hopelessly divided by events thereafter and humbled at the polls in 1962. While some of its nominal members served the regime, the best known of its leaders broke with the President. Some were European-minded and expansionist, many were defenders of colonialism and the old order. Less a party than a pressure group of small subsidized interests, opposed to serious tax reform, it had none of the antiparliamentary, small-town vulgar fascist tendencies of the obscurantist supporters of Pierre Poujade, but it looked back rather than forward and its brightest hope was to pray for a return of some of its strength, which had flowed to the UNR.

Hardly less dismal were the prospects of the *Parti républicain radical et radical socialiste*. Its fortunes had been tied to those of the Third Republic, which it had epitomized better than any other party. Its strength had shifted from town to country, its relative situation from extreme Left to Center, its religious view from laicism to acceptance of State aid to Church schools. After the Liberation it revived slowly, committing itself increasingly toward the Right, and divided by a struggle for leadership. A party of personalities, defender of *petit bourgeois* and rural interests, it was largely unprogressive. Disenchanted young leaders who had unsuccessfully tried to return it to the Left (e.g., Mendès-France) abandoned it for the PSU; those of a more conservative point of view migrated to the UNR. Despite its factions reuniting for the 1958 elections, it lost all the ground gained after 1944. Scarcely distinguishable doctrinally from the moderate Right, it suffered further defeat in 1962. With its social bases being constantly eroded, it had a considerable past, as the memory of Clemenceau or even Herriot suggested, but its future was dark and its anticipation of regaining strength in the event of the UNR's demise was probably less justified than that of the Independents.

The *Mouvement républicain populaire* waxed and waned dramatically. Republican and parliamentary, in no way allied to the old Catholic Right but intimately concerned with Christian attitudes, it was at once conservative and progressive. In agreement with the Right on the Catholic school question, it was similar to the Left in its attitude toward nationalization and social security. The Barangé law of 1951 on State aid to private schools marked its evolution toward the Right and its break with the Socialists. If it defended colonial interests and wars in Africa and the Far East, it broke with the extremist views on Algeria held by Georges Bidault, who went on to a half-insane prosecution of the OAS vendetta against de Gaulle, to exile and perhaps oblivion, living in a private world of revenge and bitterness. Consistently European in its foreign policy, and opposed to the General's lack of social policy, it had no choice but to abandon attempts to participate in his government. Unnaturally inflated after the Liberation by those who found it a useful shelter when the old

Right was in disgrace, the MRP suffered heavily in 1958 and 1962. And it too placed its hopes on the eventual breakup of the UNR.

So far as the future of parliament was concerned, probably no party was more important than the *Parti socialiste, section française de l'internationale ouvrière*. Its bureaucratic organization and disciplining of the parliamentary group were distinctive. Under both Jean Jaurès and Léon Blum it had had an honorable if unconstructive role outside the Government from 1905 to 1936. The Blum experience of 1936-1937 was destined to become a kind of socialist legend, but the party collapsed in the defeat of 1940. Though revived, its attachment to outworn Marxist formalism, its reluctance to make room for youth, and its extraordinary support of the Suez and Algerian enterprises under the Fourth Republic gave it a mixed and tarnished record. Having helped bring de Gaulle back to power in 1958, it turned away to an increasingly hostile attitude, disguised at first as "constructive opposition," and culminating in the gross misjudgment of tactics during the elections of 1962. Year after year the search continued for some way in which to regroup it and the progressive forces on the Left.

The crisis of conscience into which Guy Mollet led the Socialists in 1956, embracing policies that could not be reconciled with anything the party had stood for during its fifty years, brought forth a left-wing intellectual opposition which Socialist support of the 1958 Constitution intensified. The result was that a small group broke with the SFIO that autumn and, together with the dissident Radicals led by Mendès-France, formed an autonomous socialist party which eventually in April 1960 joined with other splinter groups to establish the *Parti socialiste unifié*. Half progressive, half orthodox, it was bedevilled by personal quarrels and doctrinaire disputes, and it seemed fated to collapse unless it could be merged in that fundamental reformation of the whole Center and Left which continued to escape realization in France.

The best-disciplined political organization under the Fifth Republic remained the Communist party. Doctrinaire, unimaginative, and rigid, it had a checkered career after it came into being at the Socialist Congress of Tours in 1920: total opposition down to the coming of the *Front populaire* in 1935, open and then clandestine treason from 1939 to 1941, Resistance and governmental participation from 1941 to 1947, insurrectionary strike actions for the next few years, and thereafter an unrequited approach to such governments as that of Mendès-France in 1954 and, finally, the electoral alliance Mollet preferred in 1962. With some evidence of greater independence of Moscow—a generic phenomenon among western Communist parties—after the fall of Khrushchev in 1964 and the succession of Waldeck Rochet that year when Maurice Thorez died, the Party still claimed something between 20 and 25 per cent of the electorate. Many supported it from habit or because the social and material integration of the workers into the prosperous post-1945 society was far from complete, and because neither the SFIO nor the PSU could appeal to the ordinary

Communist voter. Controlling the big *Confédération générale du travail* (CGT), the Party survived serious defections in 1956, squalid internal house-cleanings, a massive falling off of members, and a 10 per cent drop among the electorate after the Liberation. But while it lost ground particularly in the countryside, its hold on the urban worker remained strong.

Apart from minor groups and coalitions, the Republic's political life centered on these parties. They did not correspond to particular socio-economic groups in the nation, though factory workers tended to vote Communist, other wage earners Socialist, some small merchants and artisans for the Poujadists, and the substantial classes for the Right. But both the UNR and the MRP drew support from elements of all classes. Nor was there any fixed geographical distribution corresponding to the classic but very rough division of a century ago: the strongly Catholic and right-wing West and the republican East. The newer parties (Communist, MRP, RPF, and UNR) found their strength in the most economically advanced part of the country (i.e., roughly the North) and the older parties in the more static South, but the generalization was at best sketchy and in process of being altered by modernization of the economy. Not that the old struggle between Left and Right had been eliminated. Time had, of course, worn down the old conservatism; even the Vichy experience had not much encouraged its hopes. But reaction had doubtless anticipated gains from the course the Republic took while trapped and blackmailed by the Algerian war; the memory of the horrors of the *Front populaire* remained with the capitalist Right. If the Fifth Republic was clearly moving forward not backward, nevertheless, as Maurice Duverger observed, it was only pressure from the trade unions and the leftist parties which assured the continuance of social security, high wages, and economic planning. Controlled and moderated though it was, the struggle between Left and Right remained "fundamental."

Pressure Groups and Civil Servants

Beyond the formal structure of politics and yet close to it lay the pressure groups: veterans' organizations, banks, agricultural associations, trade unions, manufacturing associations, the winegrowers lobby, the home-brewers of alcohol, the schoolteachers, the Church, the Army. . . . Under the parliamentary Republic, the old "Republic of Pals," the activities of these groups were more obvious, perhaps. Even under the Fifth, however, they have shown tenacity of purpose in the full glare of publicity. Despite Prime Minister Debré's statistical indictment of the private distilling privileges of the *bouilleurs de cru* in 1960 (16,000 deaths annually from alcoholism, nearly $120 million lost in excise taxes), the Senate rejected the Government's bill to crack down on them, and the result was a compromise whereby some two and a half million citizens were permitted to retain their right to distill ten litres a year free of tax. A similarly controversial revocation of pensions to veterans over 65 years of age had to be rescinded in 1960. No doubt reduction of the Assembly's authority after 1958 made it less useful than it had been earlier, but interest groups still intervened in national politics, financing candidates of loosely organized parties, obtaining pre-election commitments, profiting by the competition between candidates in closely disputed districts. The deputies from Normandy still concerned themselves with apples, those from the Gironde with wine, or those from Dunkerque or Marseille with shipping.

France was slow to recognize lobbies and the word was hardly used before the North African interests took the field in force under the Fourth Republic. All such interests dressed themselves in the flag or some other suitable disguise (thus the tavern and barkeepers's trade organ was called *The Lemonade Dealer of Paris*). Among the largest were the *Ligue de l'enseignement*, the *Syndicat national des bouilleurs de cru*, and the *Fédération nationale des syndicats d'exploitants agricoles*. This last organization was a classic example of the kind of pressure group in which the small man permitted the big interests to monopolize the conduct of its affairs in return for fighting for tariff protection for him; this made the lobby's cause respectable and naturally assured a high rate of profit to the more efficient large-scale producer. The powerful *Conseil national du patronat français* (cnpf), grouping federations and unions of employers (above all, the great chemical and metallurgical industries), sometimes brought its "war chest" to bear in the name of the same small man for the same reason, although small and medium enterprise increasingly came to be directly represented by the *Confédération générale des petites et moyennes entreprises*, which survived the Poujadist invasion of its domain during the Fourth Republic and continued to bring its large numbers to bear under the Fifth. Open or secretive, the means used by such groups were varied: strikes, letter-writing campaigns, press control, representation in chambers of commerce, financial contributions to parties, and, perhaps increasingly since 1958 and the decline of parliament, direct pressure on the decision-making apparatus of the regime.

The strength of some pressure groups (for example, the farmers) was in the variety of politics of their adherents, which permitted bidding up of their support by competing parties. Some, like the cnpf or the cgt, obviously could work only one polarity of the political spectrum. Some, such as the *Comité national d'action laïque* or the *Assemblés des cardinaux et archevêques*, were still more narrowly ideological. Some were so clandestine, like the notorious banking interests—the *mur d'argent*, which had so terrified Édouard Herriot and at least contributed to his downfall in 1925 —that information on their composition and activity was virtually unobtainable. And, finally, one was so new and blatant and frightening, the Army in the politics of the Fourth Republic, that its power became a public scandal. All were favored by the shift of governments toward the less-disciplined parties of the Center and Right after the collapse of *tripartisme* in 1947. If the left-wing solidarity of the Republic until that date encouraged trade-union pressure, thereafter right-wing groups prevailed—although the colonial wars and their attendant tragedies aroused a strong left-wing movement against torture, miscarriage of justice, extension of the fighting, etc., in the final four or five years of the Fourth Republic. Under the Fifth, the authoritarian nature of the regime offered more scope to the big conservative interests, which had now come to share the dynamic economic ideas animating the administration. This might well compensate for the loss of leverage in what René Mayer once called the "Chamber of Corporations." At all events, the first President of the Fifth Republic was not infrequently seen engaged in combat with pressure groups. He gave ground to the farmers, collided with the veterans, managed the Army, held off the teachers, slapped the bishops's wrists from time to time, and yielded occasionally and reluctantly to the unions.

The style and orientation of pressure groups would shift and change, but, like the bureaucracy, lobbyists would go on forever. Also like the bureaucracy, the pressure groups often enjoyed an over-inflated reputation. For though they acted to oppose the fiscal power or the *dirigisme* (planning and control) of the State, or sought to use the State for their peculiar advantage, they also tended to cancel each other out. What distinguished their real or supposed power from that wielded by the bureaucracy was probably its negative slant. By contrast, the positive role of the bureaucracy had increased notably under the Republic. The notion of the growing power of the technocrats was doubtless exaggerated: those, for instance, who laid down the guide lines of economic planning after the Liberation were not a bureaucratic clique but an assortment of economists, statisticians, and businessmen. Moreover, the few hundred top-flight civil servants, (*grands fonctionnaires*) working closely with Ministers might emerge from the same schools (the École Polytechnique or the Faculté de Droit), but they differed in specialization, political affiliation, and age. Probably best known were the *Inspecteurs des Finances*. Drawn from the business or professional classes, rather than from the old Parisian or provincial aristocracy, they were guardians of the interests of the State, often reformers, influential through their access to the press as well as to the Government. As proconsuls in the empire, *grands fonctionnaires* had exercised considerable authority, often making policy in the absence of decision or control by Paris. Under the Fifth Republic, they were more likely to be active in financial or regional reform. Centralizers, responsive to tradition, and exponents of moderate progress, they were coming to have a role not unlike that of the old Center parties, and their place in the general arrangement of things seemed unlikely to be diminished.

The *grands fonctionnaires* constituted a *groupe dirigeant*, as Bernard Gournay called them, and it was possible to think of them as a kind of pressure group. But their activity was more obviously in the general interest, however interpreted by them, than that of other public groups, i.e., civil servants of a lower rank with a more narrowly defined function and responsibility. Thus the great mass of state employees, organized for the defense of their own well-being, constituted a series of pressure groups not greatly different from private associations. Indeed France, like every modern state, seemed certain to witness such an interplay of private and public interests organized for their own protection as would make it henceforth impossible to think of the lower bureaucracy as being very different from private-interest groups, which operated openly to impose their will. And though the *grands fonctionnaires* might appear as one polarity, and, say, the CNPF as another, in fact under the Fifth Republic the association between them was a good deal closer than that.

The Gaullist Regime without de Gaulle

Of the Republic's government, so much seemed clear. But the future of the regime was impossible to predict. "People are worried about what will happen after I go," de Gaulle remarked in the summer of 1963, "and I'm a little worried too." When that might be no one knew. The OAS killers had tried repeatedly to murder him and promised to install "a regime of bloody repression." He had survived them and intended, if his health remained good, to seek reelection in 1965. Running against him might be such a reactionary as Jean-Louis Tixier-Vignancour, a lawyer with a pedigree of anti-Gaullist activities and a violent antiparliamentary past, but not the much more important Gaston Defferre, moderate Socialist, wealthy newspaper publisher, and mayor of Marseille. Following the collapse of talks seeking to achieve electoral collaboration between Socialists, Radicals and MRP, with this man as the coalition candidate, Defferre withdrew from his forlorn task as the General's principal opponent. Should de Gaulle actually run, his election (by the people, this time) was certain, no matter who might challenge him. And the trend toward a presidential system would doubtless be still more marked. There would be no revival of parliament while he remained Chief of State. The Senate itself might well be eliminated or wholly transformed.

"Courage," Gaston Monnerville had said, "and the Republic may be saved." Whatever happened to the Senate, this seemed to be the truth. De Gaulle, as he so often said, was not eternal and France would have to get along without him. But he intended to leave such a mark as would ensure "that things will remain tomorrow as they are today." And he had implied constitutional changes to permit him to designate "the one who seems most capable to carry on what I have begun. I shall tell the French people, 'This is the one I recommend. He is the best.'" Whether this were done or not, the scrambling of the former parliamentary "Princes of the Republic" seemed doomed to frustration. The General's eventual successor would hardly wish to preside over renewed Assembly games. Defferre himself argued for a five-year presidential term, coinciding with that of the lower house, for reduction of presidential powers and for vital decision-making by the cabinet. A program not dissimilar to that intended by Debré in 1958, it might one day be realized. But it would be conditional upon thoroughgoing political reform, and still the essential regrouping of the Left (let alone Left and Center) seemed remote.

There were, nevertheless, some encouraging portents. Among the *forces nouvelles* were the political clubs, perhaps one hundred or more, of which about fifteen had serious organization and strength, e.g., the *Club des Jacobins* dating from its Radical origins under the Fourth Republic, uniting political, syndicalist and intellectual groups, or the *Club Jean Moulin*, founded in the May 13 crisis, in which many high civil servants were to be found. Little known to the public, these and such provincial clubs as the *Cercle Tocqueville* or the *Club Position* held conferences, published reviews and books, and worked for the revitalization of politics. All agreed that the axis of any new Left must be the Socialist party. Defferre himself urged these clubs to get down into the political market place, to get their hands dirty, for the general public was little affected by conferences and a new version of the July Monarchy's "political banquets." But in the task of political reconstruction, public apathy was at least matched by hard-core party reluctance to tear down historic political and religious barriers which had so long divided Frenchmen against themselves.

What was certain was that the existing system was too personal to long outlive the man who principally shaped it after 1958. The revival of politics, even the emergence of a more responsible parliament one day, was as sure. Whether important clubs, such as *Citoyens 60*, could do a great deal to prepare the country for that day no one could say. They seemed like a healthy, hopeful sign of the times. But the process of revision by which a democratic and constructive style of politics might be achieved in France, without destroying the executive stability approved by the nation and its most responsible leaders, remained hidden from view.

NINE

ECONOMIC PROGRESS AND

STUBBORN REALITIES

"Le bonheur et le malheur des hommes ne dépend pas moins de leur humeur que de la fortune."

Reputations notoriously outlive the conditions from which they spring. And not surprisingly the Fourth Republic won little recognition for the economic progress it made. Yet the recovery of France from the Second World War was remarkable. The stagnation so much associated with the collapse of her fortunes between the two wars became an historical memory. But it was also true that still under the Fifth Republic vestiges of former attitudes and former inequalities remained to cloud the otherwise quite brilliant panorama of prosperity and progress which the State so rightly prided itself upon. By no means had all the causes of previous depression been eliminated, and not every part of the nation was sharing in the general good times. There remained another France, *"la France pauvre."*

Decline and Recovery: Heritage of the Fourth Republic

A legend persisted to the effect that in almost every manner France fell behind as a great power during the nineteenth century. This was not so. Even in the realm of economic development, and by comparison with the spectacular achievements of Great Britain and Germany, France knew periods of prosperity and progress before 1914, notably during the Second Empire and after 1896 under the protectionist policy of the Republicans. From 1901 to 1913 and from 1920 to 1929, per capita industrial production increased in France at a rate higher than that for Europe as a whole. But of course, as always, the figures might be read in many ways. Between 1815 and 1914, when British and German population soared, France's population increased by a mere 10 per cent. Before 1914 about 50 per cent of Great Britain's population was industrial, 40 per cent of Germany's, and only 30 per cent of France's. The leading industrial power on the continent in 1850, France had been far outstripped by the German Empire in 1914. And in the depression decade before 1939 her production fell off, and it began to recover more slowly than that of her neighbors. Defeat, occupation, and the dislocation of the Liberation seriously delayed her recovery, of course, and as if to compound her plight France began to engage almost at once in a chain of costly imperial wars. Thus, though the ruins might be fewer than in Germany, the fundamental economic structure was probably less sound and the commitments were far greater.

The reason why the French position declined relatively during the last century is still argued over by economists, sociologists, and demographers. Although France has been envied for the multiple character of her production and her wealthy agriculture, one explanation was that her natural resources were few: too little coal in too poor quality; iron-ore deposits remote from factory and port; and such a balance of resources throughout the country as limited the benefits of industrial specialization and discouraged development of low-cost transportation. Against this argument, others said that French resources always responded to demand. The explanation of agricultural stagnation (equal inheritance laws, hence a fragmentation of the land, hence unproductiveness, shortage of labor for industry, lack of capital, and low demand) was similarly vulnerable. Nor did the view that Frenchmen starved their industry by exporting capital find favor with those who claimed that insistent demand eventually succeeds in making capital available at home. The proposition that the unprogressive family firm dominated and depressed the economy was countered by examples of progressive family enterprises, and by demonstration of the diversity of industrial organization. Insistence upon the fact of population stagnation was accepted by some observers as no more than a partial explanation. Finally, there were explanations based upon the French preference for quality goods; the entrenched class system, which tends to create inflation and thus leads to concentration upon the search for stability; the Malthusian attitude, which creates a highly protected domestic market; and inept government meddling. Possibly more persuasive was the argument that the fundamental cause lay in the lack of progressive attitudes on the part of management, labor, and consumers.

At all events, the Liberation found the country seriously weakened. Figures vary, but about 18 per cent of real property was destroyed or damaged. This was greater than the damage done during the First World War. Nearly ten thousand industrial and commercial buildings were wholly or partly ruined. Almost one and a half million houses were destroyed (more than twice the number in the previous war). More than three-quarters of a million farms had been demolished or damaged (four times more than in the 1914 war). Half the railroad locomotives, one-third of the merchant marine, three-fourths of harbor installations and freight yards were destroyed or had been seized by the enemy. Bridges were down, mines blown up or flooded, and the food supply inadequate. Inflation was endemic, the black market flourished in place of regular commerce, and the Provisional Government was unwilling to enact a program of currency reform and austerity. But it set about restoring transportation, providing power, reopening the mines, and repairing heavy industrial enterprise. With assistance from the Allied armies, transportation was virtually restored by the end of 1946. That same year coal production climbed back close to the 1938 level.

But the most significant fact was the emergence of a new spirit of dynamism in the economy. Probably it had to do with the demographic change which had its beginnings at the end of the Third Republic. Both the 1939 *Code de la famille* and the Vichy emphasis upon family seem to have encouraged a rising population curve; the Resistance similarly made its appeal to youth and a national renewal. In short, there was a perhaps inexplicable but fundamental alteration of outlook: the nation looked forward. More obviously, the new spirit was linked to a break with the introverted economic attitudes of the Third Republic, suggestions of which had been observed among various businessmen, politicians, and engineers before 1939. Under Vichy, the State reached out to organize both agriculture and industry, partly in revulsion against the old order, partly to forestall direct German intervention. Business organizations were established, run by civil servants and managers, which created a new conception of cooperation and a new vision of wider horizons. The Resistance condemned the "corporatism" of Vichy, but, for quite other objectives of economic and social democracy, continued the State intervention in business, supported both nationalization and economic pluralism, and thus encouraged the business leaders who had come to see the possibilities of breaking with the Malthusian tradition. No longer would big business seek so obviously to serve its own interests by defending small enterprise. Many business leaders were forced to lie low because of their record under the Occupation and because the old Right was in disgrace; some were prepared to go forward with the administrators and planners. There was still to be much opposition to national regulation, let alone international organization, but even the revival of the Right under the Fourth Republic did not see any great business assault upon the *dirigisme* that had followed the Liberation. The *Conseil national du patronat français* was not merely the old *Confédération générale de la production française* revived.

The Plan: Achievements and Unfinished Tasks

Postwar recovery came about, therefore, in a setting of demographic optimism with acceptance of a fully public sector of the economy (nationalized transport, fuel and power, certain aviation and motor industries, large banks and insurance companies) and a planned development of a private sector as the result of cooperation between the State, business and trade unions, and economists and technicians. Owing something to the seventeenth-century Colbertist tradition, to nineteenth-century Saint-Simonian conceptions, and to the "new men" of the late Third Republic and the experiments of Vichy, a *Commissariat général du plan de modernisation et d'équipement* was established in 1946. Headed by Jean Monnet, sometime brandy salesman, financier, inter-Allied civil servant in the two wars, and man Friday to British, American, and French governments before 1944, this agency embodied the *mystique* of planning. Surrounded by a small staff of bright young economists, Monnet virtually declared war on the old Malthusian society and informed the country that it must modernize or slip hopelessly into decadence. Hundreds of professors, industrialists, trade unionists, civil servants, and assorted experts served without salary on the twenty-five committees which made recommendations to the *Commissariat*. Attached loosely to the Ministry of Finance, this agency had limited funds and a moral authority only. Its influence, limited to the area of capital investment, was nevertheless great. Although it could compel neither Government nor private enterprise to accept its proposals, its close association with the administration and the importance of the Government to private industry in a country where the State controlled about half the national investment directly or indirectly assured it an increasing stature and power. Though its degree of success was a matter for debate, there was no doubt that it presided over the most spectacular economic advance France had registered since the Second Empire.

Equally indubitable was the fact that the Plan owed nothing to the revival of parliamentarism after the Liberation. The Resistance hopes for a new political beginning had foundered with its own fortunes on the obvious antiparliamentarism of General de Gaulle and the obviously dictatorial ambitions of the Communists. Caught between these twin authoritarianisms, the country had moved back toward the political system of the Third Republic. In the bureaucracy, therefore rather than in the political class was located the mixture of forces that supported the *mystique* of planning. The *Commissariat* was not set up by legislation or government decree. It was, in effect, a legacy of the Resistance Charter of 1944, if not of the *étatisme* of Vichy, to France under the revived parliamentary Republic.

Despite many setbacks and a starting point made even less promising by the interregnum of 1944-1946, the first Plan, 1947-1950 (but extended to 1952), had considerable success in its concentration upon restoration of basic industries: transport, steel, mining, cement, and agricultural machinery. American loans and Marshall Plan funds were indispensable to it. Other Plans followed, shifting attention to housing, schools, roads, light industry, etc. By comparison with West Germany, French recovery was slow. The Third Plan's investment and production targets were not met, 1958-1961, nor were the Fourth's likely to be in 1965. But a Fifth was already laid down, and the long-range vision of the *Commissariat* was of a French economy integrated by 1985 "in a union of Europe, perhaps of the Atlantic, perhaps even larger."

To some reformers it appeared that resistance to change and the tenacity of the old Malthusian ideas were so strong that this vision was too sanguine. Under the Fourth Republic the Assembly had often been the spokesman for the least progressive interests in the country. The wisdom of immediate post-Liberation nationalizations was disputed. They had been effected partly for moral and political reasons, partly for economic.

The public bore the cost of heavy deficits, politicians and pressure groups exploited the directorates for their own ends. If the nation came to accept the permanence of the public sector where (though the Government controlled wages, prices, and investment) the administrative councils represented consumers and employees, both parliament and the Government were sensitive to small enterprise, protecting its inefficiencies, legislating benefits for its underpaid employees. To the planners this was discouraging, and not even the Fifth Republic was able or willing to rationalize that part of the economy overnight.

It was here that proof seemed to be found of Charles Morazé's proposition: "The deep break between thought and action is the foundation of the French mind. . . ." If it was at best uncertain whether the bigger businessmen of the CNPF had altogether accepted the implications of setting course away from Malthusianism, it seemed sure that the *Confédération générale des petites et moyennes entreprises* had not. Protective of the small-family concern, fearful of regional planning and resistant to it, this powerful lobby headed by Léon Gingembre symbolized the unprogressive economic forces of the past. Although Prime Minister Debré announced his Government's intention to reduce the mass of small outlets, bars, cafés, and retailers, the little man hung on and his customers remained faithful. Indeed, the mass of shopkeepers had increased under the Fourth Republic and showed no obvious signs of being about to diminish under the Fifth. Distribution, despite all the periodic outcries that the incredibly centralized and massively wasteful system must be reformed, remained the province of the parasitic intermediary. Even the substantial family-dominated Compagnie des Machines Bull, after carving out a sizeable portion of the international market for its computers, fell victim to its antiquated management and the tough competition of the International Business Machines Corporation.

Chronic inflation was a problem of some intractability. Only part of the general European inflation, France's difficulties here had been constant since the Liberation. The delicacy of trying to halt inflation without crippling growth of the economy was underlined by the September 1963 economic stabilization plan which, the Minister of Finance said, depended on "conscience and confidence." It included price and wage freezes, reduction of public spending, tightening of credit and installment buying, tax increases, and a bond issue with tax benefits. Naturally it engendered complaints from both labor and management; the CNPF was as critical as the CGT. The Government took a firm line, but it was clear that, with prices up about 16 per cent in the previous three years, not even the powerful executive of the Fifth Republic could impose rapid solutions on so stubborn a problem. Thus the initial successes of the regime in monetary and financial policy, following upon the reforms of late 1958, were threatened. The dramatic reversal of the Fourth Republic's unfavorable export-import balance was cancelled by 1962 when again imports crept up over exports. Private investment was cut back. And a further unfavorable factor was the low public and private outlay for research—again, part of a general European phenomenon. Of 40,000 patents granted in France in 1962, only 16,000 went to Frenchmen.

Of course production figures could be made to tell a more encouraging story. Taking 1938 as the base year, the 1962 output of coal showed a 15 per cent increase; electricity nearly 400 per cent; petroleum about 400 per cent; steel almost 300 per cent; automobiles more than 600 per cent. The country's progress might be measured by the great natural-gas fields at Lacq, the oil fields there and in the Landes, but above all in the Sahara (exploited jointly with the Algerian Republic); the Lorraine steel mills; the great hydro-electric plants on the Rhine, the Rhône, and the Rance River. It was evident in the Renault Dauphines on the roads of Europe and America, in the swift electrified rail service crossing the country, in the Caravelle jet transports ranging many skies, and in the splendid transatlantic liner "France." Whether offering Dassault executive jets or bottled Source Perrier, the dynamism of some French manufacturers and merchants was apparent under the Fifth Republic.

But all too often this dynamism had come from only part of France. Doubtless the Fifth Republic was taking action to eliminate it, but a kind of schism had opened up between "static" and "dynamic" areas. The malady was very old. Modernization tended to be more marked in the north and northeast than elsewhere. Industry attracted industry, and such was the internal migration that only about a third of the country enjoyed an increasing population. This internal migration to prosperous districts, a reduction of agricultural jobs as a result of growing mechanization, and hence a low birthrate in areas where the average age remained high or grew higher, tended to widen the disparities of population and wealth between the two kinds of areas. Some stricken departments had lost more than half their population since the beginning of the Third Republic. Resistance to structural reorganization was strenuous: whether the Economic Development Commissions established regionally would be able to halt the relative and absolute decline of France west and south of a line running very roughly from Le Havre to Grenoble remained uncertain. But the rise and fall of Poujadism was instructive.

Housing was typical of problems to which both Republics paid some attention after the Liberation but which continued to defy solution. It required nearly a generation to overcome the consequences of legislation dating from the First World War, which, in an inflationary situation thereafter, kept rents permanently pegged at the 1914 level and thus discouraged building and all maintenance, let alone improvements, by landlords. As social policy, it was thoroughly misconceived, an expression of working-class and *petit bourgeois* domination in this area of activity. The Second World War merely compounded the problem. Faced with massive destructions and a rising birthrate, the Fourth Republic retained these ancient controls without being willing to overhaul the antedeluvian building industry. Relaxation of the controls where only new construction was involved had a predictable consequence: luxury buildings were put up. Thus followed further property deterioration, a racket in subletting, and despair on the part of young married couples.

Obsolescence ran at about 120,000 units annually. Construction soared by comparison with the pre-1939 situation (56,000 units in 1938, a mere 12,200 in 1947, and 290,000 in 1958) but the 1964 target of 365,000 was far below the national need. All the subsidies, special loans, projects, grants, tax exemptions, and joint public-private enterprises had not achieved more. No longer, perhaps, would the Crédit Foncier authorize (as it had done in 1951) 50 per cent of its units to be built without bathrooms, and 10 per cent without lavatories and running water. But Paris in the '60s still had only 3.2 million units for 8.5 million people. Half a million had no running water, 1.4 million no private toilets. Rent increases, new building associations, and reform of real-estate legislation promised some improvement of this serious situation. But mortgage rates of nearly 15 per cent discouraged remodeling and building, and it was hardly surprising that one apartment in three along the Avenue Foch was registered in the name of a corporation. Moreover, another generation would pass before Frenchmen learned to accept the real cost of housing, learned how to budget for it, pay and be paid the wages necessary to it. Behind the dazzling face-lifting André Malraux lavished on the formerly grimy public buildings of the capital of France, the *crise du logement* continued and the *politique* it cried out for was still not to be seen.

Employers, Employees, and the State

The response of the working class to France's post-Liberation economic development was an obvious one of disenchantment. Yet some large part of the social reforms laid down in the Resistance Charter was acquired. Trade-unionism had emerged as an important element in the Gaullist camp, having survived its interwar divisions (Communist, Socialist, and Catholic), the triumph and defeat of the *Front populaire*, the bitter rifts produced by the war in 1939-1940, and suppression by Vichy. Its two branches, the left-wing, Communist-dominated CGT and the Catholic *Confédération française des travailleurs chrétiens* claimed respectively 5.5 and .75 million members in 1945. The mood was euphoric and even self-denying: "To produce is to win the battle of democracy." But in 1946 the confidence, the unity, and the strength began to ebb. Despairing of obtaining power through parliamentary means, faced with union restiveness and strikes, the Communists went into opposition in 1947. A reformist group, claiming more than a million members, broke away from the CGT to form the CGT–*Force ouvrière* in 1948. The Communist-led insurrectional strikes of 1947-1948, beaten back by a show of force by the State, gave way to periodic work stoppages, directed simply toward compelling wage increases. Union numbers fell off drastically. Thus labor never came to express its power in an organized political manner, and that largest part of the workers which subscribed to the CGT was thereby identifying itself with a political party whose object was destruction of the regime. Yet not even revival of the political Right stripped away the gains made immediately after the Liberation; indeed the working class as a whole had some share in the general prosperity of the Fourth and Fifth Republics.

But probably because of the fact that so much of labor was attached to a party hostile to both regimes after 1947, mere material improvement failed to remove the profound and historic sense of alienation which stemmed from the Revolution. The repeated dramas of the nineteenth- and twentieth-century confrontations with the bourgeoisie had not been exorcised from the collective memory, and the bitter myth of the *Front populaire* lived on, together with a brooding sense of injustice. Neither the Fourth nor the Fifth Republic offered the worker a fair opportunity to obtain any great degree of education; the system remained hopelessly antiquated, rigid, centralized and, in a very real sense, discriminatory. If the younger businessmen who were associated with the *Jeunes patrons* were full of good intentions and Catholic idealism, their contact with the workers was hardly close and their influence in the business community at large was not noticeably impressive. Participation in various kinds of associations with employers was a repeated failure after 1944. The worker suspected, rightly, that the employers sought not to cooperate with organized labor but to dispel its organization by paternalism or whatever. In the face of evident union weakness (a majority of labor had no affiliation), nothing discouraged this undoubted intention. And though parliament under the Fourth Republic granted a sliding wage scale, the Government of the Fifth seemed not to recognize any special working-class case. Its official philosophy was that "The French people must learn the discipline of collective growth." But the doctrine of "social solidarity" meant different things to different classes, and in a system where the tax burden continued to fall heavily on the workers (although their social security was very great), with quite spectacular evasions by the wealthy and the rural, it was not reassuring to hear the Chief of State say tentatively, "If excessive disadvantages really do exist, we must of course remedy them. . . ."

In vain, then, the Government insisted that the French workers' wages compared favorably with wages in Italy, Holland, or West Germany. For men's wages rose faster than women's, skilled labor's faster than unskilled, management's faster than employees', and family allowances were outpaced by the cost of living. Strike action was common, lasting fifteen minutes or several weeks. Electricity, gas, mail delivery, garbage collection, or transportation would be cut off. Factories, schools, and offices would shut down. A perpetual battle of statistics raged among unions, management, and the Government. The workers were convinced that austerity programs struck principally at them; they knew that wage increases came only as a result of their action. The most impressive victory was won by coal (and other) miners in 1963 after a lengthy strike against the State, after the Chief of State had blundered by signing a requisitioning order and throwing his prestige into the struggle. So massive and widespread was national support that the Government dared not impose fines and imprisonments. The UNR majority pressed compromise upon Prime Minister Pompidou. Notables such as the Bishop of Arras and the Archbishop of Cambrai declared their sympathy (asked where the wage increases could be found, the irritated President replied, "We could always take up a collection in the churches"). The result was humiliation and capitulation for the regime.

But the incident emphasized more than the limitation of presidential authority: it underlined the repeated failure of both Government and unions to tackle the problem of sick industries ahead of time. Collective bargaining was hardly known in the nationalized sector; no arbitration machinery existed; even basic statistical information was not available. Neither management nor unions had prepared men to take up another occupation when unproductive mines had to be closed. The 1963 strike succeeded because of the Government's heavy-handed stupidity and the UNR's nervousness. The essential problem of educating the public and the workers to the requirements of a rational economy and social program remained. The State might impose legislation to outlaw flash strikes in transportation and public utilities (over Senate objection), but the spiral of rising Government estimates and subsidies to nationalized industry, higher rates, fares, charges, and taxes, would continue and social unrest would plague France until a master social program was evolved.

Agriculture

Agricultural problems under the Fourth and Fifth Republics were no less troubling and, on occasion, achieved a similarly dramatic presentation. The farmers' place in the nation had altered greatly during the previous century. Engels spoke of their "unmanageable stupidity," and Marx said they made up the nation "just as a sack filled with potatoes forms a sack of potatoes." They were undoubtedly fragmented and had the highest rate of illiteracy in the country, but compared with other workers they enjoyed a high standard of living. If they did not control the Third Republic, their numbers assured them that it would be responsive to their needs. Yet their relative position steadily declined. The Méline tariff of 1892 both protected the family unit and encouraged agricultural stagnation; the continued fragmentation of peasant life was undisturbed by agrarian syndicalism and welcomed by politicians Left and Right. Orators like Herriot celebrated the silent peasant as "the greatest of French philosophers" but offered no serious leadership to him. Before the fall of the Third Republic, grass-roots awakening to the need for reforming agriculture was slight; few belonged to larger regional or national associations, and fewer still were active in politics. Yet a beginning had been made, and Vichy, for all its quaint Arcadian claptrap, did nothing to weaken a growing tendency to instill the myth of peasant unity. Thus the Resistance inherited both the traditional protectiveness toward family units and the beginnings of agricultural reform. A peasant elite had begun to emerge in the 1930s, and though some were to be "lost" because of their too close association with Vichy, more survived to have an important post-Liberation role.

From 1944 to 1947 efforts were made to unite farmers in the left-wing *Confédération générale d'agriculture*, successor to the clandestine organization of the same name set up in 1943. Its object was modernization without eliminating the small farmer, its methods were cooperation and collectivism. But membership fell off under the Fourth Republic. Localism reasserted itself over centralized leadership. The component groups, notably the powerful *Fédération nationale des syndicats d'exploitants agricoles* (FNSEA) controlled by big conservative farmers, took an independent line. The big lobbyists for wheat, wine, and sugarbeet, spoke again with a loud voice. Many of the farm-machinery cooperatives disappeared. If something close to 40 per cent of the population had wrung a living from the land in 1940, not many more than 20 per cent still did so a quarter of a century later. Though the farmer's immediate post-Liberation prosperity was both real and the object of suspicion by the urban populace, his relative position plummeted thereafter. A very large proportion of the peasantry eked out a marginal existence. The variety of circumstances was great. Protection assured both survival to the inefficient and vast profits to the large-scale interests. The FNSEA both encouraged peasant protests and worked on the Government to obtain price supports. Doubtless it represented the interests of a healthy mixed farming even more effectively than the lobbyists represented the big single-crop farmers. But, though a "silent revolution" was in progress, neither the farmers' organizations nor the politicians faced up to the basic problem: to end the great disparity between rural and urban style of living, the structure of agriculture must be overhauled, the search for a single policy applicable to big and small farmers be abandoned, and the emotional myth of the small farmer as the guarantor of French stability be rejected as relic which was costly to the whole nation and was lining the pockets of those who manipulated it.

Progress had, however, been made by both the Fourth and the Fifth Republics. The *Jeunesse agricole catholique* had evolved from its conservative origins in 1929 to become a powerful force for social and agricultural reform. It sponsored the successful *Centres d'études techniques agricoles* soon after the first of these experimental groups came together in 1945 to discuss and investigate farming problems. In twenty years more than a thousand were established, above all in the most backward areas. Though regional interests might have unfortunate consequences for the nation as a whole, it was a hopeful sign that regional solidarity was coming to make inroads upon merely special interests. Rigid compartmentalization and stagnation were inevitably giving way to a rational exploitation of the land. On the other hand, the Fifth Republic still wrestled with high production costs, low prices, the fragmented character of much landholding, and the shortage of capital and technical assistance. It had to face the problem of mechanization, which encouraged a rural migration that in turn made conversion to livestock farming more difficult. It had yet to rationalize the distribution system and assure markets.

Meantime, farmers compensated for the reduction of their influence brought about by parliamentary decline by taking direct action. Their fears were aroused by emergence of the Common Market after 1957, despite a 1960 bill passed by the Assembly affirming their right to a standard of living equivalent to that of urban workers. Arson, road blocking, interruption of communications, dumping of vegetables and wine, besieging of Prefectures, and violent collisions with police and security troops characterized the discontent year after year. Though the Government in 1962 provided a land-distribution bill, recognition of cooperatives, and some protection against large-scale entrepreneurs, the problem of markets continued to produce tractor-riding demonstrations against the "misery of prosperity." Halting foreign imports, proclaiming an "Eat Apricots Week," or dumping produce in Latin America were expedients only. President de Gaulle's jibe at the Church, to the effect that the farmers would do better to protest to their Bishops than to his Prefects, since the difficulty originated with *le bon Dieu*, did not calm matters. All the same, the agrarian reform bill of 1962, denounced by both the far Right and the far Left, showed that the regime could distinguish between the young progressive farmers and the old subsidy-seeking protectionist single-crop growers. Even though it disappointed the most radical young reformers, it was still a major move toward basic agrarian renewal. Somehow agriculture had staggered through the twentieth century content to rely on what Stanley Hoffmann called assistance of "the wheelchair variety." Many farmers still looked no higher than that. But if it was true, as Gordon Wright maintained, that most peasants of a generation ago "probably had more in common with their predecessors of Balzac's time than with their successors of 1963," their ghosts seemed unlikely to return and set the clock back.

The farmers insisted that their share in the general prosperity had constantly fallen; though they made up better than 20 per cent of the nation, for instance, they purchased only 10 per cent of its automobiles. That the access their children had to higher education was not much better than about half that percentage was another grievance. And the two phenomena were not unrelated. The difficulty they had, therefore, was to see that their situation might be improved by the linking of France's economy to that of Europe. They feared that such a linking must be dependent upon a high level of industrial exports, which in turn must be assured by low-cost production dependent in some large part on low food prices. In short, the peasantry would pay.

Toward the European Common Market

But as the negotiations for a Common Market worked out it was by no means certain that this analysis had been correct. Certainly the immediate post-Liberation position of France on the international scene had not been brilliant. The effort to balance her foreign accounts at expanded levels resulted in extraordinary aid to exporters and repeated restriction on imports. She failed to fulfill obligations undertaken in adhering to the Organization for European Economic Cooperation established in 1948. As often as the trade situation improved, some new external crisis (Korea or Suez, for instance) destroyed the precarious balance. Moreover, industrial expansion necessitated coal imports, and before the Sahara fields became operative oil imports were vital. United States assistance in arms, in military infrastructure, and in servicemen's expenditures in France was substantial—the United States finally contributed about 75 per cent of the material cost of the Indo-Chinese war—but American, European, and international lending agency loans were swallowed up without effect. The benefits derived from devaluation in the 1940s were offset by inflation; the long-delayed devaluation of 1957 was both late and timid, without serious effect on the trade balance. Thus France lived beyond her means and was committed beyond her capacities.

Launched on the road toward an integrated Europe, she was apparently incapable of realizing progress in that direction. Yet the establishment in 1952 of the European Coal and Steel Community (ECSC) was a major step toward integration of the French economy. The revival of West Germany and the evidence of her renewed economic competitiveness and strength had given additional support to the schemes of Jean Monnet and others for the functional approach to European integration. Announced in May 1950 by Foreign Minister Robert Schuman, this first step had been taken despite the refusal of Great Britain to join in the plan. It had been accepted after strong opposition from Right and Left, and only after failure of the *Chambre syndicale de la sidérurgie française* campaign against it, the great steel manufacturers who had not been persuaded of the advantages of more equal access to German coking coal. The ultimate Monnet-Schuman purpose was political integration and an end to the series of western European wars, but at first the economic function of the Coal and Steel Community was more evident. Its success remained much debated. Competition from British, Japanese, Austrian, and Soviet steels was keen. But for France the lesson of the ECSC was that French industry could compete. It helped to destroy the national inferiority complex. It was a step along the road toward economic rationalization and away from the old Malthusianism of the recent past.

If this functional approach to European unity fell on evil days after 1953, the impetus behind it never faltered. And after intensive activity and much maneuvering, the Six of the Coal and Steel Community moved in 1955 to set up both a European atomic energy pool and an economic community. Both schemes were embodied in the treaties signed in Rome in 1957. Euratom, destined to relative obscurity, depended as the ECSC did on a Council of Ministers representing the six states (Belgium, Holland, Luxembourg, West Germany, Italy, and France), the Common Assembly of parliamentary delegates, and the Court of Justice. That France played an important part was indicated by the Frenchmen who served as the first three presidents of Euratom's Executive Commission and her contribution of 30 per cent of its budget.

Euratom hoped by 1980 to be able to supply 25 per cent of the Six's energy requirements, but the European Economic Community (EEC) was more immediately important. Its negotiation had been difficult. Though France was more confident of her ability to compete than she had been in 1950, special interests nevertheless imposed conditions for French participation. Significantly, the Common Market's Commission was not a supranational body of technicians like the ECSC's High Authority. Ministers were more powerful here than in the Coal and Steel Community; on important issues weighted majorities were required. France insisted on successive stages toward achievement of the ultimate common market, on recognition of national exceptions, special consideration for agriculture, harmonization of national wages and welfare costs, special taxes and quantitative restrictions on imports, export subsidies, participation of her Overseas Territories, and so forth. Some observers suspected that she wished only to shore up an uncertain economy behind a still larger tariff wall. But, again, the experiment was to show that French manufacture could compete, and it was the French who pressed for speedier dismantling of the Common Market's internal tariffs. With some 26 per cent of the Market's population, they manufactured about 28 per cent of its goods, and their rate of industrial growth was second only to that of Italy.

But agriculture posed a more intractable problem. With 47 per cent of the Market's cultivable land, France had in fact been led to ratification of the Rome Treaties largely because of her need for a wider market for agricultural produce. Years of discussion brought agreement on a free market for such produce by 1970, but the mechanics were greatly disputed. Deadlocked on the French demands for guarantees for beef and dairy products, the EEC was threatened with breakup by the President of the Fifth Republic. Before the 1963 ultimatum expired, the Germans obtained acceptance of a compromise by which they accepted common prices and policies on these items in return for French agreement to a lower Common Market external tariff. Still another conflict over cereals led to the same threats and, at the close of 1964, agreement upon a compromise wheat price. Thus was solved the basic dispute between France's relatively low-cost, surplus-producing agriculture and West Germany's inefficient high-cost agriculture. For France it was a great success; for Germany, an immediate defeat but, doubtless, an impetus toward serious agricultural reform; for Europe, an important stage on the road to full economic union. But every effort by the other EEC partners to tie France down to acceptance of supranational institutions was fiercely resisted, and once more in 1965 the agricultural question led to Gaullist threats to withdraw from the Common Market rather then see the parliamentary organs of EEC strengthened.

More dramatic than the Franco-German economic confrontation had been the French rejection of Great Britain's belated attempt to join the EEC. The problems of reconciling British agriculture and Commonwealth agreements with the policies of the Six were real, and the British record of opposition to the Common Market had been lamentable. But President de Gaulle's lofty refusal to pursue negotiations further in January 1963 was motivated less by fear of having to accommodate New Zealand butter and English bacon and eggs than by the political implications of admitting into "Little Europe" so insular and un-European a nation, one so obviously bound not to the European idea but to the Atlantic Community and to the United States. Amidst the international uproar he had provoked, the President observed with wry detachment that "perhaps in fifty years" the English would enter the Common Market, "but doubtless I shall no longer be here." As for the immediate disarray, "Nobody will quit the Common Market," he predicted accurately. "Italy, for example: We send her iron and coal, and we buy her pasta and Fiats. She's very happy."

In this mixture of confidence and disdain was to be seen not only a great man's arrogance but the new confidence and buoyancy of the French economy, committed to cooperation in a supranational market. The EEC was far from settling its last problems. The last internal tariff reductions would be difficult, and those with the United States and the outside world lengthy and tough. But each passing year made it less likely that France or any of the Six could seriously intend some new threat to withdraw. Nevertheless the General's hostility to the basic supranational implications of the Common Market portended, in his time, an endless series of such threats. No one could be sure that, whatever the cost to French agriculture, one of them might not be carried out.

The French Republic had abandoned its stagnant economic past and committed itself to a great continental experiment. Its own economy was far from having resolved all its problems. Yet much had been done under the Fourth and Fifth Republics to rationalize what had so lately seemed a Malthusian system impervious to progress and condemned by the weight of the past. The *mystique* of the Plan and of the Common Market was strong. Bringing economic realities into line with it would require a discipline, a courage, a self-denial, and an adaptability not hitherto known. But if French material expectations outran both domestic productivity and the possibilities of a labyrinthine distribution system, if economic justice remained still an unrealized ideal, the crust of the old nineteenth and early twentieth century society had been shattered forever.

Whatever the future of *dirigisme*, the State would not renounce entirely the positive role it had come to have. From both labor and the CNPF complaints were loud against fixed wages, ceiling prices, and artificially stabilized currency. But while the CNPF continued to sound occasionally like economic Bourbons who had learned and forgotten nothing, and labor continued to act out a hostile alienated role rooted in its historic experience, the mass of French citizenry might hope for at least some continued measure of *dirigisme* until the eternal quest for unity within the nation seemed more nearly in sight.

TEN

THE NATION, THE ARMY, AND

"THE WORLD AS IT IS"

"Les querelles ne dureraient pas longtemps si le tort n'était que d'un côté."

The myth of the martial virtues of the French, of their taste for expansion and glory, has survived with astonishing tenacity. A mere handful of names known to history has sufficed to support this conception. This has been the fate of many peoples, but possibly none has a more misleading reputation here than the people of France. The past was certainly not without its portion of great feats of arms and the will to dominate. Across more than four hundred years the glitter and dash of Francis I, challenging both England and the Empire, had not faded; nor the memory of Louis XIV lifting his kingdom to hegemony over continental Europe. Only 150 years ago, Bonaparte, having electrified and terrified the civilized world with the deeds of the French in arms, retired to exile and his final task of giving the myth a form and a personal identification still felt beneath the dome of the Invalides.

Retreat from Glory: Before 1944

Frenchmen celebrated their leaders' victories as their own; they certainly bled for them. Even in the twentieth century they commemorated, as did every people involved, the bitter victories of the First World War. But it could not be shown that they had sought out, as a people, the paths leading to such glory. No doubt combative shouts were heard both before and after that November day in 1095 when Urban preached the crusade at Clermont. Even in July 1870 a popular martial note was sounded, supporting the reckless challenge to Prussia, and in August 1914 the French, too, toasted the brilliant lightning decisions no one was to win. The descent on Port Said in November 1956 awakened a last militant enthusiasm which, however, like the mood of 1870 if not that of 1914, arose from the sense of profound national humiliation and collapsed as swiftly. They were momentary excitements, not deep commitments to adventurous external policies. After Francis I, moreover, came the introverted preoccupations which almost destroyed the unity of France in civil war. Before the Sun King was the unglorious (though not unambitious), healing reign of Henry of Navarre. And after it was the passive *immobilisme* of Louis XV, *le bien aimé's* age, a time of inquiry and self-concern when an empire was almost completely lost. Though the record showed Louis XVIII intervening in Spain, Louis Philippe hesitating about the Belgian ambitions of some around him, and Napoleon III seeking the restoration of continental prestige, the nineteenth century was, in Europe at least, devoid of the French hegemonist impulse. The twentieth offered after 1918 and before 1947 a sometimes melancholy catalog of confused purposes and uncertain will.

The French under the Republic of 1875 appeared to have their eyes fixed less upon the "blue line of the Vosges" than upon their own gardens. To the imperialists it seemed notorious that the country should so little concern itself with the deeds of its civil and military proconsuls; to Foreign Ministers and Premiers it sometimes seemed a blessing. Paul Cambon told Théophile Delcassé in 1899 that his accounting to the Chamber of Deputies was the first such survey of foreign affairs offered parliament by a Minister in twenty years. Though Jules Ferry was pulled down, it was not entirely clear why he fell. If parliament roused itself to seek information, it could readily be put off. "You will judge me," said Foreign Minister Jean Cruppi in 1911 as he launched the country on a perhaps nearly disastrous expedition to Fez, "by my acts." And, as one critical Senator put it in protest, "The Minister is more powerful than Louis XIV and less responsible." It seemed so often that the great issues in the nation were neither foreign nor colonial but domestic. It was the judgment of Maurice Barrès as Deputy that in foreign affairs "a professional competence is necessary; if it is a question of the Army, the Navy, foreign policy, one has to be familiar with our Government's talks with various other governments. I am not a presumptuous chatterer. . . . I leave the responsibility to them." The national instinct to withdraw from the discussion of and from responsibility for foreign affairs asserted itself before 1914 and, again, before 1939—that is to say, in situations quite different, where the positions and obligations of France were quite different. In the 1910 elections less than 10 per cent of the candidates declared their positive stand on foreign affairs; in 1914 the issue of the Three Years' military service law was not properly discussed in the context of Europe's armed peace and was in fact largely rejected by the electorate. Though the Republic was distraught and divided in 1939, the mood of withdrawal was profound. "Our obligations toward Czechoslovakia?" the Deputy Jean Montigny remarked some two months before Hitler destroyed the state finally. "Circumstances, alas! have released us from them." Or, as Flandin put it, less crudely, "Peace is never lost while we have the will to keep it."

By 1939, of course, the Republic had suffered a series of shocks which created a new mood of futility, something far more serious for a great nation than mere preoccupation with domestic troubles. Worse still, the sense of inferiority and incapacity had by then become established in the area of government, from which, for instance in 1914, it had always been absent. It had not been surprising to hear the Socialist Charles Bonnier say in 1911, "The real war that must interest us is social war: there there is no ambiguity and all blows fall upon the real enemy. That is the foreign policy and the diplomacy of the working class." What was alarming was to have this preoccupation with the social question (but from the other side of the barricades) similarly adduced by the Right, 25 years later, to justify the flight from a heavy national responsibility; above all, to have Ministers both before and after a declaration of war convinced that unless the war were ended quickly by negotiation the interests of the nation— not least, its social stability—would be violently overthrown. The time when governments had, as Jean-Baptiste Duroselle pointed out, taken advantage of public indifference to foreign affairs in order to act decisively was temporarily ended. The familiar proposition that a strong external policy was espoused by the Left before 1875 and by the Right thereafter had broken down around 1935-1936. If Léon Blum on the Left and Louis Marin on the Right supported stopping Hitler by force, in every sector of the Chamber were to be found the advocates of peace at almost any price. What marked this point in time was not so much Paul Faure's "To save peace I would not hesitate to plunge into garbage cans," nor even the Moderates' denunciation of "this mad and stupid adventure." Rather it was the wartime Premier's despairing, "What do you want me to do? Now we have to go on to the end. If the house falls, it will fall on us."

The climate of 1939 was to be explained by something more than a long-standing tradition of indifference in France to the external scene. To long-established territorial satiety and consequent lack of national ambition (the frontier rectifications in the nineteenth century were not major, the few manifestations of expansionism minor and fleeting) had been added a deep-seated yearning for deliverance from war. On the Left it was obviously more intense than the spirit that had characterized the old Second International; on the Right it was both new and virulent: "There is only one more hope for France," Alain Laubreaux remarked, "a short and disastrous war." This violent pacifism followed from the exhaustion of 1914-1918, the sense of having failed in 1919 to secure the peace at the conference table, the awareness of demographic decline and the obvious failure after 1929 to retain relative standing among the industrial powers, the realization of profound social schism existing within the country, the virtual breakdown of the political system, the contradictory but significant external pulls of foreign ideologies, and the very real demoralization brought about by the circumstances in which France was pushed toward war by Great Britain, whose record in foreign affairs since 1918 at least had been so hostile to France and whose preparations for the battle were so evidently inadequate.

Emmanuel Mounier commented that the whole country was "living tensed toward a negative end: to destroy a man, to destroy a regime," when all its political, economic, and social problems remained to be solved. "A crusade is not external." He was wrong. There may have been those in 1939 who thought, as the Girondins thought in 1792, that war would solve many questions; it is much less certain that the nation was in the condition he described. Despite the war, because of the war even, national "introversion" had by no means disappeared. Doubtless France was given little time, and scarcely more leadership, to adapt. A fundamental command error, following out of a strategic conception intimately allied to the lessons of 1914-1918 and the consequences drawn from that war's aftermath, and a daring enemy plan of attack, which depended in fact upon this French sclerosis for success, prevented any second chance to overcome the moral and military deficiency of the nation. If the stunning defeat of 1940 produced an incredulous movement of resurgence in the Empire, resistance was quickly snuffed out; the Free French enterprise was at best an uncertain adventure.

The real rally was to the inward-looking policy of the Marshal; that was his finest hour, a pathetic reenactment on the national stage of his role in 1917, founded this time not on mutiny but on defeat, directed not to crushing the enemy but to surviving and even collaborating with him. Never before or since were the domestic preoccupations of the French so obviously encouraged by their Government. And the moment of profound emotion at this old man's message to turn back upon the good earth swiftly passed. If the French rediscovered the *patrie*, they also rediscovered their old divisions. The Occupation opened up fresh ones. Above all, the war would not leave France alone. It bankrupted implacably the policies of all who had opposed the adventure of General de Gaulle. And by 1944 there was something approaching a new consensus around this man's conception of France and her destiny. The reverse of the Marshal's introverted policy, it was to command a national following not much longer than his had done.

The Rough Road Back, 1944-1958

Perhaps more accurately, the Gaullist policy of 1944 drew its following not merely from the conception of greatness reborn, which was largely the General's special contribution, but from the Resistance conception of internal rebirth which, theoretically at least, had been absorbed into the Liberation as a whole. What the immediate postwar years seemed to show was that neither part of this ambition could be achieved by traditional practices. A policy of accommodation and relaxation in the economic sphere led to serious shortages, maldistribution of goods, and inflation. The pursuit of classic Third Republic policy in foreign and colonial affairs was quickly revealed to be impossible or illusory. Postwar Russia was not the Russia of 1935, let alone that of 1891. If the memory of Mers el Kébir and other painful incidents was muted, Great Britain was not ready to do more than commemorate the Entente of 1904 in the Treaty of Dunkirk, 1947; preaching Europe, she put her trust in America. As for assuring French security by dismembering Germany and possessing the mines of the Saar, France's Anglo-American allies would have none of it but the Saar proposal, because it was clear to them that the problem was not a revived Germany but an expansionist Russia, and the Germany they revived against this threat naturally condemned the Saar scheme.

Above all, the French hope of complete colonial restoration was denied. Though the British had promised their aid to achieve it, their rivalry was traditional and their intentions, principally in the Middle East, suspect. The United States' hostility to colonialism was notorious, not least concerning North Africa. Whatever the designs of or encouragements given to nationalist uprisings by these two allies, France readily resorted to the slogan with which she had so often explained massive failures from 1792 to 1940, "Nous sommes trahis," except that in the colonial sphere, from Syria to Algeria, 1945-1962, the explanation for the rising of native forces hostile to France might have more direct reference to the Americans or the British, e.g., "It smells of oil."

At all events, two or three years after the Liberation it was clear that the road back in politics was open, but that the road back in foreign and colonial policy was barred. Rejection of the European Defense Community would be a resentful acknowledgment of this fact; Suez a disastrous confirmation; Bizerte a bitter, barren expression of hostility to it. Whether Frenchmen sought to return to the ways of introversion is debatable. There were occasions under the Fourth Republic when this seemed so, and the phenomenon of neutralism was found in distinguished, if small, segments of the nation. But it could be argued either way. Moreover, if the enthusiasm of 1944 had departed—as de Gaulle, the symbol of the national hope that France would regain her place in the world, had departed in January 1940—more positive forces existed. Stemming out of reform movements under the Third Republic, out of Vichy and the Resistance both, were men who conceived of the national destiny being accomplished by means other than those of the past. They were given powerful assistance (negatively) by the Soviet Union and (positively) by the United States. Foreign Minister Bidault's discovery in the spring of 1947 that Stalin would not support France's claim to the Saar, like Thorez's support of working-class demands and endorsement of Moscow's policy against France, brought down *tripartisme* and swung the Republic clearly into the American camp. And the United States was by then becoming convinced that it had no choice but to commit itself economically and militarily to western Europe. Thus, though it was undoubtedly true that the fragility of cabinets discouraged major policy decisions before 1958, the conditions of the Cold War played directly into the hands of politicians, civil servants, businessmen, or technicians who conceived of foreign policy as implying the closest links with a European community.

Initiatives came not from the Government, J.-B. Duroselle maintained, but from the intelligentsia outside it. This, then, was a kind of positive counterpart to the initiatives taken in the Empire by the proconsuls (the irreparable acts committed in Saigon in 1946, or the deposition of the Sultan in 1953), the resulting damage from which it was the unhappy task of the Ministers in Paris to limit short of total disaster. But to make such a distinction, where these foreign-policy initiatives were concerned, between the intelligentsia and the cabinets was perhaps to suggest that governments were not normally influenced from that quarter. Yet if Bidault, for instance, had not found time to peruse Jean Monnet's plan for a coal and steel community, Robert Schuman did—and though the scheme was dramatic and pregnant with consequences for western Europe, one might wonder whether it was brought forward in a manner different from that in which civil servants had brought forward ideas under the Third Republic. The Schuman plan was surely no more differently conceived than, say, the *Front populaire's* ill-fated reforms for Algeria. In this sense, it was not easy to see that the governmental record on foreign-policy decision-making was so negative. Even if the Rome treaties of 1957 were regarded as an example of Duroselle's conclusion that the Fourth Republic's policy was only "as a general rule" the "carrying on what already existed," still the element of a certain positive governmental commitment was not lacking. Moreover, it would be difficult to show that Governments accepted the intelligentsia's initiatives primarily for economic reasons. It would not even be possible to show that all the intelligentsia had put economic motivation before political. "There is only one way to end wars between nations," Monnet remarked in the spring of 1950: "that is to merge them into one."

But if a degree of positive decision-making, on strongly political grounds (French strength and rank being intimately related to the economic recovery of France and Europe), be granted to the Fourth Republic, still it was true that the old Third Republic tradition of flight from responsibility in foreign policy had not entirely disappeared. The French accepted the Anglo-American view in 1948 that Germany must be reunited and revived, and even put forward the proposal of a European Army in 1950, but successive Governments delayed putting the ensuing European Defense Community to parliamentary vote and then permitted it to be rejected in an emotional upsurge of anti-German speeches. The subsequent French acceptance of German rearmament within NATO in the autumn of 1954 was the price paid for Premier Mendès-France's and parliament's reluctance to commit the country to Europe. His fear that France was not yet economically strong enough to undertake and maintain her rank in EDC had joined with the old Germanophobia of the revived Right. Yet everyone knew that one way or another West Germany would be armed by the Americans. France might veto a method proposed; she was powerless to prevent the act itself. In a very real sense, therefore, she had to take a positive attitude during the London negotiations which brought Bonn into Western European Union and NATO. But she was also able to insist upon solution of the Saar problem as a condition of her agreement. And though in the October 1955 plebiscite Saarlanders rejected the French plan for Europeanization of their territory (and in the December elections chose Germany over France), what made the whole German settlement acceptable was a growing awareness by this time that the caricature of helpless

France threatened by mighty Germany no longer accorded with the facts. In a word, France had not originally chosen Europe; she had had it thrust upon her. She had proposed making Europe in a certain way, in 1950, to avoid an otherwise "inevitable" reappearance of German hegemony, only to find that her newly discovered economic strength and ability to compete in foreign markets assured her own military might, made the Germans more receptive to partnership, and enhanced the position both of France and Europe vis-à-vis the United States.

This happy outcome would seem evident after 1958. Three or four years earlier, it was less so. Sir Winston Churchill might write Mendès-France in January 1955 to say, "Your courage and vitality have given me an impression of French leadership which I had not sustained since the days of Clemenceau," but this and his reference to "all the vehement and self-centred groups" opposing German rearmament were less the compliment intended to Mendès-France than a contemptuous commentary on the Fourth Republic. The EDC mess had reduced French stock in London and Washington to zero; the French reaction tended toward self-pity. "And so we are told that the world is sick and tired of our hesitations," Jacques Madaule noted. "If such hesitations were justified, nobody cares. Sentiment doesn't count in politics. And so we are left alone, face to face with our destiny." Yet the mood passed. Though the Soviet Union denounced the alliance of 1944 and thus made the French search for an end to the Cold War through a Summit conference the more insistent, a certain confidence was reviving. If Poujadism suggested the worst kind of introversion, the old hostility to Germany was ebbing, the devolution of empire was beginning to concentrate more attention upon Europe. As Mendès-France (himself a casualty of the Republic's troubled first decade) put it, "a rejuvenated dynamic France" was foreshadowed and "the painful, difficult phase of reconstruction" was drawing to a close by the end of 1955.

For the Fourth Republic, however, the tragedy was that precisely at this juncture a deepening commitment to the Algerian war deflected resources to and focused attention upon a ruinous struggle hopelessly distorted and misinterpreted even by those who had declared that France must make a choice among the courses of action open to her at home and abroad. The result was that European policy leading to the Rome treaties was overshadowed by the colonial imbroglio. Seeking its strength in Europe's economic union, the regime seemed condemned to dissipate it in North Africa. Constantly criticized by friend and foe, France grew bitter again; opinion divided or simply became indifferent. The State drifted toward incoherence.

Argument about the degree of introversion of the French people is probably not fruitful. No doubt the profoundest concerns of every people are domestic; doubtless in moments of crisis a nation may either rally to an external challenge or "withdraw into its grief." The history of France showed examples of both reactions; the Fourth Republic seemed to be an exception only because its life was so short, because the rising tide of confidence was overwhelmed by the last great colonial war. It might be difficult to show that the indifference of Frenchmen to the struggle in Indo-China had been greater than the indifference of Englishmen to the struggle in Malaya or the indifference of Americans to the war in Korea: each army complained about such attitudes. It might be equally difficult to show that the French were more indifferent to Europe than were the British, let alone the Americans. What is certainly true, however, is that the Governments of the Fourth Republic, so precariously based, were compelled to give much attention to foreign policy, if only because the problem of internal reconstruction, not to mention defense, could be accomplished best by intimate participation in reconstructing Europe. As Alfred Grosser put it, this was a policy of "necessity," whereas the policies of General de Gaulle, whether in 1944 or 1958, were those of "taste." All of them, however, were in fact directed toward adapting France to the conditions of the world as it was after the Second World War.

De Gaulle: Politique de Grandeur

The Fourth Republic drew to its close in a welter of hostile acts and the humiliating acceptance of Anglo-American "good offices" in its external relations. Nearly fourteen years had passed since the General entered liberated Paris. His task in those days had been herculean: to consolidate his claim to represent France; to increase French participation in clearing the national territory, to regain full control of the Empire; to play the Russian card against the American; to ensure dismemberment of Germany and cooperation with Great Britain; to remake the constitution, reshape political life, and revive the economy. Neither his own (disputed) authority nor the country's plight permitted him to achieve this. He failed in Syria and Indo-China. Above all, though he won full external recognition for himself, he failed in politics—"I asked him to help in the reconstruction of France," he wrote of Herriot; "he informed me that he would dedicate himself to the restoration of the Radical party." Thus de Gaulle could not succeed in the principal task of foreign policy.

In June 1958 everything was different. The politicians had run their course and permitted the Army to put the General back in power in order to save the Republic from the Army. Though the State's finances were shaky, the country was economically healthy. Though hectored by her allies, France was a pillar of the western alliance. De Gaulle had a control and a base far stronger than in 1944. Despite the perils of Algeria, the over-all prospects were brighter. His task was to pursue his (he would say France's) goals while liquidating the troubles because of which Army and nation, however confused their intents, had accepted him. By the spring of 1962, despite nearly four more years of North African war in steadily more barbaric conditions, his position had been repeatedly upheld and confirmed, not least by his courage, moderation, and resolve. France by then was enjoying an authority not known since 1918, pursuing a *politique de grandeur* directed, as de Gaulle said in 1964, "from consideration of

France's higher interests, which is something quite different from the immediate advantage of the French people." The style was unquestionably
personal and authoritarian, the preoccupation with foreign policy infinitely more obvious than that of the previous regime. The nation may
not have cared greatly for this emphasis, but it could scarcely avoid a thrill
of pride that its international stock had risen so high.

The twentieth century was iconoclastic, reluctant to believe in "great
men." But outside some such category, de Gaulle would be incomprehensible. Moreover, though his style superficially suggested the past, in fact
he was modern. His intense concern with the State might appear antique,
but he had long ago freed himself from the reactionary nostalgia of the
Action Française. For him, France was at once the historic French State
and an idealized being which to be itself must be "in the front rank."
This idea of the nation was matched by a conception of himself—
equally powerful and equally incapable of rational analysis—as the instrument of destiny. "There was no one else to do this thing but me," he
remarked once of his original act of rebellion. "I did it because I had
to." As this instrument, he sought not to return to a golden age but
to adapt to and bring under control "the world as it is" and what he
called "*la force des choses.*" With him, then, the Fourth Republic's search
for a role in Europe and for equality with Great Britain in the Atlantic
alliance's directorate was given an added dimension and a powerful new
impulse. Standing on the solid economic achievements of the former
regime, his natural authority magnified by success in the Algerian negotiation, he showed himself to be probably the ablest practitioner of
cabinet policy since Bismarck. With him, the whole activity of the State
was directed toward pursuit of a strong foreign policy. For this, in the
contemporary world, he knew that the State required more than an able
diplomacy, a strong military force, and a reliable police; it needed to grow
in economic, scientific, and technological power, and it needed to shoulder
a heavy burden of responsibility around the globe among the underdevel-
oped peoples. For de Gaulle, as for Bismarck and other classical statesmen, the world was a chessboard on which only a handful of great players
maneuvered perpetually. The goal was unchanging, but the conditions of
play had doubtless become more complicated since 1890. In his own way,
de Gaulle was quite as flexible as the great Chancellor; whether he would
be, in infinitely less favorable and more complicated circumstances, as successful the future alone would tell. But it did not seem likely.

In 1958, then, the *politique de grandeur* had to be pursued in the light
not only of de Gaulle's own failures fourteen years before but of the experience of the Fourth Republic. That Republic had had no more love
for the United Nations than had the Third for the old League of Nations,
yet it had felt compelled to work with it and in it, if only to avoid condemnation by it on the colonial problem. The Fifth Republic, with its
colonial problem well in hand, quickly communicated the President's view
that the UN had long since ceased to be more than a Babel where, say, the

impudence of Ghana was exceeded only by the demagogy of the Soviet Union. De Gaulle therefore dismissed it as *"le machin,"* or *"les nations dites unies,"* refused to pay its peacekeeping bills and on occasion had his representative stage walkouts. Such a forum for windy speeches and gratuitous insults from a rapidly expanding number of nationalist, grasping, economically, militarily, and politically chaotic, noisy little states—as he saw it—was no place in which to conduct the affairs of the world. Nor did de Gaulle return to that illusion of the Fourth Republic: the Summit Conference. As long as Europe was tied to American protection, no concessions on Germany would be made by the Soviet Union; moreover, to make Europe one day independent of the United States, France needed the goodwill and cooperation of West Germany. Thus the Summit idea seemed doubly condemned for some time to come.

More positively, de Gaulle made a direct bid for "rank" in Washington and London, September 1958. This demand for admission to a "directorship" in the Atlantic alliance failed, and was to lead to repeated threats that NATO as organized in 1949 could not survive without fundamental reorganization. These were no more than a vociferous following-through of the complaints made by the last Governments of the Fourth Republic, but the Fifth Republic systematically reduced its participation within NATO, withdrawing most of its military forces, most of it air power, and all of its naval units, forbidding American nuclear weapons on French soil unless placed under French control (a condition the United States refused). Admitting publicly that NATO was "indispensable" while the Soviet threat existed, the President maintained that the conditions of 1949 had disappeared, that the Republic must remain "the master" in its own house, and that the treaty should be renegotiated before its expiry in 1969. Whether the days of "the American general staff" (as French critics called the NATO command) were numbered, Europe's revival had in any event made basic changes in the old treaty inevitable.

In this assault on NATO in the name of France, de Gaulle was again carrying out a policy of independent nuclear development initiated by the Fourth Republic. First considered in late 1954, the decision to explode a French bomb was taken by the Gaillard cabinet in 1958, and the first explosion detonated in February 1960. Soon after his return to power, de Gaulle had spelled out his intention to create a nuclear *force de frappe*. Against international protests, atmosphere testing in the Sahara grounds continued in 1961, and underground tests thereafter. Inevitably he rejected the Geneva Test Ban Treaty (also President Kennedy's secret last-minute offer to assist France with nuclear development if she would sign), proceeded with plans for hydrogen bomb tests in the Tuamotu Islands southeast of Tahiti, laid down nuclear-powered submarines, and assailed his domestic critics as "the voices of *immobilisme* and demagogy," "the same sort of laggards and scatterbrains" who had opposed new weapons before 1914 and 1939. Small and costly (though Gaullists argued that the cost amounted to only one-half the subsidies paid to agriculture), the nuclear force was not intended as a substitute for American protection. Though the argument that "France should defend herself with her own arms, for her own ends, and in her own way" had been handed to France by Dulles's notorious threat of "agonizing reappraisal," de Gaulle knew the United States would not abandon Europe; the argument was merely useful to create popular support for this expensive prestige instrument, which might be useful to "trigger" American nuclear intervention in a European cause from which Washington might otherwise retreat. Unfortunately, however, the heavy cost of the striking force involved drastic cuts in conventional forces which the Americans wished France to develop, lest the Soviets, with their massive conventional armies, be able to blackmail the United States in Europe into acceptance of, say, a coup in Berlin—the very situation the nuclear force was designed to render impossible.

This striking force was in many ways a logical weapon. In 1945 de Gaulle had learned how hard it was to make one's political voice heard without having a first-class weapon in hand. The Fourth Republic had discovered as much, and had come to fear that the security it enjoyed beneath the American umbrella without essential political independence might, once the Soviet Union had nuclear weapons, be withdrawn. Hence the decision to proceed independently. But there was also the possibility that the Fifth Republic's insistence upon a nuclear arms was directed partly toward the reformation of the Army and to its return to the traditional place it had occupied in the nation. The quite extraordinary crisis this Army had lived through from 1940 to 1962 had left it sorely tried in body and soul. The Gaullist emphasis upon nuclear forces was not merely the price paid for getting the Army out of North Africa and reoriented again to continental Europe, but it might be seen as the symbol of strength and prestige this famous and now mauled professional force required to rally around.

The Tragedy of the Army

In 1939, when so much in Europe was doubtful, men scarcely doubted the French Army. Yet a year later the wreck of it fought a valiant retreat or was swept helter-skelter across Flanders and France under the broiling sun before the Wehrmacht. The defeat was complete; the notion that it was principally from the Army that the demand for armistice had come was humiliating. What was saved clandestinely under Vichy was not permitted to reopen hostilities when the enemy came into unoccupied zone in 1942. Between the older generation and the younger a spiritual divide opened up. In Syria, Frenchman fought Frenchman. Having opposed the Anglo-Americans in North Africa, French forces then went on to join them against the Axis. Even in the Italian and French campaigns, 1943-1945, the contribution by France was small. The sense of having not greatly contributed to the victory bore on the Army as it did on the nation. Moreover, victory brought inevitable purging in the ranks of the officers.

And then this only half-reformed instrument was committed to futile slaughter on behalf of colonial causes. Young, proud, ardent, often brilliant, and always slowly promoted and poorly paid, its officers were brought face to face with the dramas of conscience the nation was reluctant to recognize. If the country expected sacrifices of them, it was also ready to surrender the ground fought for and abandon the native populations who had given the Army their trust. Command errors, as in Indo-China, deepened the military *malaise*; scandals in political circles, even touching matters for which men were giving their lives far from France, increased the sense of alienation. The civil-military rift, so evident in Weygand and so masked by Gamelin under the Third Republic, widened under the Fourth. The Army had long looked upon itself as the embodiment of all that was best in the nation, but only with the Dreyfus Affair did it begin to question political decisions. Only in the 1930s did certain elements establish connections with civilian action groups opposed to the regime. Only in 1940 did Weygand openly question political decisions and threaten disobedience if the Army did not have its way; only then, too, did his upstart opponent de Gaulle defy the legal Government and raise the standard of rebellion against it. But it was the peculiar conditions of modern warfare, the blurring of the frontiers separating war, politics, and ideology, and the experience of revolutionary and psychological war waged by Communists in Indo-China that served to convince the young generation of a higher duty to the nation than traditional obedience.

By 1958 the Army was becoming what Jacques Fauvet called "the biggest party in France." And that spring it acted and had its way with the civil authorities. Paradoxically the man it brought to power had had an unhappy love affair with the Army; his writings were full of contempt for the routine spirit which prevailed in it between the wars. Perhaps Weygand never fully understood or accepted the consequences of *his* political act; de Gaulle, however, had taken to politics in Paul Reynaud's cabinet with alacrity. As the country staggered to disaster in 1940, de Gaulle's almost cruel confrontation of the aged, dispirited commander-in-chief of the Army betrayed a vaulting ambition. With the sentence of death passed on him at Toulouse, de Gaulle's connections with the old Army ended forever; indeed they had been severed before that. "I went in silence over to the Marshal, who was dining in the same room, to present my respects," he recalled of his eve of departure from stricken France. "He shook me by the hand without a word. I was not to see him again, ever."

In 1944-1945 de Gaulle fought hard for American re-equipment of the Army. But he was a statesman then; he had crossed to the other bank that he had long ago eyed. Though Leclerc had been with him almost from the first hour, de Lattre de Tassigny and Juin had served Vichy as late as 1942; Pétain's death sentence in 1945 he had merely commuted to life imprisonment, and if Weygand escaped trial, others—notably General Dentz—perished in ignoble conditions in prison. The old Army had no love for de Gaulle. But by 1958 all that belonged to the past. What he and the colonels or hesitant generals had in common was their contempt for the Fourth Republic. On their implicit but equivocal pact the regime was brought down and the Fifth Republic established. If most of the Army remained obedient to the Government thereafter, its mood was "*attentiste*." The issue of *Algérie française* had brought de Gaulle back, and his final rejection of it, as impossible to sustain, occasioned a minority rebellion against him in which the military ringleaders sought desperately to attach their cause once more to that of the western struggle against communism. Perhaps this extraordinary man alone saved the Republic from overthrow once again. How de Gaulle encouraged this Army after June 1958, pacified it, misled and "betrayed" it, disciplined it, and confronted it in a struggle to the death, but always saved its honor was not the least remarkable part of four years ending in the collapse of murderous opposition to the State with which embittered military men and civilians disgraced themselves. Only in the April 1961 revolt did he publicly thrash the "partisan, ambitious, and fanatical" rebel generals; only amidst sickening Secret Army atrocities did he wish to execute General Jouhaud and dissolve in fury the tribunal that had sentenced the OAS leader, General Salan, merely to life imprisonment because of "extenuating circumstances." Careless of civilian opponents of the war, who suffered severely at the hands of civil and military justice, he repeatedly protected the Army, some of whose officers repeatedly sought to destroy him. With the Algerian cease-fire he sealed the dossiers on military torture and murder.

After 1962 the President's task was, as he said, "to turn the Algerian page." Thirty years before, he had called on the "military elite" to become conscious of "the pre-eminent role it has to play, and to concentrate anew upon its one and only duty, which is to prepare itself for war." Nothing indicated that he conceived of the Army's place under the Fifth Republic in other terms. The psychological and revolutionary lessons learned in the East must be forgotten, and this long-exiled Army be brought back to Europe and reintegrated into society. If he did not dispute the Army-Nation equation, he rejected a political role for the military—his own extraordinary career underlined the temptations and dangers of such an ambition. Though Juin bitterly criticized him for losing Algeria, the Marshal finally came in 1964 to concede the "flagrant disobedience" of the generals' revolt and recommend "a frank return to our tradition" of obedience. Some who had opposed the Republic's Algerian policy by word were restored to commands; the principal rebels remained in prison; lesser offenders were amnestied from time to time. Some of those who had taken part in the various assassination plots against the General were executed. Time alone would heal the wounds. Ultimately de Gaulle would never win the Army to him, for he had ended its illusions. His object was rather to win it back to France, to cement the bonds between it and the nation, to create confidence between it and the Government by displaying executive authority and assuming direct presidential responsibility for and control of military policy. Whether the reduction of traditional arms (hence a weakening of the Army-Nation idea so dear to the officer corps), and the professional role symbolized by the nuclear force would find military approval was uncertain. As a conception of the defense policy of France, it had its military critics just as the General's earlier writings had had a generation before. But it was military statesmanship of a high order.

In Search of Europe: Global Strategy

Whether it was French or European statesmanship was another question. Considered as merely French policy, the nuclear arm might not necessarily open the way to a larger voice in NATO for France, as a great conventional Army certainly would. In conditions where France's European allies remained protected by the American nuclear umbrella, it was far from sure that the French weapon could "trigger" the American (although the possibility might deter Russian action). And the United States continued to refuse to create a tripartite nuclear directorate within NATO. Thus the advantages accruing to France from this military policy remained, for the moment at least, slight. But the President also hoped that the establishment of French nuclear power would help to disengage Europe from the Atlantic alliance's toils. Like the Fourth Republic, the Fifth assumed an ambiguous attitude toward Europe, both asserting French leadership in Western European Union and asserting WEU's claim to equality in NATO, that is, both seeking to make use of Europe to increase the stature of France and seeking to put forward the claims of Europe as a "third force" in the world. The evident American rejection of de Gaulle's 1958 demand for a three-power nuclear directorate within NATO appeared to shift French policy toward Europe, although, as under the Fourth Republic, the dualism of approaches to "rank" remained. What was certain in 1965 was that the General or some Gaullist successor would, were the existing French regime not changed, end France's "subordination" in NATO by 1969 and thus destroy the Atlantic Alliance as it had been known.

The creation of Europe implied above all a Franco-German partnership, and the Fifth Republic inherited the fruitful work accomplished between 1950 and 1958. For five years thereafter relations were close. Such was the General's personal ascendancy over the old Chancellor that France rapidly became the dominant partner (which the ephemeral governments of the Fourth Republic had never been). Adenauer's suspicions faded as he took the measure of de Gaulle's intransigence on Berlin and Germany vis-à-vis the Soviet Union, and thus he reluctantly supported the French plan for a Europe not of merged sovereignties but of cooperating fatherlands. Adenauer's tour of France in the summer of 1962 was merely politely received, but de Gaulle's triumphal progress from Munich to Hamburg that September seemed to mark the rehabilitation of Germany. His memorized speeches in German ("Sie sind ein grosses Volk"), his somewhat indiscriminate sweeping of the Nazi period under the same rug with the collisions of 1870 and 1914, created sensational enthusiasm. The treaty signed in Paris, January 22, 1963, pledging cooperation in foreign, defense, and cultural affairs, was said to cap more than a dozen years of constructive approaches and also, as Adenauer put it, to end "four hundred years of quarrels, disputes, and wars." Though French parliamentary ratification was not without both opposition and abstention, public opinion was favorable. It seemed a remarkable turn of events since the harsh words of the EDC debate less than a decade before. Yet, though it rested on more than a merely admiring Adenauer–de Gaulle friendship, the accord unquestionably depended upon German acceptance of French predominance. And after the long-delayed retirement of Adenauer that autumn, it was evident that Bonn would henceforth be less amenable to the General's conceptions of Europe and European defense and more obviously oriented to Washington and the Atlantic alliance. No less intransigent on Berlin and the conditions of German unity than de Gaulle, Chancellor Erhard was, however, both willing to talk with the Soviets and skeptical of the Gaullist thesis that only a strong, independent western Europe, free of doctrinaire American anti-communism, could relax Soviet fears and achieve unity with a liberalized eastern Europe. Moreover, the record of France's seeking an Atlantic nuclear directorship suggested the limitation of her commitment to the European idea, as, of course, did the President's rejection of all supranational institutions. And although France finally secured abandonment of the United States' proposal for a "so-called multilateral atomic force," the scheme had divided her from her new German friend.

By 1963, then, French policy in Europe was apparently blocked. Relations with Great Britain were cool following the abrupt rejection of British application for Common Market membership during the President's January press conference. Backed by the other Five of the EEC, Great Britain had appeared certain to enter and de Gaulle resigned to it. Whatever he owed to the British, he had had many rows with them during the war, had indeed come close to being politically broken then by Churchill and the Americans. The British postwar record of refusing to make any serious political commitment to Europe was flagrant; of selling arms to Tunisia while the Algerian war continued, less than friendly; of hectoring the limping Fourth Republic, annoying; of seeming to be the United States' favorite satellite, discouraging; and of approaching the Common Market after vainly trying to counter it with the European Free Trade Association, suspicious. Nevertheless from 1960 through 1962 negotiations proceeded. Though Adenauer and de Gaulle hoped to achieve their "Europe of fatherlands" before British entry, Belgium and Holland in particular insisted both on a higher degree of integration and on participation of Great Britain in the political talks. The quarrel became shrill, and it was then, in 1962, that the President resorted to his preferred method of bilateral agreement when he turned to Bonn, speaking rather loosely of "organic cooperation" as the basis for "the union of our two countries." It is possible that when Prime Minister Macmillan talked with him at

Rambouillet in December de Gaulle still had not made up his mind. But immediately following, Macmillan agreed in Nassau to President Kennedy's plan for merging of Great Britain's nuclear force in a multilateral force under American command, thus giving the General the pretext at least for vetoing British membership in Europe. Having confirmed her "insular, maritime" preference for "a colossal Atlantic Community under American dependence and leadership which would soon completely swallow up the European Community," Great Britain was excluded.

Underlying all this was de Gaulle's profound conception of the permanence of the nation state and the essential unity of Europe. Men and creeds passed, but the State and its inherent policies never changed. "The banner of ideology," he remarked, "in reality covers only ambitions. And I believe that it has been thus since the world was born." So Great Britain might cooperate with Europe, might construct a Channel tunnel to France or even collaborate on such a project as a supersonic jet transport, but she was essentially an Atlantic thalassocracy. So, still more, was the Soviet Union essentially historic Russia, a European state with European ambitions. De Gaulle was neither intimidated by Soviet threats about Berlin ("this uproar of imprecations and demands"), nor taken off guard by periodic Soviet cordiality. One day Russia would be ready to do business with a strong France and a strong Europe; in the meantime all negotiations would be futile and dangerous. Finally, the General viewed the United States steadily not only through the veil of a quarter of a century of American opposition, sneers, and hostility, from Roosevelt through Johnson, tempered by moments of sentimental goodwill and his own brief paternal regard for John F. Kennedy. If he was perfectly sincere in assuring the Congress in 1960 that France had made a moral choice "to be on the side of the free peoples," his sense of history told him that the United States' interests could never be those of France and Europe: it was in the nature of things that the United States seek to control Europe economically and militarily, and that was intolerable. A loyal ally, as the Cuban crisis of 1962 proved (de Gaulle's point in swiftly backing Kennedy was to show that in the last analysis the ally most immediately threatened must be supported in its decision), France would remain a difficult ally, pursuing her national interest quite coldly and logically, as nation states must.

By 1963 the prospects of achieving European unity were cheerless. Between the "Europe of fatherlands" conception and the design of the integrationists a considerable gap existed. It might be narrowing, with the integrationists giving ground, but in the meantime the Fifth Republic struck out on another course for itself (and in the name of a Europe still unorganized and incapable therefore of acting in its own interests) to compel recognition of its independence by the United States above all. The attempts to intervene in the Vietnam war, though doubtless a justifiable effort to mediate a tragic conflict, were, like the recognition of the People's Republic of China in 1964, controversial and daring, as the outcry in the West made clear. As always, the President made the distinction between China and the Communist dictatorship which currently ruled it. To say that the West must come to terms with Peking was undeniably realistic. What was striking, however, was that de Gaulle sought immediate negotiation in Asia whereas he refused it with the Soviet Union over Europe: in short, France, with no strength of her own, was quite ruthlessly seeking to commit an unwilling America (which alone had the strength to negotiate) to a course of action from which France would emerge with great prestige. It was a brilliant exercise, logical and emotionally appealing, but there was no certainty that this role of *le cavalier seul* would succeed. Nor was there assurance that France could establish her primacy in Europe and her independence of the United States by the program of economic, scientific, military, and cultural assistance to which the Fifth Republic was committed from Mexico to Persia, from Greece to Japan. A vast effort, it illustrated the flexibility of method essential to the President's policy. Quite cynically, it depended upon the incessant underlining of United States' errors around the globe and the consequent implication that French leadership was the only intelligent alternative. De Gaulle might be able to commit his successors to this same course; but equally he might compel them one day to choose between the approaches taken and the burdens assumed.

Foreign Policy and the Nation

Certainly the foreign policy of the Fifth Republic displayed an imaginativeness and boldness shot through with shiftings and contradictions of tactics. The President reversed himself frequently, or pursued two different lines of thought simultaneously. Thus the policy of dismemberment of Germany was followed by the policy of "organic union" with Germany; the policy of Russian alliance gave way to the policy of intransigence; the talk of "yellow peril" in 1959 was superseded by recognition of Peking in 1964; the incessant criticism of the United States was matched by loyalty to the Atlantic alliance. Apparently mystifying, the *politique de grandeur* was mobile but severely logical if its premises were accepted. It was both personal and supported by a group of extremely intelligent professional diplomats; it was apparently not debated in the Government, which, indeed, was sometimes informed of its policies at press conferences. Whether the country fully supported the policy was more difficult to say. A foreign policy conceived entirely *politically*, not imposed by either military or economic considerations but rather turning both to account, it was greatly appealing to a nation whose descent into the abyss of 1940-1944 had been so swift and whose subsequent trials were so multifarious and insistent: it echoed historic nationalist aspirations, adopted the idiom of radical reformism, and suggested at least a Catholic conservatism. It struck a profound chord of anti-Americanism in France and a reassuring note of French superiority to the rival barbarisms of East and West. All too often, the clear-sighted truths of the President's observations were lost beneath the xenophobic shafts which betrayed his own impatience and frustration and delighted his still-wounded compatriots.

The future of the General's policy was unpredictable. Though the country largely applauded him, it remained uncomprehending of his subtleties, critical of the high cost of the *"mission humaine"* undertaken in the world, and ever ready to blame its domestic ills upon this enormous charge. If there was an opposition press, the great dailies continued their tradition of failing to discuss France's foreign policy and to communicate more than an inkling of foreign opinion about it. Indeed the mass media, state-controlled or private, had a record of obscurantism on the issues of foreign policy exceeded only by their irresponsibility toward the drama of the colonial wars. Unprepared for the devolution of empire, the public had sustained massive shocks when the facts became known and reacted by displaying indifference and parochial self-concern. Unprepared for the resistance met by the Fifth Republic's external policies, it blamed the foreigner and gave its attention to domestic reforms. Assembly debates were infrequent, after the fact, and incapable of affecting policy: some of the opposition was excluded by the elections, much of it was tainted with the failure of the Fourth Republic. Moreover, critics of the policy of *le cavalier seul*, such as Paul Reynaud, preached an integration in the Atlantic Community which made little appeal to the nation. The General's principal political challenger, Gaston Defferre, was more critical of the means than of the ends of the Gaullist policy, gave relatively little attention to foreign affairs (since this was not an issue on which political capital could be made), and in any event suggested a vaguely socialist policy for Europe which would not greatly eliminate difficulties with the United States or even West Germany. Defferre's withdrawal in 1965 made the speculation academic.

Beyond the intangible quantity of prestige, the gains of the Fifth Republic's policy were evidently small. To the paradox of France's claim to lead Europe but refusal to permit Europe to be created in a manner acceptable to other Europeans was added the coolness (however justified) toward Great Britain, which drove her steadily back on the United States and thus reduced the flexibility of approach to *grandeur* which the President sought. As spectacle, the Gaullist diplomacy was undeniably imposing. But without concrete successes it would not survive. Those who came after de Gaulle would be unable to resist domestic pressures for a limitation of the enterprise, even if they chose to resist the pressures from the integrationists and the Americans. Without this man's extraordinary authority, they would nevertheless have to offer the nation something not unlike the sense of pride and well-being he had twice restored to them. And they would be unable to exact the same cost. Here, then, as elsewhere, the future hung upon the possibility of attaching the nation to the regime once the charismatic figure had departed.

ELEVEN

TODAY, TOMORROW, AND

THE DAY AFTER

"Ce n'est pas assez d'avoir de grandes qualités, il faut en avoir l'économie."

More than one hundred years ago, while living in Sorrento, Tocqueville reflected somewhat morosely on the unfinished Revolution, the last act of which had been so often proclaimed and which nevertheless remained so elusive as regime succeeded regime. "As we go on, its end seems farther off and shrouded in greater darkness. Shall we ever . . . attain a more complete and more far-reaching social transformation than our fathers foresaw and desired, and than we ourselves are able to foresee; or are we not destined simply to end in a condition of intermittent anarchy, the well-known chronic and incurable complaint of old peoples? As for me, I am unable to say; I do not know when this long voyage will be ended; I am weary of seeing the shore in each successive mirage, and I often ask myself whether the *terra firma* we are seeking does really exist, and whether we are not doomed to rove upon the seas forever!" * Since that winter day late in 1850 the fortunes of France had not ceased to revolve, and how many lesser Tocquevilles had given way from time to time to similarly somber thoughts? In the mind's eye the parade of triumphs and defeats, shocks and shiftings of direction stretched backward and forward from that point in time when he set those words down while sojourning along the Italian shore.

To these swings of destiny's pendulum, the French reacted both with self-pity and with realism. Brilliant and sensitive, they took their failures hard, magnified their cause and, sometimes at least, sought the source of their misfortunes outside themselves. In the twentieth century particularly, the notion that they were doomed to suffer alone on behalf of the general cause stirred their sense of injustice and impelled them to withdrawal. Yet they also responded to challenges flung down. If they flagged momentarily beneath the blows raining down in 1917, they endured; if they blundered and were "deserted" at Suez, they finally found their way out of the colonial tunnel; if they had slipped into economic stagnation, they had within themselves the intellectual resources and boldness which led them

* *The Recollections of Alexis de Tocqueville*. Trans. by A. T. de Mattos, ed. by J. P. Mayer. (New York: Meridian Books, 1959), pp. 68-69.

to renovation. And it was the genius of this analytical and articulate people to be able to link together the tasks of defending their independence, of assuring their post-colonial *mission humaine* in the world, and of concentrating upon their economic expansion which was the essential foundation of the other two. Doubtless this persuasive harmonization of tasks was more readily and more authoritatively achieved by the "elective monarchy" of the Fifth Republic than it might be by whatever style of government succeeded, but there was reason to think that the national acceptance of the program could survive.

Impelled by the international conditions of their prosperity and the revival of their prestige, the French might well return to the goal of equality and cooperation with their great neighbors (rather than of European primacy, if not splendid isolation), and they appeared unlikely to lower their eyes from the wider horizons to which the Fourth and Fifth Republics had raised them. As the European idea had survived and disentangled itself from the Nazi perversion of it, so it might win new adherents once the place of France had been acknowledged in the great capitals of the world. But until that rank had been fully secured, no leaders would easily return France to the discipline of international bodies or a supranational European organization where her voice was not to be heeded. The essential introversion of both Vichy and the Resistance was history; the economic conditions that had suggested abdication to the Third Republic had either gone or were under attack; the education of a new generation in foreign affairs was at least under way. But precisely because no other state in recent times had been so preoccupied in the classic way with foreign policy, because it was the deepest thought of the presidency of Charles de Gaulle, some adjustment in thought and action was inevitable. What this man had achieved—still more, what he had asserted—could be lost, but it would certainly be struggled for by those who came after.

Less certain would be the legacy of internal reforms accomplished. Though bold economic and financial reforms had combined with the surge of confidence in 1958 to propel the economy forward on the path planned by the Fourth Republic, the Fifth Republic inherited the unsolved problems of fiscal injustice, deferred regional reform, inflated subsidies, labyrinthine distribution, and lagging wages. In some areas hardly more than a beginning assault had been mounted; in many the approach was piecemeal. Reformist thought had been tainted by its association with Vichy, and weakened after the Liberation by the return of the old parties and pressure groups to the Assembly regime. The social question was still posed. The alienation of the working class, that grim inheritance from the nineteenth century, continued to proclaim the social lag in a country rapidly industrializing itself away from the comfortable formula of a well-balanced economy. Like regional tensions, social tensions lay scarcely beneath the surface, as the dreary permanence of the Communist vote made plain. If the Republic had understood 90 or so years before what it must do to attach the nation to it politically, it still had not solved the problem of attaching it socially. As both the Fourth and the Fifth Republics showed, the tiresome squabble about state assistance to separate schools still occasioned outcry and even resignation, yet clearly the real problem was rather to advance the cause of social mobility by thoroughly democratizing the educational system. Much had been achieved since the Liberation; more remained to be done. The burden of the past—whether family resistance to education because it might alienate the next generation from the regional, occupational, and social patterns so long unchanging; or whether the style of education, rhetorical, individualistic, fiercely analytical, and too little scientific—weighed on the whole nation. Boileau's ruling dictum, *"Ce que l'on conçoit bien s'énonce clairement,"* was an incomplete educational philosophy for the later twentieth century.

In a larger sense, even, the national education remained unsatisfactory. The problem of *civisme* was as acute as ever. If the *Jeunes patrons* had shown the way toward some new ideal of responsibility among the business class, and if the labor movement was abandoning its militant and sterile ideology for economic demands and a share in high-level management, there were signs that still both parties conceived of their interests as something less than complementary and of their relationships to the State as essentially defensive (or, periodically, offensive). No doubt the working class was beginning to emerge from its ghetto, business from behind its protective tariff, the farmer from his dependency upon subsidy, and the shopkeeper from his little fortress erected against the State, but the ghost of Alain lingered on with its message of resistance and its ideal of atomistic egoism. And to these older problems was added the problem of the Army. Whether it was finished as a political force remained uncertain. Offered a renewed continental role, with an independent nuclear weapon of some significance, a mechanized *force de manoeuvre* to strike with both conventional and nuclear arms, and a national defense force, all to be sustained by selective service and heavy credits, it nevertheless had its memories to live down, its bitterness and its lessons of subversive warfare learned far from Europe. For less coherent regimes such an Army might still appear to hold an authority not lightly to be disregarded.

Nor would the moral crises sustained in the more than two decades after 1940 be easily forgotten. The twentieth century had been hard on the intellectuals; the record showed both deep involvement in and total rejection of the ideological conflicts of their time. In France, perhaps, their situation had been as painful as anywhere. The Algerian war had driven them into a series of opposed camps. More depressing than the rallying of the Academic Right to the forlorn cause was the intransigent hostility of the Left to Army and State, a comprehensible protest against the barbarism committed in the name of France matched by an unreasoning justification of, or indifference to, the barbarism to which she was subjected. Indeed, the alienation of the intellectual Left from the regime was a permanent phenomenon after 1939, marked by tentative attachments to the Soviet world (at least until 1956) and unsparing denunciation of the horrors of American civilization. Thus was surrendered a position of potential importance vis-à-vis the political Left, and the internal dialogue of France was rendered the poorer. And, as so much of the post-Liberation period showed, a great part of the intelligentsia simply abandoned the field for completely apolitical pursuits. Moreover, this withdrawal of the intellectuals had its much wider counterpart in the nation at large, which ended by abdicating responsibility for troubling deeds done on its behalf, refusing to seek or believe evidence of them, and taking refuge in its own parochial pursuits. Although many individuals and organizations braved the persecution of the Army and the State in order to speak out against this moral gangrene, millions more turned aside. Vainly the counsel for Secret Army defendants pointed their finger at "the people of France" in whose name St. Cyr "terrorists" had been "pushed over the edge of this pit of destruction." The nation had turned away; and then, apart from a few such exceptional cases which went to trial, the record was closed. Upon this scene of justice corrupted and miscarried, violence and hatred of a murderous kind introduced into all levels of public and private life, the curtain descended. In the silence that followed, it was difficult to guess what the ultimate effects might be.

What was missing in this Fifth Republic was inspiration and participation. It was the flame that burned low. Despite the charismatic person of the General and his oracular pronouncements (growing steadily less so after 1962), despite the ceremonies staged with theatrical flamboyance by André Malraux (such as the torchlight memorial service for the martyred Resistance hero Jean Moulin), the regime lacked a mystique. What fascinated the nation was the spectacle of its world role; what concerned it principally was its well-being; what it knew was that the regime could not last in its present form. Since the first hour, the old parties had waited like discredited but inevitable heirs in the drawing room below. Though they had aged in the process, it was less certain that they had matured. Though the old Right had largely disappeared, no new united Left had emerged and the Center remained fragmented. Yet nothing was so certain as the fact that the political parties must one day succeed to the responsibilities assumed unilaterally by the executive after 1958. The reduction of ideological militancy in the unions might be a hopeful sign for the non-Communist Left; so, too, the activities of student and non-political discussion groups. Above all, the people, so long absent from the Republics, must be reintegrated through the political system and the process of debate and compromise on national issues be regenerated in the nation. How this was to be accomplished, however, was unclear. But unless popular participation were achieved by the parties, France would once more see the small "political class" of 15,000 or 20,000 establish its ascendancy and parliament become again a closed arena in which meaningless games are played and pressure groups operate, while the bureaucracy (which must in any event make an increasingly large number of technical decisions) encroaches steadily on the governmental domain.

Authority in the General's regime was conferred by plebiscite and was so loftily situated that problems assumed crisis proportion before the Government intervened. It was so personal that the regime sank no roots in the country. It was distant (save for television broadcasts and village square encounters), unwilling to accept direct support (the cry of "Help me!" in 1961 was followed by police assault upon demonstrators against the Secret Army in 1962), too mindful of powerful interests to avoid contempt. The parties' hostility to the regime and the General's triumph over them had destroyed their role as intermediaries: the notables took their causes directly to the administration; failing to obtain a hearing, various groups resorted to strikes or even violence. In short, though the nature of authority had altered in the Republic, and the connection between the people and the State appeared closer than ever before, in fact the connection was verbal and exceptional. As always, a true dialogue between the nation and its Government remained to be established. If the parties reorganized themselves, left behind the ideological baggage of the nineteenth century, eschewed a policy of revenge against the executive for the years of parliamentary eclipse, and followed that true course of coalition politics which gradually blunts the sharpness of party differences, then the Fifth Republic might flourish independent of the extraordinary man who brought it into being. Then the nation might awaken from its paralyzed stance somewhere between apathy and rebellion.

It seemed almost inconceivable that, having in a number of ways made such progress away from the negations and abdications of the last century, France would not now step forward to take full responsibility for her fortunes once more. For France, after all, *was* more than the historic State and its long record of achievements—more, too, than her great men, living or dead. France was also almost fifty million Frenchmen, aware of their talents, unafraid of the century, and with the ghosts of former defeats and unhappy days banished to the limbo of the past.

Chosen, not entirely by chance, from the mass of books that come to mind, the following titles concentrate upon works available in English. Readers who have no direct acquaintance with France and the French ought perhaps to begin by finding out what they look like. An attractive portrait is in Sir Denis W. Brogan and the Editors of *Life* magazine, *France* (New York, 1960). More conventional is Martin Hürlimann, *France* (New York, 1951 rev. ed. 1958). Magnificent aerial views of the country are in Marc Vincent, *et al.*, *Au dessus de la France* (Paris, 1958). Hilda Ormsby, *France, a Regional and Economic Geography* (London, 1931; rev. ed., 1950) or E. Estyn Evans, *France: A Geographical Introduction* (London, 1959) are useful studies of the land. Standard guides are in the *Guide bleu* and Michelin series.

Histories come in various forms, styles, and points of view. An excellent interpretative narrative account with much bibliographical material is Gordon Wright, *France in Modern Times: 1760 to the Present* (Chicago & London, 1960). A very good brief account of the whole span of French history is Herbert Butterfield, *et al.*, *A Short History of France from Early Times to 1958* (Cambridge, England, 1959), though inclined to be uneven and episodic. One of the best of histories since 1715 is Alfred Cobban, *A History of Modern France* (rev. ed. in 3 vols., Baltimore, 1962-65). John P. T. Bury, *France 1814-1940* (New York, 1949) is straightforward and reliable, Denis W. Brogan, *The French Nation from Napoleon to Pétain, 1814-1940* (New York, 1957) characteristically urbane. The elegant plates in André Maurois, *An Illustrated History of France* (New York, 1960) offer a romanticized view.

On the Third Republic, Brogan's *France Under the Republic: the Development of Modern France* (New York, 1940) remains the best English account, and Jacques Chastenet, *Histoire de la Troisième République*, 7 vols. (Paris, 1952-63) the fullest. For the 1930s, Alexander Werth, *The Twilight of France 1933-1940: A Journalist's Chronicle* (New York, 1942) is still worth reading. Arnold Wolfers, *Britain and France between Two Wars: Conflicting Strategies of Peace Since Versailles* (New York, 1940) is dated but nonetheless illuminating. On the unhappy war of 1939-40, Colonel Adolphe Goutard, *1940: la guerre des occasions perdues* (Paris, 1956) is critical and sound, much better than its truncated English translation, *The Battle of France, 1940* (New York, 1958). Jacques Benoist-Méchin, *Soixante jours qui ébranlèrent l'Occident*, 3 vols. (Paris, 1956) is scintillating and distorted; the English version *Sixty Days that Shook the West. The Fall of France: 1940* (New York, 1963) has been badly reduced and edited to add fresh distortions of another kind. On

166

Vichy, Robert Aron, *The Vichy Regime 1940-44* (New York, 1958), slightly shorter than the French original, is readable and generally unpolemical. Aron's *The History of the Liberation, June 1944-May 1945*, 2 vols. (New York, 1962-64) is a lively account. Three foreign journalists' views of the Fourth Republic may be mentioned: Herbert Lüthy's brilliant *France Against Herself* (New York, 1955), Alexander Werth's long, leftist chronicle, *France 1940-1955* (New York, 1955) and David Schoenbrun's chatty *As France Goes* (New York, 1957). They are full of the judgments that madden Frenchmen; an antidote is Raymond Aron's *France, Steadfast and Changing: The Fourth to the Fifth Republic* (Cambridge, Mass., 1960). Useful papers by various hands are in Edward Mead Earle, ed., *Modern France: Problems of the Third and Fourth Republics* (Princeton, 1950). A helpful outline is Robert Lacour-Gayet, *La France au XXe Siècle* (Paris & New York, [1954]). Donald C. McKay, *The United States and France* (Cambridge, Mass., 1951) remains of interest. But the two most valuable books are probably David Thomson's superb study, *Democracy in France since 1870* (4th ed., New York, 1964) and the fine symposium of Stanley Hoffmann, *et al.*, *In Search of France* (Cambridge, Mass., 1963).

On the French character, Carleton J. H. Hayes, *France, A Nation of Patriots* (New York, 1930) is by no means entirely obsolete. The same is true of Salvador de Madariaga, *Englishmen, Frenchmen, Spaniards* (New York, 1929) and Friedrich Sieburg, *Who Are These French?* (New York, 1932)—all of which, however, have conclusions displeasing to their subject. André Siegfried's *France, A Study in Nationality* (New Haven, 1930) and his later essay on the French in *Nations Have Souls* (New York, 1952) doubtless present more acceptable views. Pierre Maillaud, *France* (New York, 1942) is short and perceptive, Charles Morazé, *The French and the Republic* (Ithaca, N.Y., 1958) eccentric and dazzling as well as sometimes just maddening and wrongheaded. Edward R. Tannenbaum's *The New France* (Chicago, 1961) is an original and illuminating study, as is Laurence Wylie's splendid *Village in the Vaucluse* (Cambridge, Mass., 1957). Wylie's essay, and that of Jesse R. Pitts in *In Search of France*, are similarly important. I have borrowed quite shamelessly from nearly all of these.

On the cultural life of the French, Ernest Robert Curtius, *The Civilization of France* (New York, 1932) and Georges Duby & Robert Mandrou, *A History of French Civilization* (New York, 1964) are of lasting value. Helpful essays are in Julian Park, ed., *The Culture of France in Our Time* (Ithaca, N.Y., 1954). R. L. Graeme Ritchie, ed., *France, A Companion to French Studies* (London, 1937; rev. ed., 1951) is reliable. Geoffrey Brereton, *A Short History of French Literature* (London, 1962) and the encyclopedic *Oxford Companion to French Literature* (New York, 1959) offer the long and the short of it. Henri Peyre, *The Contemporary French Novel* (New York, 1955) and Martin Turnell's *The Novel in France* (New York, 1950) and *The Art of French Fiction* (New York, 1959) are intelligent criticisms. Emile Bouvier, *Les lettres françaises au XXe siècle* (Paris, 1962) offers a general panorama. Laurent Le Sage, *The French New Novel: An Introduction and a Sampler* (Penn State, 1962) and Germaine Brée's anthology, *Twentieth Century French Literature* (New York, 1962) are handy guides.

On the problem of the intellectuals and the State there is a large literature. Herbert Tint, *The Decline of French Patriotism 1870-1940* (London, 1964) is a rather disappointing sketch; Michael Curtis, *Three Against the Third Republic: Sorel, Barrès, and Maurras* (Princeton, 1959) an illuminating comparison of these major figures; Edward R. Tannenbaum, *The Action Française: Die-Hard Reactionaries in Twentieth-Century France* (New York, 1962) and Eugen Weber, *Action Française: Royalism and Reaction in Twentieth-Century France* (Stanford, 1962) important and readable works of distinction. Paul Sérant, *Le Romantisme fasciste: Étude sur l'oeuvre politique de quelques écrivains français* (Paris, 1959) is exactly what the title suggests, as is the very sound study of the far Left, David Caute, *Communism and the French Intellectuals 1914-1960* (London, 1964).

For modern French painting, there are, among so many others, Maurice Raynal, *et al.*, *History of Modern Painting from Picasso to Surrealism*, 3 vols. (Geneva, 1950), Jean Laymarie, *French Painting: The Nineteenth Century* (Geneva, 1962), and Werner Haftmann, *Painting in the Twentieth Century* (New York, 1960). The special issue on "Contemporary Art," *Yale French Studies*, Nos. 19-20 (Spring 1957-Winter 1958) contains essays of interest. Pierre Lavedan, *French Architecture* (Baltimore, 1956) is a good survey. Nikolaus Pevsner, *Pioneers of Modern Design from William Morris to Walter Gropius* (Baltimore, 1960), Michel Ragon, *Le Livre de l'architecture moderne* (Paris, 1958), Jurgen Joedicke, *A History of Modern Architecture* (New York, 1959) and Reyner Banham, *Theory and Design in the First Machine Age* (London, 1960) all have excellent plates. For Auguste Perret and Tony Garnier, see H. R. Hitchcock, *Architecture: Nineteenth and Twentieth Centuries* (Baltimore, 1958); for Le Corbusier, the enthusiastic Peter Blake, *The Master Builders* (New York, 1960) and Françoise Choay, *Le Corbusier* (New York, 1960).

Paul Collaer, *A History of Modern Music* (Cleveland, 1961) is a useful general account. Rollo H. Myers, "Music" in *The Culture of Modern France* is a brief discussion. On the theatre, there are two issues of *Yale French Studies*, No. 5 (1950) and No. 14 (Winter, 1954-55) which are informative. Harold Hobson, *The French Theatre of Today: An English View* (London, 1953) discusses Sartre, Montherlant, Anouilh, etc., and Leonard C. Pronko, *Avant-Garde: The Experimental Theater in France* (Berkeley, 1962) deals with Beckett, Ionesco, and others. Georges Sadoul, *Histoire générale du cinéma*, 6 vols. (Paris, 1948-54) runs to 1945. His *Histoire du cinéma français 1890-1962* (Paris, 1962) and Penelope Houston's *The Contemporary Cinema* (Baltimore, 1963) are up to date.

Educational reform is discussed briefly in John F. Cramer & George S. Browne, *Contemporary Education: A Comparative Study of National Systems* (New York, 1956). Georges Duvau, *Les Instituteurs* (Paris, 1957) is an urbane, brief account. See also "French Education: Why Jeannot Can Read," *Yale French Studies*, No. 22 (Winter-Spring, 1958-59), and the penetrating, witty analysis by J. G. Weightman, "The Sorbonne," *Encounter*, XVI (June 1961), 28-42.

On religion, Adrien Dansette, *Religious History of Modern France*, 2 vols. (New York, 1961) is a fair general survey since the Revolution. His *Destin du Catholicisme français 1926-1956* (Paris, 1957) and William Bosworth, *Catholicism and Crisis in Modern France: French Catholic Groups at the Threshold of the Fifth Republic* (Princeton, 1962) deal with the recent period.

Stephen H. Roberts, *History of French Colonial Policy (1870-1925)*, 2 vols.

(New York, 1929) has not yet been superseded. An important era is treated in Thomas F. Power, *Jules Ferry and the Renaissance of French Imperialism* (New York, 1944) and in Frederick L. Schuman, *War and Diplomacy in the French Republic* (New York, 1931), a series of acute essays on foreign and colonial policy and diplomacy. The literature on the decline of empire is of course vast and polemical. Among various accounts of the Indo-China tragedy may be mentioned Donald Lancaster, *The Emancipation of Indo-China* (New York, 1961), Edgar O'Ballance, *The Indo-China War, 1945-1954* (London, 1965), and Jules Roy, *Dien Bien Phu* (New York, 1965). See also the forthcoming John F. Cady, *Buddhist Lands in Southeast Asia* (Englewood Cliffs, N.J., Spectrum Books). On North Africa, Roger Le Tourneau, *Evolution politique de l'Afrique du Nord musulmane 1920-1961* (Paris, 1962) is an orthodox, cautious study, Lorna Hahn, *North Africa: Nationalism to Nationhood* (Washington, D.C., 1960) a serviceable narrative, Nevill Barbour, ed., *A Survey of North West Africa [The Maghrib]* (New York, 1959; rev. ed., 1962) a comprehensive handbook, Charles F. Gallagher, *The United States and North Africa* (Cambridge, Mass., 1963) and Richard Brace, *Morocco, Algeria, Tunisia* (Englewood Cliffs, N.J., 1964) excellent analyses. More specifically on the Algerian rebellion, Dorothy Pickles, *Algeria and France, from Colonialism to Cooperation* (New York, 1963) is succinct and fair. Edward Behr, *The Algerian Problem* (New York, 1961) and Joseph Kraft, *The Struggle for Algeria* (Garden City, N.Y., 1961) are intelligent journalists' accounts. To the inhuman aspects of the war, Pierre Vidal-Naquet, *Torture: Cancer of Democracy. France and Algeria 1954-62* (Baltimore, 1963) offers a brief introduction.

On the political system, at least as it was traditionally, see D. W. S. Lidderdale, *The Parliament of France* (New York, 1951), Maurice Duverger, *The French Political System* (Chicago, 1958), and Nathan Leites, *On the Game of Politics in France* (Stanford, 1959). For the Fourth Republic, the essential book is Philip Williams, *Crisis and Compromise: Politics in the Fourth Republic* (London, 1964). On the coming of the Fifth, see Williams and Martin Harrison, *De Gaulle's Republic* (London, 1960) and Alexander Werth, *The de Gaulle Revolution* (London, 1960). Dorothy Pickles, *The Fifth French Republic: Institutions and Politics* (New York, rev. ed., 1962) is reliable, J. A. Laponce, *The Government of the Fifth Republic: French Political Parties and the Constitution* (Berkeley, 1961) sound, and Maurice Duverger, *La Cinquième République* (Paris, 3rd ed., 1963) probably the best general analysis. Important studies appear regularly in the *Revue française de science politique*, far too numerous to be singled out here, and in the *Cahiers de la Fondation nationale des sciences politiques*. Georges A. Lavau, "Political Pressures by Interest Groups in France," in Henry W. Ehrmann, ed., *Interest Groups on Four Continents* (Pittsburgh, 1958), pp. 60-95, is a useful introduction, and Jean Meynaud, *Les Groupes de pression en France* (Paris, 1958) is fundamental.

Studies of Charles de Gaulle are numerous. Of three works in English, Alden Hatch, *The de Gaulle Nobody Knows, An Intimate Biography of Charles de Gaulle* (New York, 1960) is less appalling than the title, Stanley Clark, *The Man Who Is France: The Story of Charles de Gaulle* (New York, 1960 rev. ed. 1963) worse, and Duncan Grinnell-Milne, *The Triumph of Integrity: A Portrait of Charles de Gaulle* (New York, 1962) much better. All have serious failings. Among recent French studies, J.-R. Tournoux, *Pétain et de*

Gaulle (Paris, 1964) is especially illuminating; Robert Aron, *Charles de Gaulle* (Paris, 1964) and Paul-Marie de la Gorce, *De Gaulle entre deux mondes: une vie et une époque* (Paris, 1964) are sensible, François Mauriac, *De Gaulle* (Paris, 1964) enthusiastic; and Alfred Fabre-Luce, *The Trial of Charles de Gaulle* (London, 1963), a brilliant attack. André Passeron, *De Gaulle parle* (Paris, 1962) and Ernest Mignon, *Les Mots du Général* (Paris, 1962) are useful collections. But of course the basic source remains the superb writings of the man, above all the revealing essays in *The Edge of the Sword* (New York, 1960) and the three splendid volumes of *War Memoirs* (New York, 1955-60).

On the general problem of the economy, Shepard B. Clough, *France: A History of National Economics 1789-1939* (New York, 1939) is useful. Warren C. Baum, *The French Economy and the State* (Princeton, 1958) is less hopeful than John Sheahan, *Promotion and Control of Industry in Postwar France* (Cambridge, Mass., 1963) or Charles P. Kindelberger's excellent essay, "The Postwar Resurgence of the French Economy," in *In Search of France*, pp. 118-47, to which I am much indebted. David S. Landes, "French Business and Businessmen: A Social and Cultural Analysis," in *Modern France* and Henry W. Ehrmann's fine study of *Organized Business in France* (Princeton, 1957) have a worthy counterpart in Val Lorwin, *The French Labor Movement* (Cambridge, Mass., 1954). On agriculture, Jacques Fauvet and Henri Mendras, eds., *Les Paysans et la politique dans la France contemporaine* (Paris, 1958) is an important symposium, and Gordon Wright, *Rural Revolution in France: The Peasantry in the Twentieth Century* (Stanford, 1964) is scholarly and readable. Among the many studies of European integration, Emile Benoit, *Europe At Sixes and Sevens: The Common Market, the Free Trade Association and the United States* (New York, 1961), Hans A. Schmitt, *The Path to European Union: From the Marshall Plan to the Common Market* (Baton Rouge, 1962), Leon Lindberg, *The Political Dynamics of European Economic Integration* (Stanford, 1963), and Miriam Camps, *What Kind of Europe? The Community since De Gaulle's Veto* (New York, 1965) may be mentioned. A thoughtful and disturbing report on the darker aspects of the recent success story is Paul-Marie de la Gorce, *La France pauvre* (Paris, 1965).

On foreign policy, the works of Schuman and Wolfers referred to above cover the Third Republic. For the Fourth, see Jean-Baptiste Duroselle's trenchant analysis, "Changes in French Foreign Policy Since 1945," in *In Search of France*, 305-58, the detailed study by Alfred Grosser, *La IVᵉ République et sa politique extérieure* (Paris, 1961), and Edgar S. Furniss, Jr., *France, Troubled Ally: De Gaulle's Heritage and Prospects* (New York, 1960). On the Fifth, Duroselle's essay is excellent, Grosser's *La Politique extérieure de la Vᵉ République* (Paris, 1965) is penetrating, and Paul Reynaud, *The Foreign Policy of Charles de Gaulle, A Critical Assessment* (New York, 1964) is an attack. Nora Beloff, *The General Says No: Britain's Exclusion from Europe* (Baltimore, 1963) is a critical narrative by a knowledgable journalist.

For the Army, Richard D. Challener, *The French Theory of the Nation in Arms, 1866-1939* (New York, 1955) is a sound analysis, Raoul Girardet, *La Société militaire dans la France contemporaine* (1815-1939) (Paris, 1953) a thoughtful background essay, and Paul-Marie de la Gorce, *The French Army: A Military-Political History* (New York, 1963) a readable study of recent times, to be supplemented by James H. Meisel, *The Fall of the Republic: Military Revolt in France* (Ann Arbor, Mich., 1962) and Edgar Furniss, Jr.,

De Gaulle and the French Army: A Crisis in Civil-Military Relations (New York, 1964), both of them excellent. Philip C. Bankwitz, "Maxime Weygand and the Army-Nation Concept in the Modern French Army," *French Historical Studies*, II (Fall, 1961), 157-89, is first-rate, and Girardet, ed., *La Crise militaire française 1945-1962: aspects sociologiques et idéologiques* (Paris, 1964) is similarly important.

Obviously, much material on the contemporary scene is to be found only in newspapers and periodical literature. And where the French press is largely inaccessible, English-speaking readers will doubtless depend a good deal on the foreign correspondents reporting from France, whether for the *New Statesman*, the *New York Times*, or the *New Yorker*, to whom, as to others, I myself am greatly indebted.

INDEX